The NASHVILLE CHRONICLES

The Making of Robert Altman's Masterpiece

JAN STUART

SIMON & SCHUSTER *New York London Toronto Sydney Singapore*

SIMON & SCHUSTER
Rockefeller Center
1230 Avenue of the Americas
New York, NY 10020

Designed by Bonni Leon Berman

Manufactured in the United States of America

1   3   5   7   9   10   8   6   4   2

Library of Congress Cataloging-in-Publication Data

Stuart, Jan.
The Nashville chronicles : the making of Robert Altman's masterpiece / Jan Stuart.
p.   cm.
Includes index.
1. Nashville (Motion picture)   2. Altman, Robert, 1925–   I. Title.

PN1997.N332 S78 2000
791.43'72—dc21   00-061875

ISBN 0-684-86543-2

Acknowledgments

As many times as I don my journalist's hat, I never cease to be filled with wonder and surprise when people who did not know me when they got out of bed that morning are relaying potentially sensitive information to me just a few hours later.

In assembling a book of this anecdotal nature, that wonder is enhanced by the weight of humility and responsibility that overtakes one whenever strangers open their homes, personal papers and daily lives to a writer. Anyone who has sat through even one generic celebrity interview in some irrelevant hotel suite knows this is nothing to be sneezed at.

Perhaps it is gilding the lily to thank Robert Altman for making available his experiences, files, and persnickety humor with such trust and abandon. *The Nashville Chronicles* is itself a gesture of gratitude for his lead in taking moviegoers down roads that few other directors know exist. The thirty-year rebellion that is the Altman film canon stands as a reproach to all the times that I have ever abandoned a writing project midstream, buying into the hooey of corporate suits with M.B.A.s who insist that no one out there would be interested.

The families that Altman pulls together for his movies, however transitory, are a testament to his own daring and love of play. For a year and a half, I was made an honorary member of the *Nashville* family, which is about as close to a movie fan's dream as it gets. While one tries to resist the clannish tendency to play favorites, there are a few but for whom these chronicles would not have made it past the starting line, let alone completion.

Somewhere on a fifteenth-story office perch above New York's Park Avenue lurk two such folk: a young woman of boundless energy, diplomacy, and never-say-die resourcefulness named Wren Arthur and a young man of gentle but potent goodwill named Joshua Astrachan. If they had a dime for every phone request they granted and every minute indulging my needs with files, photos, videos, addresses, phone numbers, Xeroxes, desks, proper lighting, and sympathy, they could start their own production company.

I would recommend to Wren and Josh that they appoint Joan Tewkesbury, Henry and Lois Gibson, Ronee Blakley, Bill Myers, and Christina Crowe to the board of such a company, so there would be at least one other movie mill besides Sandcastle 5 where graciousness, heart, and generosity were understood to be as essential to creativity as caffeine and chutzpah. Their enthusiasm, embracing spirit, and implicit appreciation of the need for documenting film history carried me over many a pothole.

Among the others to whom I am especially indebted for the fullness with which they shared their homes, workplaces, and memory banks are Kathryn Altman, Geraldine Chaplin, Martin Starger (thank you Darren), Lily Tomlin and her indefatigable assistant Judy Van Herben, Richard Baskin, Michael Murphy, Kelly Marshall Fine, and Karen Black. Ned Beatty went the extra mile on my behalf, quite literally, as did captivating raconteurs and all-around good souls David Hayward, Allan Nicholls, Keith Carradine, Alan Rudolph, Bert Remsen, Robert Doqui, Tommy Thompson, Jeff Goldblum, Harry Haun, and Dennis Hill. I deeply regret that the telephone and Internet had to be my conduit to such accomplished individuals as the redoubtable Barbara Harris, Sue Barton, Scott Glenn, Elliott Gould, Timothy Brown, James Dan Calvert, Julie Christie, Sam Cohn, Robert Harders, Wayne Simpson, Tom Stoppard, Richard Perry, David Picker, Richard Portman, and Pauline Kael, but their stories came through with candor, sensitivity, and a nose for irony that would seem to be a prerequisite for tenting in the Altman camp.

For contributing unique documents and information to the bounty of research materials on *Nashville*, I must thank Jim Webb, Donna Deitch, Damien Bona, and Eugene Wyatt, along with my assistants Mark Wood, Beth Whittaker, and Lisa Timmel. I am grateful as well to Lois Smith at PMK, Cheryl Weinstein at Simon & Schuster, and Lowell Dubrinsky at Sandcastle 5 for their part in seeing me through the muck and mire.

The enlivening hospitality of all of my hosts during the interview and writing process was above and beyond the call of friendship or blood ties. I am beholden to John Wesson, Gary Murphy and Jason LaPadura, Dennis and Toren Charnoff, Lee Meihls, Kannan Jagannathan, and the staff at Nashville's evocatively weathered Savage House Inn, which Altman should bear in mind for locations if he ever reconsiders a sequel to *Nashville* or contemplates a remake of *Suddenly, Last Summer*.

There were enough well-wishers and fire-stokers to fill the Grand Old Opry, where I would want to reserve the onstage VIP bleachers for my beloved amigos Suresa Dundes, Joe Koenenn, and the heroic Jed Mattes, whose collective grace under fire and participatory gusto infuse every page of this book. The next time I make it to Tennessee, I also intend to bring back a haul of Goo-Goo Clusters for Ellis Kreuger, Jack MacBean, Jonathan Green, Anne Stockwell, Jade Wu, Tom Ross, Gail Campton, Joel Kaye, Lloyd Williams, Gray Foy, John Epperson, James Morrison, Mark O'Donnell, Justin Ross, Paul Steinberg, George Mott, Judy Pansullo, Paul Iappini, Stefan Killen, Eric Myers, Arlene Chai, Micah Cramer, Bonnie Kaplan, Steven Greco, Paul Colford, Jennifer Krauss, John Anderson, Jack Schwartz, Tim Cusick, Frank Watson, and the Friends of 15th Street and Mt. Toby, whose encouragement, feedback, and leading kept me afloat.

To close off my thanks where all of the following essentially begins for me, I must bow in honor to Helene Keyssar, who first opened my eyes to the incomparable pleasure of a Robert Altman flick. For a generation of theater and communications students, she has transformed critical inquiry into a heady Tilt-a-whirl ride. If it were to someday emerge that Helene and Joan Tewkesbury were separated at birth, it wouldn't surprise me in the least.

For Edith and Carl,
who always knew a good movie
when they saw one

The
NASHVILLE
CHRONICLES

Introduction

One night in 1945, Robert Altman sat in a twin-engine plane 3,500 feet in the air. A pilot cadet on an advanced training session, he hovered in a backseat while his instructor, a veteran flier by the name of Lang, piloted in front with a student officer named Allen. Together, the trio comprised the right wing of a three-plane formation over Frederick, Oklahoma.

Altman was nineteen when World War II entered its final act and the Air Force captured his imagination. Forty-five years later, he would pause to wonder why in the world they were doing night formation, a strategy he insisted was rarely if ever employed in the war. For whatever reason, Lang, Allen, and Altman were in the sky, it was dark, and the young trainee from Kansas City had neglected to buckle himself in properly.

This oversight registered itself plainly enough when, within minutes of hitting the desired altitude, the pilot in the center plane was overcome by vertigo. Thinking the aircraft to his left was coming at him, he veered right toward Lang, Allen, and Altman. Seeing this, Lang abruptly pushed the controls down, sending the plane into a roll. Within seconds, they spiraled into a power dive headed straight for the ground. Altman was tossed from his seat, his body banging and knocking without mercy about the rear of the plane.

Lang cut the power precipitously, throwing the plane into a pullback that upped the g force with great severity. Amid the frenzy, Altman was mentally able to remove himself from the situation long enough to take stock and arrive at the conclusion that he had come to the end. And as he did, a calm took over. Terror vanished, and elation took its place.

The euphoria would be short-lived. As Altman was hurtled back by the g force, Lang showed signs of regaining control. Having giddily resigned himself to an early demise, the bruised trainee became aware that his instructor might yet reverse their fate. Now faced with the possibility of survival, however minuscule, Altman became terrified.

The plane swooped close to the ground. The tops of trees rushed at them, scaring the bejesus out of everyone else in the skewed formation. Altman's instructor screamed, "Cocksucker!" at the other pilot through his radio, then called in for an emergency landing. Throwing what was left of caution to the wind, Lang ignored the standard landing pattern and brought the plane down with nerve-rattling speed.

When he attempts today to explain the perverse joy that swept over him at that moment when death seemed a certainty, the veteran Altman merely says, "I heard from people that when something is inevitable, you kind of giggle and give into it."

The sheer exhilaration of the young flier's close shave would eventually galvanize his life as a pilot of motion pictures. "I try to get in a little over my head, try to get in trouble, try to keep myself frightened," he told *The Washington Post* in 1975. When I reminded him of that remark twenty-four years later, he nodded and said, "There's a lot of survival connected to that. If you succeed at one thing, you've broken the back of the myth that it's impossible to do. So I try to recreate the chaos in which I've succeeded before."

For the better part of the last thirty years, Altman has endeavored to plunge himself over and again into chaotic work excursions and potentially fatal career forays that would spell curtains for filmmakers of weaker heart, resolve, and inspiration. And he has thrown thousands of daredevil actors, writers, editors, technicians, cooks, and bottle washers into the backseat, asking them in advance to kindly unfasten their seatbelts.

When United Artists asked Altman in 1973 to take on a script they hoped to produce about the country-music industry, it might have been politic to say yes. His reservoirs of goodwill among the studio mucky-mucks sorely needed replenishing. By the mid-seventies, Altman had engendered a bad-boy reputation among film moguls, just as he had among the TV producers for whom he wrote and directed weekly series in the fifties and sixties, when he had raised many a blood-pressure count with his lackadaisical respect for the script and a perverse penchant for killing off major characters after only six or seven installments. In dramatic contrast with Alfred Hitchcock, one of his short-time television employers who famously preplanned each frame of his movies within an inch of their celluloid lives, Altman regarded storyboards as straitjacketing and scripts as disposable.

Robert Altman. (*Jim Coe*)

His iconoclast's temperament could be tolerated, even venerated, when the results were as lucrative as they were with *MASH*. Since that Korean War romp certified Altman as a Hollywood player in 1970, however, he had worn out the welcome mat with a string of critical darlings (*McCabe & Mrs. Miller, The Long Goodbye, Thieves Like Us,* and *California Split*) that flipped Hollywood genres on their heads and alienated the moviegoing public.

Rather than accept the studio's Nashville script, Altman chucked it back at them, balking at the quality of the writing. In another year, he would begin production on another scenario set amid the country-music business, a wildly ambitious epic of shit-kicking music and country-fried politics. It would be written by a former Broadway-musical gypsy with no résumé to show for herself in either arena, star twenty-four actors of whom only one was organically related to the music (who would nevertheless compose their own songs and write much of their own dialogue), and engage the help of thousands of Tennessee residents who would willingly park their suspicions of Tinseltown interlopers at the gate for the possibility of free hot dogs and trips to Disneyland. And all for a price tag that would insult the per-picture salary requirements of today's third-tier stars. *Nashville* would be his masterpiece.

Regardless of whether one were seduced by it or bemused by it, whether one combed the nooks and crannies of Pauline Kael's labyrinthine rave in advance or walked in cold, no one who saw *Nashville* when it opened in 1975 was quite prepared for what he got. It was a country-and-western concert, a political campaign, a character study (with particular emphasis on the eccentric meaning of "character"), a travelogue, an assassination thriller, a satirical comedy about the peculiar natures of celebrity, race, class, sex, and popular culture in America. And the damn thing rarely sat still, as if the director had tapped into the restlessness of the era and used it as an energy source. When one considers the films that could be said to speak to the zeitgeist of the seventies, *Nashville* holds an unassailable spot at the top of the list.

Acolytes of Altman would say they knew he had it in him all

along, but even they would be caught off guard by what came out. Here, in varying degrees, were the prankster spirit of *MASH,* the insolence of *Brewster McCloud,* the ambling gait and catch-as-catch-can looseness of *McCabe & Mrs. Miller.* With *Nashville,* however, deconstructing the genre film was no longer an end unto itself for the director. Altman was hunting bigger game, nothing less than an epic pronouncement on the state of the union. All at once, there was a new sense of purpose and weight behind the sly jokes. The improvisational acting method had settled in and settled down, abetted by a fleet pair of editor's scissors and a hyperalert ear tuned to the sounds and rhythms of an itinerant city. No other film in Altman's loop-the-loop career employed his go-for-the-chaos philosophy of filmmaking with greater consequence—and keener foresight—than did this giddy cross-pollination of showbiz posturing and political grandstanding. What had struck some as a short attention span in his earlier films had matured and coalesced into a 360-degree view of the world that would become securely identified as Altmanesque.

Interviewing Altman upon the occasion of the release of *The Gingerbread Man* in 1998 (shortly after he had successfully battled the studio to retain control over the final cut), I asked him if, given the opportunity, he could make *Nashville* today. He responded with an unhesitating No. When I asked why, he replied, "I wouldn't have the courage."

It seemed an odd response at the time, not only as he had just weathered yet one more battle with the studio moneymen to keep his latest baby from harm's way, but because it seemed that every movie he had ever made had required *cojones* of Trojan proportions. As I began to talk to the cast and crew of *Nashville* over the following year, however, the breadth of kamikaze-style nerve that propelled this picture began to crystallize.

If only as a feat of improvisational legerdemain, *Nashville*'s fragmentary portrait of five days in the life of the country-music business was without precedent. It was a spectacular reproach to the Hollywood studio system of honing a script. While Joan Tewkesbury's meticulously wrought screenplay offered the actors an exhaustive blueprint with which to construct their characters, Altman encouraged them to embroider with as much detail from their own lives as was required to make them at home with their assignments. Nourished by the director's generally unflappable, occasionally volatile, personality, the reward was an often unlikely merging of actor and role that would inspire startling turns and fuel some provocative psychodramas on the set. In a number of instances, as so often happened with Altman films, the resulting performances would launch an actor's career or endure as that performer's watershed achievement.

Impressionistic in form and kaleidoscopic in its attentions to two dozen characters, *Nashville* would inspire analogies to artists as far-flung as Fellini, Chekhov, Dos Passos, Joyce, and Doctorow. For all its ostensible literary pedigree, *Nashville*'s uniquely self-referential deployment of a large ensemble cast would find a largely ignored parallel in the genesis and thematic content of a groundbreaking Broadway musical that premiered the same month.

Like *A Chorus Line,* which evolved its text from the histories of many of the dancers who would comprise its original cast, *Nashville* used show-business aspirants as a microcosm of American ambition. *A Chorus Line* concealed its origins as a support-group hash-session for dancers by assuming the shape of an audition like no audition ever known: a soul-bearing tête-à-tête between director and performer. Since Altman disdains auditions, most of the actors in *Nashville* landed their parts through similarly unorthodox, if less probing, encounters.

Given the movie's intensely collaborative genesis, the *Nashville* that emerges under Altman's stewardship is a crazy quilt of American regionalism that conceals the disparate histories of its participants. When you unthread the seams, you find that Robert Altman's *Nashville* is at least as much about Ronee Blakley's Caldwell, Idaho, Thomas Hal Phillips's Kossuth, Mississippi, Robert Doqui's Stillwater, Oklahoma, Ned Beatty's Louisville, Allen Garfield's Newark, Lily Tomlin's Detroit, Shelley Duvall's Houston, Richard Baskin's Los Angeles, and Barbara Harris's Second City, Chicago.

Newsweek sniffed out something to this effect when, tossing one more literary lion into the talk soup of hyperbole, it quoted Walt Whitman's *Leaves of Grass* to kick off a cover story on the film. To Altman, however, the sound of his countrymen's music was more dissonant than celebratory. Beneath all the tunes in *Nashville,* the director heard America caterwauling. (Director Wim Wenders would later refer to it as a "movie about noise.") There was so much cacophony, indeed, that Altman had to devise a special multitrack stereo system to sort it all out.

While *Nashville* traffics in plain folk alongside its country luminaries, it is less a populist tract in the Whitman spirit than a democratic film in the literal sense of having the capacity to observe all sides of the behavioral coin. Good people misbehave, unpleasant people redeem themselves. Or they don't. Those who would be inclined to canonize Lily Tomlin's Linnea Reese and Keenan Wynn's Mr. Green while filing Henry Gibson's Haven Hamilton and Keith Carradine's Tom Frank in the discard bin need to look again.

Film is a director's medium. With what we have come to know of this particular director in the twenty-five years since the making of *Nashville,* we can readily make the claim that Robert Altman's pawprints are all over this movie. Yet one cannot underestimate the tempering hand of its screenwriter, Joan Tewkesbury, in *Nashville*'s dogged reluctance to reduce its people to masks of farce or melodrama, hero or heavy. Altman has always been drawn to working with women, partly because he loves them and partly because he must sense on some level that they complement his vision. If one is able to sift out the actors' contributions from *Nashville*—a treacherous task at best—one finds a heady fusion of the director's and the screenwriter's sensibilities: his acerbity and her wariness, his cynicism and her empathy, his his-ness and her her-ness.

Nashville would be an astonishment if only for its brazenly promiscuous structure and the manner in which order was fashioned from a (deceptively) improvised process. It wouldn't take long after its release for observers to note that it was doubly remarkable as a harbinger of things to come in both the musical and political fronts it was assaulting.

When Altman and company set up shop in Nashville in June of 1974, it was a burg in transition. The city's skyline, defined by two forlorn towers, reflected the once low-reaching ambitions of its music business. (When I asked Altman what he thought of the town, he simply said, "I couldn't find it.") The Ryman Auditorium, the city's beloved nineteenth-century gospel tabernacle and the original locale of *Nashville*'s violent climax, had just lost its famous tenant of thirty-one years. The Grand Ole Opry had relocated to the sprawling Opryland theme park way off in the burbs, another refugee from the crumbling of Downtown, U.S.A.

Prodded by the breakout triumph of such new-generation singers as Loretta Lynn, Tammy Wynette, and Roger Miller, country music was beginning to bust out of the cluster of cozy houses that surrounded Nashville's lower Broadway. Musicians, songwriters, record producers, and publishers of all stripes descended from New York and Los Angeles to this burgeoning Emerald City of entertainment and high finance. Banks muscled in, hotels happened, more towers. By the 1990s, country music had expanded its demographic appeal to reach the well-heeled and well-educated of America's urban culture, making it the second hottest-selling genre in the recording business.

It would also give Bible-printing, long the city's number-one industry, a run for its money. Country music, with its twangy paeans to trailer-park Jobs making the best of a raw deal, provided a fittingly moral voice for such an aggressively devout population.

Nashville was also a victim of its new dawning. With the big-city infusion, came big-city marijuana, cocaine, and pharmaceuticals. When beloved Opry banjo picker David "Stringbean" Akeman and his wife were murdered at home by intruders on November 11, 1973, it seemed as if the other shoe had dropped with a bang. Decades before the bombing of the Federal building in Oklahoma City rendered "America's loss of innocence" an overworked cliché, Nashville was experiencing its own loss of innocence.

And so was its music. When I visited Nashville's redoubtable Exit/In club in the spring of 1999, a stunning lineup of young country performers under the banner "New Western Beat" seemed determined to regain a purity of musicianship that was sacrificed with the Garth-ing and Wynonna-zation of country. Sitting at the Grand Ole Opry two nights later, I couldn't help feel how unfortunate it was that *Nashville* was rejected out of hand by many of the big country stars of the day, who felt they were being trashed. The scruffy, seat-of-the-pants, let's-try-this kind of riffing with which *Nashville* came together seemed to have more in common with the roots of country music than what was going on at the Opry. *Nashville,* in its own insolent, inauthentic way, was a tribute.

But then Altman never intended to make a movie "about" Nashville. The tainted purity of Nashville's music business in 1974 merely trained an X ray on the cavities lurking behind the nation's ever-optimistic Gleem smile. *Nashville* would be, as Altman defended his picture upon its release, his "metaphor for America." This was an America burnt out by the scandal of Watergate and a war in Vietnam that turned a disaffected youth against the government. Twenty-five years later, it was a country struggling to shake off the scandal of Monicagate and a cultural war that saw a disaffected youth turned against itself. Anyone trying to make sense of the shootings at Columbine High School— a national obsession at the time this introduction was being written—would be very interested to see an early scene in *Nashville* in which a grinning parade of overrouged JonBenet Ramseys twirl major artillery as if to the manner born.

Assassination and politics came into the scenario almost as an afterthought. Between Martin Luther King, the Kennedys, and *The Parallax View,* political executions were already old news when *Nashville* premiered in June of 1975. Typically, Altman had a new wrinkle: An assassin's bullet would strike, not a politician, but a music star. John Lennon's precedent-setting murder would not occur for another five years.

The assassination of Barbara Jean was Altman's curveball, tossed into an elaborately contrived campaign for an alternative presidential candidate whose down-home populism would be likened at the time to George Wallace and, later on, to Ross Perot. "Metacontemporary" was the word used to describe the prescience of *Nashville* by its second assistant director, Altman prodigy Alan Rudolph, who was not alone in speculating that the film presaged the election of Jimmy Carter a year after its release. HAS FACT BECOME FICTION IN '76 RACE? fretted a headline in a *TV Guide* column by Kevin Phillips, who joined the *Village Voice*'s Alexander Cockburn and James Ridgeway in accusing the president-to-be of running a "*Nashville* candidacy"—"all vagueness, posturing, packaging."

Carter was, perhaps, a mere cameo actor in the grand two-part Washington miniseries that has played itself out in the years between the filming of *Nashville* and its recent twenty-fifth anniversary. There are so many public personages invoked over the course of Altman's Opryland epic, so many tides forecasted, so many topical Pandora's boxes sprung, so many great literary stylists echoed, so many issues prodded, that it is possible to conclude, as one letter writer did in the *New York Review of Books,* that the movie is hollow at its core, and that its director has no opinions, no "ideas."

Those who subscribe to that line of thinking have been conned by the sheer crush of expectations with which the movie was saddled upon its premiere. Joyce? Dos Passos? Chehkov? To quote John Lennon, "Get back, Jojo." Altman never asked to join that club. While the man who made *Nashville* is proud of his achievement, he dismisses outright any claims to masterpiece status. Beneath the portentous wrapping of scale, length, and blood-stained Old Glory is an entertainment, one whose pleasure quotient only increases with repeated viewings. Altman, his antennae always cocked for bullshit, prefers to call it his *Grand Motel*.

The reality is somewhere between Vicki Baum soap and Kurt Vonnegut pop sociology. *Nashville* is one of the greatest tabula rasae ever to enjoy the imprimatur of a major Hollywood studio. You bring your baggage when you walk into Altman's motel, and you check out with baggage that may or may not be your own. *Nashville* kicks in with an auto pileup, and works its way up to a collision of politics and show business. And when crashing is inevitable, as Altman said, the best course may be simply to giggle and give into it.

Prologue

The air was filled with the smoky Fourth of July perfume of bar-becued red meat. It was the summer of 1974, a sizzler even by Tennessee standards. Taking shade under the wooded cover of a suburban Nashville home, a platoon of actors huddled around film director Robert Altman, expectant, eager, ready to burn up the road. Like so many sojourners to Nashville before and since, they had come there in Jeeps, caravans, convertibles, and 727s, serenaded by country-and-western tunes played on the radio. Except for a few veterans of television's early years, they were a young group, hovering in their seemingly indefatigable twenties and thirties. Many knew what was in store from working on pre-vious Altman films, although just as many had never worked with him before. For a handful, it was their first picture alto-gether. They were about to be spoiled for life.

This preshoot holiday cookout was the first time Altman's dirty two dozen (minus Karen Black) were assembled in the same place. It was the premier festivity of what for many would be an ongoing two-month party. Other directors might think twice be-fore conducting a cast meeting on such a kick-back occasion, but Altman liked to fudge the distinction between work and play whenever he could. Some of the best on-camera moments came out of off-camera downtimes such as this. Consequently, he had become very adept at taking notes with a spatula in one hand and a scotch in the other.

He welcomed his actors. "More than anything I want you to have a good time this summer," he told them, setting the priori-ties. "You've all read the script. Now I want you to put it down and forget about it."

Meeting adjourned. The veterans smiled. The neophytes blanched. Some of them had already memorized their lines.

In spite of Altman's injunction, the script would offer the ac-tors an essential compass for the journey they were to take in the coming two months. And despite the aura of randomness which informed the movie that emerged from that journey, each of their twenty-four characters provided a singular and indivisible strand that could not be removed without unraveling the whole.

Who were these people, and why were they in the same story? Here was a deceptively eccentric group portrait of American celebrity as it was coming to be defined in the final quarter of the twentieth century: the royalty of politics, pop music, and the movies. They were the chosen few who carried their trains, the self-anointed who aspired to the throne, the peasants with their noses pressed against the castle windows hoping for a glimpse. And regardless of which group one identified with, they could be viewed with reverence, ridicule, compassion, indifference, irritation, wonder or, most likely, some combination thereof.

The famous director was cooking steaks for his actors on the Fourth of July to level the playing field. Some actors would have

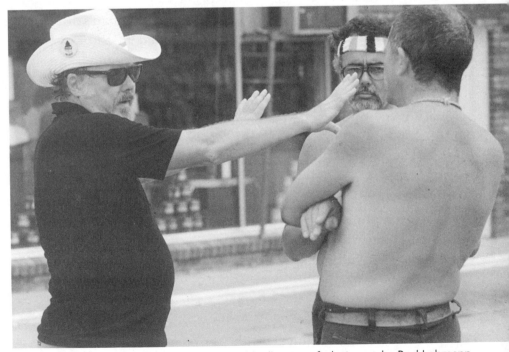

Altman (left) discusses a scene with director of photography Paul Lohmann (right) and assistant director Tommy Thompson. (*Jim Coe*)

more lines, some would have more songs, many would suffer the bruising disappointment of seeing their best stuff sacrificed in the cutting room. But there were to be no stars, no divas pulling rank. And that equitable worker-ant division of labor would reflect itself in the audience's experience of the characters. While there would never be any question of the social hierarchy that determined a character's actions, our sense of who was chasing after whom in *Nashville*'s circular golden-goose chain of ambition-seekers would rarely be that cut-and-dry.

In this manner, a reigning country queen could be holding an airport crowd in her thrall one moment and crawling before her manager-husband in another. A farmer's wife with dreams of cutting a record could be snubbed by the country queen's understudy one day and upstage them both the next. A groupie from Los Angeles could walk into a Nashville music club on the arm of the son of a Grand Ole Opry star and walk out with a biker she'd never met before. A journalist who has been bounced out of a country singer's recording session could end up sleeping with a folk singer, who would end up sleeping with a gospel singer, whose district-attorney husband is in bed politically with the campaign handler of a presidential candidate who is using them all.

It was, in short, the antithesis of what is often called the high-concept picture, the movie that can be summed up in two sentences in terms readily available to a pre-Pokémon age group. Over the sixty days that followed this Fourth of July weekend roast, hundreds of firecrackers exploded before a Panavision camera. For every dud, and God knows there were duds, there were dozens of comets and star-bursts. As with any pyrotechnic display, the desired elements could be programmed in advance, but the final outcome would be left to the forces of nature and chance.

Somehow, it worked. Big-time. And somehow, it all got done before Labor Day. It had to. Altman was working on one tight-assed budget. The last thing he needed was to spring for one more holiday barbecue.

CHAPTER ONE

ROBERT ALTMAN GOES TO A JOHN DENVER CONCERT

(Wherein a Horny Young Actor Writes a Love Song and Elvis Presley's Booking Agent Sells His First Movie)

"Robert Altman is like a good sheriff in a bad town."
—TOM WAITS

WHEN PEOPLE SPEAK OF ROBERT ALTMAN'S old Lion's Gate offices in Westwood, dammit if you don't usually hear a sigh trail after. For those who drifted in and out during its glory days from late sixties to the late seventies, Lion's Gate was an oasis. Part production office, part salon, part saloon, it evolved into a drop-in center that provided actors succor and a sense of community in an isolating industry town. It was the nurturing mom-and-pop watering hole we all embroider in our memories as we grouse about how impersonal human transaction has become. Like Woodstock, it could only have happened then.

Altman named his former production company with the offhandedness of someone who is used to shrugging off gems of dialogue out of thin air moments before the camera rolls. His attorney was pressing him for a name so he could incorporate. Robert Altman Productions? No, not that, Altman said, characteristically shunning the obvious. Staring up at him from his desk was a book about Vancouver, where he had just shot *That Cold Day in the Park.* On its cover, a photo of the Lion's Gate Bridge. He looked at the picture and announced, "We'll call it Lion's Gate."

As with so many beloved sanctuaries, Lion's Gate had its origins in turbulence. During the mid-sixties, Altman had signed a year's contract with Universal, during which he directed episodes of *Kraft Suspense Theatre.* At Universal, as in his earlier television jobs, Altman was invariably locking horns with "the suits," who were always checking over their shoulders to see what the sponsors were going to think. It couldn't have helped matters that Altman's chief boss and nemesis, Roy Huggins, named names before the House UnAmerican Activities Committee in 1952.

While at Universal, Altman forged an alliance with a producer named Ray Wagner. Together, they rented a two-story complex at 1334 Westwood Boulevard, two blocks south of Wilshire, and planted the seeds of what would become Lion's Gate. One of their maiden efforts was a novel that Altman had acquired from a dentist named John Haase who lived down the block from him. Titled *Me and the Arch-kook Petulia,* it concerned a divorced doctor and his relationship with an eccentric, free-spirited young woman.

The project soon collapsed amid a dispute over Altman's work on *Nightwatch,* a TV cop-show pilot with Carroll O'Connor. The partnership finally split in a rancorous deal that gave Altman sole rights to the ill-fated TV series and Wagner rights to the Haase book. Altman watched ruefully from afar as the freewheeling script he had so closely nurtured with writer Barbara Turner was handed over to writer Lawrence B. Marcus and director Richard

Lester. The resultant film, *Petulia,* would be deemed one of the defining screen comedies of the late sixties.

Left with the lease on 1334 Westwood, Altman transformed the two-story commercial complex into a fantasy of masculine Old World charm: dark plank floors, wrought iron fixtures, distressed plaster walls, scalloped cornices atop the doors. Ignoring city ordinances, Altman converted one of the garages in the back alleyway into an illegal screening room. Upstairs were offices for Altman's chief *consiglieri:* line producer Robert Eggenweiler, whom he knew from his Universal days, and assistant director Tommy Thompson, a friend and associate dating back to Altman's stint helming *Whirlybirds* for Desilu in the fifties. Eventually, Altman installed an apartment upstairs for himself as well.

On the main floor, three adjacent rooms with separate entrances spilled out onto a courtyard, where one could enjoy the services of a barber, a travel agent, and a sandalmaker. One room was the prowling grounds of Altman's production-office watchdog and jack-of-all-trades, Scott Bushnell. Altman presided in the rear office next to a white-mantel fireplace, a few sofas, and a pool table. Visitors would reach him by entering a warm central re-

Actor Scott Glenn, one of the Lion's Gate denizens.
(*Jim Coe*)

ception room furnished with more couches and a bar. "It was like a men's club that admitted women," recalls Thompson. "Actors would come in the evening, the bar was open, and they'd schmooze."

"It was just sort of a hangout place for friends of Bob's," remembers actor Scott Glenn. "Very often when I would finish work at the end of the day or my martial arts classes in Santa Monica, I'd just drop by Lion's Gate to see who was there. People would be sitting around reading poetry or bullshitting with Bob about football. Gary Busey might be playing a guitar. It wasn't about careers or networking, like now I'm meeting Bob Altman and I'm going to get a job.'"

Despite Altman's concerted efforts to take the business out of doing business, visitors would frequently walk out with employment. Half the fun of going to Lion's Gate, though, was not knowing what you were going to walk *into* once you stepped in the courtyard.

In 1972, a young man with a budding reputation as an assistant director received a call from Tommy Thompson, wondering if he might be interested in being second assistant on an Altman film to be called *The Long Goodbye*. The prospect, Alan Rudolph, couldn't have been less enthusiastic. He hadn't yet seen *MASH,* a cinematic epiphany of 1970 that invariably converted the nonbelievers, and he gleaned a vague notion from *That Cold Day in the Park* that Altman was "some guy from Canada."

Rudolph viewed the offer as a demotion. Moreover, he had been unimpressed with the regimentation and lack of creative input that were an a.d.'s lot. If that weren't enough, he had just come from a sour interview for an a.d. position in which he was told he would have to cut his hair.

For young men surviving the early seventies, hair was an issue. *Hair* was a Broadway hit. Hair was how you aligned yourself along the cultural divide that separated good soldiers and conscientious objectors, love-it-or-leave-it patriots and Hanoi Janes, Archie Bunkers and effete intellectual snobs. Since Altman's own sympathies leaned toward the rebel, Lion's Gate would occasionally take on the unshorn appearance of a young anarchists' league. Even Altman and Thompson brandished unstatesman-like beards that, transformed to a wintry gray as the years passed, made them resemble the fabled Smith Brothers on the cough drop box.

Thompson finally flattered Rudolph enough to get him in for a chat, but not before the reluctant a.d. explained tersely over the phone that he had long hair and had no intentions of cutting it. ("Not knowing," Rudolph later confessed, "I was walking in to the two people for whom I probably couldn't have hair long enough.") Rudolph arrived at Lion's Gate, wandering uncertainly into Thompson's office. Thompson, whose fondness for a good jest was honed during his years producing for Lucille Ball, introduced himself as Altman. "He was having fun with me," re-

Altman flanked by *Nashville*'s second assistant director Alan Rudolph (left) and first assistant director Tommy Thompson (right). (*Jim Coe*)

calls Rudolph. "We talked a bit, then he laughed and said, 'I'm not really Altman. But why don't you come and meet him?' So I followed Tommy in. Bob was at his desk. He looks up from his desk, and the first thing he says to me is, 'Cut your hair.'"

The year before, a twenty-one-year-old college dropout with hair reaching well below his shoulders sauntered into Lion's Gate. Unlike his father and older brother, he hadn't had much in the way of acting experience. But the entertainment business looked as if it might be rescuing him from an aimless hippie existence. He had tagged along with his older half-brother to an audition for the Los Angeles company of *Hair* and had walked out with a lead role. Now he'd heard that Robert Altman had a role in a new picture called *McCabe & Mrs. Miller* for a sweet cowboy who meets a bad end. And sweetness, if you ask those who worked with him, was second nature to Keith Carradine.

The actor recalls his first meeting with the director. "He was up in his apartment in his robe and bathroom slippers, unwrapping some package he'd just received from Colombia . . . I didn't know what *that* was," he said, chuckling conspiratorially at the ubiquitousness of marijuana at Altman's social gatherings. "And he'd unwrap this package, which turned out to be pre-Columbian art, sort of glance at me, ask me questions. 'So, did you read the script?' I'd say, 'Yeah.' 'Did you like the part?' 'Yeah, seems great.' ''Dja like to play it?' I said, 'Yeah.' He said, offhandedly, 'Okay.' And then he added, 'I don't know about the hair.' That was my audition."

In this instance, Altman wasn't kidding about the hair. He needed a cowboy with heart. Soon after *McCabe*, he would need a bank robber with heart, circa 1930s, for *Thieves Like Us*. So Carradine was once again drafted to play an ill-fated Altman character.

One Sunday two or three weeks into the filming of *Thieves Like Us* in Mississippi, Altman gave a party for the cast and crew. It was a weekend idyll of the sort that would become an Altman staple during the making of *Nashville*. Carradine recalls, "It was hot, and he had this wonderful big house that he was renting, set upon a hilltop with a knoll of grass rolling away into the trees. [In a subsequent interview, Kathryn Altman insisted the house belonged to *Thieves* producer Jerry Bick]. We were sitting there relaxing, and I took my guitar, which was something I almost always did in those days. I was never much good at the Top Forty. I could only play what I had written."

Breaking into a reedy, unvarnished tenor, Carradine serenaded the party with two of his original songs. The first was a folky anthem written for a Robert Aldrich movie he'd recently made with Lee Marvin and Ernest Borgnine called *Emperor of the North*. The song, with its blue-afternoon melody and Woody Guthrie–redolent sentiments, was perfectly tailored to this Depression-era tale of tramping on the railroads. (Aldrich opted in favor of the bland Hollywood studio composer Frank De Vol). The lyric to "It Don't Worry Me" was a hobo's wrinkle on all those bowl-of-cherries numbers about smiling down hard times.

> The price of bread may worry some,
> But it don't worry me
> And tax relief may never come
> But it don't worry me
> Economy's depressed, not me.
> My spirit's high as it can be.
> And you might say that I ain't free
> But it don't worry me.

The second song spoke of freedom as well, but the emotional terrain it chartered was far more confessional. "I'm Easy" was written during the run of *Hair*. Carradine was pushing twenty at the time and trying to get to first base with one of his costars, the "Frank Mills" girl Shelley Plimpton. He had his work cut out, as she was seeing another guy.

> It's not my way to love you just when no one's lookin'
> It's not my way to take your hand if I'm not sure
> It's not my way to let you see what's goin' on inside of me

Keith Carradine in *Nashville*. His songs "I'm Easy" and "It Don't Worry Me"
helped inspire Altman to make a movie.

When it's love you won't be needing, you're not free.
Please stop pullin' at my sleeve if you're just playin',
If you won't take the things you make me want to give
I never cared too much for games, and this one's drivin' me insane
You're not half as free to wander as you claim.
But I'm easy, I'm easy
Give the word, I'll play your game as though that's how it ought to be
Because I'm easy.

"I just wanted to get laid," admitted Carradine twenty-nine
years later. He got his wish. Carradine and Plimpton were an
item for a few short months, long enough for his girlfriend to be-

come pregnant. Their baby, Martha Plimpton, would grow up to carry on in her parents' theatrical tradition.

Altman was dazzled by the numbers that Carradine sang for his party guests. "When I heard them I knew I wanted to base a whole movie around them, a movie that would simply give me an excuse to put them in," said the director.

If you inspect Joan Tewkesbury's earliest scripts for *Nashville*, you will find that "It Don't Worry Me" and "I'm Easy" are the only "original" songs included. There is a sense of the screenplay having been constructed around the songs, which recur amid a jukebox menu of country warhorses such as "Okie from Muskogee" and "D–I–V–O–R–C–E." Altman would soon scuttle the country standards in favor of a completely original score, of which Carradine's contributions (along with Ronee Blakley's) provide the most potent musical moments. And as if the director's faith needed any more vindication, "I'm Easy" would succeed in garnering *Nashville* its sole Oscar.

KEITH CARRADINE'S teenage love call would also turn the tide for a picture that no one was begging to buy. Least of all Altman's early seventies benefactor, United Artists.

Now vaunted as the grand patriarch sage of today's independent American directors, Altman and his particular brand of individualism were not always viewed by the industry with the sort of affection they are accorded today. In theory, the seventies in which Altman's film career came of age should have been welcoming. Emboldened by the political tumult of the sixties and an atmosphere of protest that triggered such profitable orgies of alienation as *Easy Rider, Medium Cool, If . . .,* and *Joe,* Hollywood was suddenly convulsed by fits of daring that would pass almost as quickly as they appeared.

It was a director's decade, hospitable to the rabble rouser who glommed on to Hollywood's temporary seizures to make big-screen personal statements the likes of which had never been seen before and would not be seen again for some time to come.

It helped, of course, if you had already proved you could play to the great unwashed. Mike Nichols could be green-lighted for a corrosive skewering of the male ego called *Carnal Knowledge,* having made the box office (and record stores) ring with a sleek crowd pleaser called *The Graduate.* Francis Ford Coppola was entitled to dissect Watergate-era paranoia in *The Conversation,* but his passion for that unsettling art film had to be put on the back burner till *The Godfather* shot its way into the popular vernacular. Stanley Kubrick could get his satire of ultraviolence, *A Clockwork Orange,* underwritten by the same studio that produced George Cukor's *A Star Is Born,* but not before altering the zeitgeist with such wide-screen spectacles as *Spartacus* and *2001: A Space Odyssey.* The welcome mat that Altman had earned with the grand slam of *MASH* (a Fox release) in 1970 was already fraying by 1973. Altman had thrown United Artists a curveball with his patently irreverent treatment of the Raymond Chandler's *The Long Goodbye.* They had hoped for a smoothly turned film noir, with a shot of seventies Technicolor. What they got was a quirky tone poem on the dissolute fringe culture of contemporary L.A., with Elliott Gould as the most laid-back Philip Marlowe in the history of film.

The film had followed a rocky road to realization. Peter Bogdanovich, who had been set to direct the film for United Artists, hoped to land more conventionally tough-guy actors like Robert Mitchum and Lee Marvin in the Philip Marlowe role. He was not enamored of Elliott Gould, the favored Marlowe of U.A. production chief David Picker. Bogdanovich would soon be replaced by Robert Altman, who had no doubt in his mind that Elliott Gould "was" Marlowe.

The shooting itself was fraught with potholes. Sterling Hayden had serious drinking problems, and Gould almost drowned in a climactic scene in which Marlowe tries to pull Hayden's suicidal character in from the ocean. When the picture premiered in Los Angeles, it was almost singlehandedly killed by *Los Angeles Times* critic Charles Champlin.

Elliott Gould recalls, "I didn't realize we were taking on not only an Establishment but a tradition of the character. It opened in L.A. with a poor campaign; it was unclear and dishonest, in terms of what Bob was making. By putting it in the present he had really broken the mold."

Altman pulled the picture and redesigned the ad campaign for New York. With help from an ecstatic Pauline Kael review in *The New Yorker,* the film did respectably well.

The experience, however, had not endeared the director to the studio execs, who were now threatening to put the brakes on Altman's imminent adaptation of Edward Anderson's 1937 novel, *Thieves Like Us,* a somber piece about bank robbers on the lam from prison. It had been filmed once before in a souped-up version by Nicholas Ray in 1948 as *They Live by Night,* but Altman wanted to hug tighter to the book. That meant more character development, mood, and period nuance, less romanticism and in-your-face action of the sort that jiggles the box-office receipts.

Instead, U.A. was eager for him to take a crack at a script called *The Great Southern Amusement Company.* The film company had been scouting for projects for their record division. This star vehicle set in the arena of country music seemed just the ticket for the screen debut of Welsh sensation Tom Jones, who had kicked up some sound-track paydirt with Burt Bacharach and Hal David's title song for *What's New, Pussycat?*

Altman took one look at it and recoiled. "It was a movie script!" he grumbled, damning it with the lowest insult he could imagine. But he was intrigued by the milieu it depicted. Loretta Lynn had been featured on the cover of *Newsweek* that fall, and suddenly everyone, it seemed, was bonkers for country music.

So this is what he told them: You get my cast and crew to Jackson, Mississippi, to do *Thieves Like Us,* and I'll deliver a Nashville picture.

United Artists would underwrite research trips to Nashville for *Thieves Like Us* neophyte screenwriter Joan Tewkesbury. But they would soon begin to feel as if their hopes of whipping up a suitable hit-parade film project for their record division had come a cropper. "A downer," U.A. production head David Picker is purported to have said in looking over Altman's *Nashville* proposal. "This is not a movie."

No one is certain anymore as to what precisely David Picker was given to inspect. It is not even clear whether he actually saw Tewkesbury's first screenplay, or a treatment. Altman has a history of finagling movie deals on the basis of little more than chutzpah and a title. This was famously the case with *3 Women,* birthed in a troubling time in which Altman's wife Kathryn was ailing. Altman was in serious need of work as well. He had just pulled out of a Middle East war drama to star Peter Falk, *Easy and Hard Ways Out,* over an argument with the movie's headstrong young producer, David Geffen, who wanted to set the film somewhere else.

Altman woke up in the middle of the night from a disturbing dream. "I woke up with this idea,"Altman recalls. "I took this pad at the side of my bed and wrote it down. Put it back. Went back to sleep. I woke up again, wrote something else down, the names of the actors who would star in it. The title, *3 Women.* Put it down and went back to sleep. I woke up again and two of my production people were in the bedroom. And I said 'Go to Palm Springs and try to find me a place that looks—.' And of course I don't keep a notepad by my bed. I hadn't written anything down. I woke up and this thing was so vivid that it worked. But I had no story. I knew the actors, knew it took place in the desert. I called this woman who worked for me and said I had come across a short story last night that sounds like it might be a pretty good genre piece. She said, 'It sounds good; can you get the rights?' I said, 'Yeah, I think so.' I went into Alan Ladd, who had just taken over Fox, and he said, 'Go ahead, make it.' And I think within eleven days we were in Palm Springs filming."

Picker, who now considers *Nashville* to be one of Altman's finest pictures, recalls his response to the material with decided reluctance: "There were probably a lot of reasons why we didn't go forward with *Nashville.* I do have a vague recollection of reading something that didn't make a lot of sense. It didn't get a lot of serious consideration because at that time it was unformed."

Picker also disputes the notion that *Nashville* would have been part of a trade for securing *Thieves Like Us,* as the latter picture was the guaranteed second half of a two-picture deal with *The Long Goodbye.* He does concede that U.A. was reeling from the fallout of those films, which were critically lauded but whose box office performance ranged from tepid to rotten. "It did not leave a very good taste in either Bob's mouth, or ours. *Thieves Like Us,* which I'm sure he thinks should have been treated better, was a disaster. *The Long Goodbye* was the source of—" He stops himself, then says, "It was very painful. I don't want to get into it. I'll save it for my book."

After U.A.'s swift goodbye, Altman received a New York party invitation out of the blue from lounge singer Jane Morgan. He didn't know the performer, or her producer husband Jerry Weintraub. But the director's reputation on the East Coast was still solid enough to sustain his positioning on the A party list. And the timing clicked. Altman was in town. Altman liked a good party. Altman went.

The occasion was to celebrate the Carnegie Hall headlining debut of an on-the-brink folk singer with an early Beatles bob and a Huck Finn smile named John Denver. It was not Denver, however, but the show's opening act that set Altman thinking. Until recently, Bill and Taffy Danoff had been two-thirds of a folk trio called Fat Chance, of whom Denver comprised the final third. Once Denver decided to split off on his own, the Danoffs regrouped and went on to spin out such low-octane ditties as "Afternoon Delight."

At the party afterward, Altman told Weintraub he had a *Nashville* script that would be perfect for the duo if he could only get it off and running. Weintraub volunteered to look at the script, and something about it spoke to him.

Perhaps it spoke to his roots in the music business, dealing as it did with small people with big ambitions who muscle up to country legends. Weintraub was all of twenty-three when, as a junior talent agent for MCA, he finagled his way to the attention of Elvis Presley's manager, Colonel Tom Parker. Some people dreamed of seeing Elvis sing live, some dreamed of meeting him, others dreamed of sleeping with Elvis. Weintraub had dreams of big signs in front of Madison Square Garden that read JERRY WEINTRAUB PRESENTS ELVIS PRESLEY. He was determined to produce Presley even if it meant having to phone Parker every day for a year to win his trust. Which he did.

At the time Altman met Weintraub, the now-multimillionaire tour producer of Elvis and Sinatra was angling to get into the movie business. The mandate that Altman handed Weintraub was, in essence, the same one that Colonel Parker had thrown at the young-pup agent sixteen years earlier. "I gave him whatever I had," says Altman, "and said, 'Get this picture made.'" Parker had needed one million to get Elvis on the road and gave Weintraub two days to find it. Altman needed at least twice that much, and Weintraub delivered it in three days. That, at least, was the mythology according to Altman, but it made for good copy.

In truth, it would take Weintraub a little longer to pull it together. And once again, *Nashville* inched a step closer to reality through the unwitting link of John Denver.

Martin Starger was the president of programming at ABC when Jerry Weintraub first made his acquaintance. "Jerry was and is a great salesman," insists Starger, who at the time had formed the network's entertainment division. "He convinced my manager of talent, Frank Brill, that John Denver was going to be a big star. We didn't know who the hell John Denver was at that point."

ABC signed Denver to a deal for specials, and the singer soon fulfilled Weintraub's prophecy to the profit of all concerned. By the time he approached Starger with what he claimed was a wonderful idea for a movie, Starger knew to take his friend seriously.

In order to keep Starger on board as the president of the entertainment division, ABC had offered him a three-year carte blanche deal: They would underwrite a movie of his own choice for which they would own the television rights. It was with this in mind that Weintraub pitched *Nashville*.

Starger responded to the proposal with cautious enthusiasm,

the caution being reserved for its director. "He had made a couple of movies that didn't work after *MASH* and was getting a reputation of 'God, he's imposssible, he's this, he's that, all kinds of
problems. He carries a lot of baggage.' I didn't know personally
any of that. It's easy to say now, but I was very taken with Joan
Tewkesbury's script. It seemed to me that it was right for the time."

Altman had been around the block enough to know the value
of a couple of cocktails in a beautiful setting. Inviting Starger and
Weintraub to his oceanfront home in Malibu, Altman played a
tape of Carradine singing "I'm Easy" and "It Don't Worry Me."
The producers were captivated. Starger, still antsy, laid out his
concerns: that Altman would be uncontrollable and go over
budget.

"We made the deal. I said, Jerry, you have to be on top of it,
that it comes in on budget. And the first dollars over the budget,
were it to go over, were to be out of Bob's salary."

"It was really Bob who produced that movie, economically

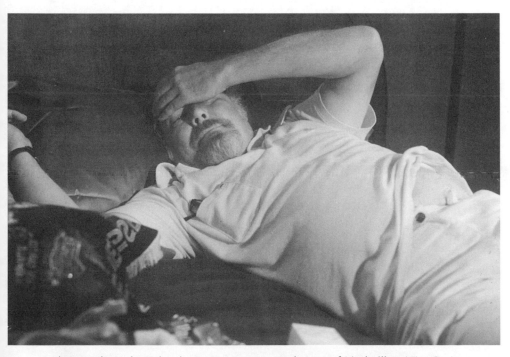

Altman takes a breather between scenes on the set of *Nashville*. (*Jim Coe*)

speaking," claims Sam Cohn, his agent of twenty-five years. "Marty was in effect the studio executive."

Nashville was sold. For $2.2 million, Robert Altman, "producer," would have to employ twenty-four lead actors and an untolled number of supporting actors, a screenwriter, a cinematographer, a music director, an editor, a sound editor, recording mixers, graphic artists, production assistants, teamsters, a publicist, not to mention a presidential campaign and rights to fifteen original songs and God knows what else would come down the pike before this damn movie got done. Upping the ante, his paycheck was on the line, possibly along with his credibility and his career.

Robert Altman had learned a lot of filmmaking skills way back when in Kansas City. He had learned how to gamble, as well. Now he was going to have to learn how to be a magician.

CHAPTER TWO

JOAN GOES TO MUSIC CITY

*(Wherein Peter Pan's Understudy Flies into
Never-Never Land and Gets Stuck in Traffic)*

THE EXIT/IN SITS TODAY IN the same place where it has always sat, just past the bend where Church Street turns into Elliston Place. You'll find it a few feet down from T.G.I.F.'s and a few feet up from an olde English pub. Just across the way is a takeout joint called the New York Deli, featuring a typical hybrid of over-stuffed pizzas, hoagies, and what-you-will that is someone's idea of how people eat on the fly in Manhattan. If you're staying downtown, getting there is a five dollar cab ride, past a listless parade of warehouses, train tracks, storefronts, and parking lots serving nowhere in particular.

Nashville is the sort of place in which, if the ad tells you the show starts at 7:00, people arrive at 7:00. Should you get to the Exit/In fifteen minutes early, you'll think you've gotten the wrong night. The lights are way, way up, exposing a spartan black box of a space riddled with small, Formica-top tables with fake-wood veneers. The chairs are still ass-upward on the tabletops. The smell of ammonia taints the air, but not so much as a mop or a pail is around to claim responsibility.

Congregating around high chairs toward the back are a cluster of skinny men and women clad in the tight black pants, vests, and cowboy boots of certified musicians. They are swigging Diet Cokes and waiting their turn while a trio rehearses up on the stage. "Say it with flowers at my wedding," croons a curly-topped fellow to a country rock beat, "and I won't forget to put roses on your grave." Behind the bar, a barely legal kid with shoulder-length brown hair hoists a glass and spritzes a soda for one of the musicians. Should you ask him if there is a show tonight, he'll grin conspiratorially and say, "In theory."

Blanketing the right wall is an Opry-buffet menu of singers and spielers given a Jay Leno infusion: Johnny Cash, Muddy Waters, Ronnie Milsap, Billy Joel, Jimmy Buffett, Odetta, Steve Martin, Dan Fogelberg, Harry Chapin, Kris Kristofferson, Cheech and Chong, Dr. Hook, the Ramones, and on and on. At 6:45 P.M., it's hard to imagine any of these folks creating magic in this overlit mine shaft of a room.

Then 7:00 P.M. rolls around and, as if someone waved a wand, the chairs come down, the audience files in, the glaring lights above give way to candles glowing from netted glass bowls on the tables. On cue, a pretty waitress swoops in to satisfy everyone's beverage need, and the place crackles with possibilities.

Joan Tewkesbury smelled those possibilities one spring evening in 1973. It was a different Exit/In then. The stage was over against the long wall, just beneath where the honor roll is now plastered. The bar was in another corner. Wooden banquettes and paneling, long gone, gave the place a kitschy, warrenlike warmth. More people smoked then, more drank hard liquor. Still, the essential Exit/In hasn't changed. One comes here now, as did Tewkesbury back then, to catch the hot young country-music dreamers cut their teeth.

Arriving by herself, the thirty-seven-year-old film-director wannabe from Redlands, California, took a seat in the back row, just as Lily Tomlin's Linnea Reese would do in the script that Tewkesbury had come to research. The room was filthy with industry types that night, overfed music producers battling over million-dollar contract negotiations and attempting to hit on the waitresses. Onstage a group called Barefoot Jerry played their

Keith Carradine, Cristina Raines, and Allan Nicholls perform
"Since You've Gone" at the Exit/In.

guitars meaningfully while singing "the words to this song don't
mean a thing." Radio mikes picked up their self-effacing message
from the din and spun it out live across the airwaves.

As Tewkesbury cocked an ear to filter the music and chatter, a
middle-aged black man sidled up to her and extended a hand.
James Broadway, he said, making her acquaintance. Broadway
told her that he had recently gotten out of jail, where he had
served twenty-six years for murder. He said he killed the man his
wife had been sleeping with, then studied law while in jail to help
get himself out. His new gig was working two back-to-back shifts
as a nurse at a local hospital. He would come to the Exit/In after
his second shift finished at eleven and stay till they threw him out
at four in the morning. Didn't much like to sleep, he said. Considered it a waste of time.

Broadway shoved a joint up her sleeve, then asked his table companion what her story was. When Tewkesbury explained she was a writer, he responded, "You should come with me to the prison, they'll give you stories." I'll bet they will, she thought, shifting her attention toward a young woman at a nearby table who was zoning out on a recreational drug of the moment.

Tewkesbury sipped her beer, and drank in the room.

THIS WAS not the first time that Joan Tewkesbury had come to Nashville. Back in the fall of seventy-three, she had gone down to soak up some atmosphere at the behest of Robert Altman. It was a kind of reconnaissance mission: go, do, take notes. He had initially asked her if she had any interest in tinkering with a cruddy script called *The Great Southern Amusement Company.* She responded with the sort of leathery, shoot-from-the-hip frankness that had ingratiated her to the salty Altman. "I don't want to rewrite anyone else's material," she said, and that was that.

Tewkesbury had her own fish to fry. In months prior, she had whipped up a screenplay about the disillusionment of divorce called *After Ever After.* In it, she charted with comedic bravado the breakdown of her nine-year marriage to land developer Robert Maguire. She wanted to direct the film, and she wanted Geraldine Chaplin to play the character Tewkesbury had modeled on herself.

The script impressed Altman, who nurtured Tewkesbury's aspirations, as he soon would those of his second assistant director Alan Rudolph, and, twenty-five years later, those of a young script supervisor named Anne Rapp. The latter would repay his investment with the screenplays for *Cookie's Fortune* and *Dr. T and the Women.* Mentoring young talent has always been an Altman specialty. "It invigorates him," attests Sam Cohn. "Besides, he's done every job there is to do on a movie from his Kansas City days. He knows that if the whole crew was on a bus and it got into an accident, he could take over and do it himself."

Altman flew Chaplin in from Switzerland. He and Tewkesbury

Nashville screenwriter Joan Tewkesbury on the set.

were instantly enamored of the twenty-eight-year-old daughter of Charles and Oona O'Neill Chaplin. Chaplin stayed with Tewkesbury, who took the actress on a tour of all the major sites of her married life.

It was to no avail. Altman couldn't scare up the funds to finance his unknown female auteur. He would have significantly better luck negotiating the directing debut of Alan Rudolph, *Welcome to L.A.*, which starred Chaplin. Acknowledging defeat, he returned to Tewkesbury and asked, "Do you mind not starting at the top?"

The director was about to head up to Vancouver to launch the filming of *McCabe & Mrs. Miller.* He recalls his conversation with Tewskesbury. "She said, 'I want to observe.' I said nobody can observe, a person can't go on a movie set and observe. You'll observe nothing. And you'll be in the way and you'll get nothing out of it. The only way is to have to work."

Altman made a skeptical Tewkesbury his script girl, saying,

"I think you can do it. You're quiet." It was a suitable trial by fire. In typically Altmanesque fashion, the script was an ever-metamorphosing creature, with dialogue being made up by actors in rehearsals, the night before shoots, on the spot. Toughened by three summers of a high-intensity rehearsal regimen with the University of Southern California theater department that demanded dramaturgical know-how in combination with a capacity for thinking on one's feet, Tewkesbury proved up to the task of the impulsive rewrites.

When Altman is happy with his team members, he tends to move them right into his next picture. Tewkesbury was asked back, with a promotion.

A *Thieves Like Us* script by Calder Willingham had been kicking around, but Altman didn't think much of it. Instead, he asked Tewkesbury to dispense with it altogether and transcribe Anderson's novel into script form as accurately as possible. (Willingham is cocredited with the screenplay, by contractual obligation.) As Tewkesbury launched into that project, Altman turned his gaze toward Nashville. Country music? What did he know? He was from Kansas City, a jazz lover with a curiosity for opera and classical and just about anything else musical. When it came to country-speak, the man was illiterate.

Altman turned to Tewkesbury and asked her if she knew anything about country-western music.

"No."

"Would you like to learn?"

"NASHVILLE THE city is at least ostensibly controlled by its men," wrote Helene Keyssar, "but *Nashville* the movie is made whole and compelling by its women." If, like so many writers, Joan Tewkesbury likes to see herself in all of her characters, it is the women of *Nashville* who most reveal their inventor. Except for a willowy, glass unicorn of a singer named Barbara Jean, these women are survivors: ambitious, shrewd, plucky, resourceful, sexy, assertive, acerbic, tireless, mildly eccentric, in

varying measures foolish and deluded, and, if not utterly independent, at least yearning to breathe free in a big way.

All of this, give or take, also described Joan Tewkesbury when
she fell into the writing of *Nashville*. In many ways, her résumé
for the task was perfect: a helter-skelter track of Tinseltown ambition and hopes, not all of them her own. Born in 1936, Joan
was one of a generation of Hollywood daughters whose mothers
had determined while they were still in swaddling clothes that
they would grow to become Shirley Temple. By the time she was
three, she was hustled into that pint-sized primer in sado-
masochism known as dancing classes.

Condemned to daily classes at the Maglin Dancing School for
the duration of her adolescence, the young Joan yearned for a
normal childhood. At ten, she was cast with thirty-five other little
girls in a Margaret O'Brien vehicle called *The Unfinished Dance*, a
title that would provide an apt portent of her future as a hoofer.
Injuries sustained in an automobile accident as a teenager would
scuttle Tewkesbury's budding career, but not before two encounters that later would be key to the evolution of *Nashville*. As she
left high school, Jerome Robbins came to California to cast *Peter
Pan*. The eighteen-year-old Tewkesbury, as it happened, was
about the same height and weight as the show's star, Mary Martin. She was signed as Martin's stand-in, which consisted primar-
ily of playing guinea pig to test the flying apparatus for the star.
By way of reward, she got to play an ostrich.

Martin and her sexually closeted husband, Richard Halliday
would provide the prototype for the asexual axis between
Nashville's reigning country princess, Barbara Jean, and her ma-
jordomo spouse, Barnett.

"Mary was being pursued by all the wrong men," claims
Tewkesbury. "Halliday took her aside at the swimming pool and
said, 'You want a career, I'll build you a career. I need an heir.'
And he oversaw every degree of Mary's career. He was the business of the business.

"Throughout history there have been the backup men or
women to the stars' careers. They stand in the wings and mouth

the words to the songs. For example, Carol Burnett and her husband of the time, Joe Hamilton. Or the reverse of that, Martha Mitchell and her husband, John. All of these strong ladies are able to have a driving force that will take care of the business, the bad publicity. I don't want the political signs up behind my wife, I don't want this, I have to have that. A lot of that is coming from the diva, only the diva doesn't want to be seen in a bad light. So these guys take the heat so she is left to do whatever they do. And that is the cash register. "

The other encounter would come around 1960, after Tewkesbury enrolled in the University of Southern California on a theater arts scholarship. She was not above subsidizing her grant with the occasional chorus-girl gig. "I was doing chi-kunka-chi-

Gwen Welles as showbiz hopeful Sueleen Gay, inspired by Joan Tewkesbury's chorus-girl days in San Francisco.

kunka in Day-Glo bra and pants at the Village, a club in San Francisco. I'd had knee surgery so I couldn't do the other kind of dancing anymore, but I was choreographing for this line of girls. We were the opening act for Bud Abbott and Lou Costello, Dagmar, Johnny Ray. Just a bunch of dopey girls."

One of the dopey girls would provide the impetus for Sueleen Gay, the dreamstruck counter waitress whose jaw-dropping lack of talent made her the antithesis of her idol, Barbara Jean. "This girl looked like milk and honey, she was so beautiful. Could not sing for shit. Yet she was convinced she was going to be a singer. *Playboy* would come around to try and get her to take the five hundred dollars to do the centerfold, and she would say very honestly, 'When I take off my bra my tits just fall to my knees.' (She had these huge tits.) But every dime she earned went for these singing lessons that weren't going to work."

Tewkesbury piled up the units at USC without ever getting the degree, grabbing teaching jobs wherever they would let her. While at USC, she starred in *Guys and Dolls* opposite one of her students, a budding composer and performer named Richard Baskin. Years later, Baskin would become the musical director of *Nashville,* albeit through very different channels.

When Baskin first saw a script for *Nashville,* he never made the connection that the writer and his old student teacher were one and the same, as Tewkesbury was going by her married name in those USC days. In the years that Tewkesbury was married to Robert Maguire, raising two small children and living in the San Fernando Valley, she turned her attention from teaching to acting and directing workshop productions.

Her most rigorous training, an experience which would season her later on for her first Altman assignment, was a performance-intensive USC summer theater program helmed by John Blankenship that required its actors to do sixteen shows in repertory over four weeks. "You did four shows a day, and when you weren't doing the four shows, you were learning your lines for the next week." Tewkesbury returned for three summers of this punishment, with her two kids in tow.

One evening she went to check out a new movie that would charge her up like nothing had done since the original stage cast of *West Side Story* came to town. It was *MASH*. The spontaneity and immediacy of Altman's ragtag ensemble connected to her own experiments as a director, which leaned toward the then-cutting-edge trend of luring audiences around streets, parking lots, and storefronts for site-specific performances.

"I had a sense of participating with all those folks in that campground, wherever it was, in the middle of the Malibu mountains. And I said, 'Okay, Jesus, I don't know how to do this, but if I'm going to work for somebody, that's who I want to work with.'"

"It was at the point in her life where she was thinking, There is more to life than this," recalls Michael Murphy, who was becoming friends with Tewkesbury at the time. Murphy, a cast member from *MASH* and one of the Altman reliable since the director cast him on an episode of *Combat!*, suggested that she come down and participate in a little theater group in the Valley that he was a part of. Soon she was directing Murphy in workshop productions.

In one of the productions, Murphy's character listened passively as a woman played by Mariette Hartley yammered away nonstop for fifty minutes. One night, Robert Altman came to see the show.

Tewkesbury figured that was entrée enough. She phoned up his secretary, made an appointment, went in, and said, "I don't know exactly what I can do here. I have danced, acted. I've sold coffee on commercials. I want to work in film."

Barely a year later, as she was tweaking her screenplay for *Thieves Like Us*, Altman sent her to check out Nashville.

THE TRIP was a bust.

It was a chaperoned journey, lasting all of three days. When you burrow into a new town—particularly one as remote from Joan Tewkesbury's post-Woodstock consciousness as Nashville—

it helps to have contacts. Tewkesbury grabbed Bill and Taffy Danoff, whom Altman had met through Jerry Weintraub. They knew people, and were accustomed from their touring days with John Denver to having a fifth wheel.

The Danoffs arranged for Tewkesbury to hook up with a public relations mucky-muck from ASCAP, who took the three on the official tour of the city. It was like being herded around Moscow by Intourist, before glasnost.

"It was bullshit," recalls Tewkesbury. "We went to see ASCAP. Like who cares? To the country-western museum, where Patsy Cline's hairpins are displayed. And of course the Grand Ole Opry, the Ryman Auditorium. Every time you'd ask a question that was outside the party line—where do they play rock and roll?—they would get you back to Patsy Cline's hairpins."

Tewkesbury returned to L.A. empty-handed. She told Altman that the only way she was going to get anything useful would be if she were to go back again, by herself.

Winter came and went. And one day in spring, as Tewkesbury idled on the set of *Thieves Like Us* in Jackson, Mississippi, she and Altman figured it was as good a time as any for her to return to Music City.

She arrived at Nashville Airport amid chaos. Everyone was jockeying to catch a sighting of some unidentified visiting celebrity arriving in a private airplane. The airport was a hubbub of travelers and their welcome wagons, news hounds, and music fans. Tewkesbury finally rescued her bags and extracted herself from the crush, only to become ensnared in a traffic jam that backed up the freeway from the scene of an automobile accident.

Tewkesbury had a different strategy up her sleeve for visit number two. She was going to set out on her own, abetted by a few phone numbers of recording studio secretaries courtesy of Bill and Taffy. Using the Danoffs name as an entrée, she found out who was recording that week. Doors opened. Folks smiled and waved sweetly at this long-maned hippie chick from L.A. as she wandered in and out of recording sessions, where she met session musicians named after barnyard animals, like Pig, Mule, and Rooster. Wherever she went, she scrawled notes on her yellow legal pad. Opal from the BBC, the gate crashing Geraldine Chaplin character, was being born—albeit in a more retiring disguise.

Among those whom Joan/Opal observed was Loretta Lynn, singing in tandem with Conway Twitty. She was struck by the contrast between the singer's diminutive stature and enormous discipline. "It was one of the most exciting things I've ever seen in my life. And I came across a very important piece of information. Loretta Lynn spends a lot of time in the hospital. I asked why, and they said, 'She works too hard.'"

The revelation had particular resonance for Tewkesbury, reminding her of her Broadway-gypsy days with Martin. "Mary would literally go home at night and stay in bed till five o'clock

Lily Tomlin sings "Yes I Do" with the Fisk University Jubilee Singers, a gospel choir Joan Tewkesbury heard during a research trip to Nashville.

the next afternoon before going back to the theater. That became her whole frame of reference."

At a recording studio specializing in gospel music, Tewkesbury was electrified by group after group, tripping out on the spirit and speaking in tongues. One of them, the Fisk University Jubilee Singers, would be enlisted as Lily Tomlin's choir in the opening and closing of *Nashville*. While there, she hooked up with two hip young music engineers. She returned day after day, grilling them on every facet of the music business. When she asked them where to go to hear the happening music, they uttered two words, like a mantra: *exit in*.

JOAN TEWKESBURY sat in her chair in the rear of the Exit/In, drinking in the room and reflecting. She was finally in the midst of divorce from her husband after nine wayward years. She scandalized her chums by asking him to take care of the kids so she could strike out on her own: one didn't do such things in the pre–*Kramer vs. Kramer* era of the early seventies. More than anything, she recalls feeling it was a period of relief, a period of release.

As she sat in that music barn, she realized all at once that she had found her movie. Here, so it seemed, was the nucleus of the circular city that was Nashville. Anyone you saw at breakfast you'd inevitably see, later in the day, as if they had all been thrown back together by the centrifugal force of the city's ever-turning wheel. Somewhere in all of this was an overlapping circle of characters, butting up against one another through a linear series of events that would be shaped by her five-day visit.

And as she realized this, she also understood that she could not separate her experience of these people from the heady tide of events that was propelling her own course. The whoosh of independence that finally brought her to Nashville would inform so many of the characters who would begin to be born in the coming days. They would have names like Linnea, and Opal, and Winifred, and Sueleen, and L.A. Joan, and Mary, and Connie. They would all be on a mission of reinvention, attempting to catapult themselves away from the familiar and into something new. And as they did, they would be encountering smooth, charming men with a talent for manipulation, guys who called themselves Tom and Delbert and Haven and Triplette and Wade and the Tricycle Man and Hal Phillip Walker.

Joan Tewkesbury got up from her chair at the Exit/In. She bade so long to James Broadway, so long to the chick zoning out on drugs, so long to Barefoot Jerry. Grabbing her bag, she headed toward the door and exited into *Nashville*.

CHAPTER THREE

WILL THE CIRCLE BE UNBROKEN?

(Wherein Joan Tewkesbury Maps Dramatis Personae, Robert Altman Plots an Assassination, and a Production Designer Walks)

AFTER JOAN TEWKESBURY LEFT THE EXIT/IN, she made a beeline back to her hotel and banged out some words on a typewriter. "It was my version of a Joan Didion essay where she had been in a hotel room in Hawaii when the war broke out in Vietnam. Only I was in Nashville, looking at all the insanity of this silly town. Thinking about the separation of leaving my children, yet knowing there was something extremely potent at this moment in time in this city. Stringbean had been murdered, the English rock groups were coming in to check out the town, the politics of the country were in such a strange state. I couldn't get a grip on the material till I got a grip on the geography of the city. That pulled it together for me. I knew that Bob worked great within these constructs."

She phoned Altman, saying, "Your movie is in here somewhere. I'm not certain how it's going to translate. But I have a way to do this. It's a single story, without telling a single story." He responded, with mock impatience, "Yeah, yeah, sure."

When she next saw him, she showed him photos of a few potential locations, explaining how the city was built in a circle and how people's lives would naturally overlap on a daily basis. That struck a chord with Altman, who, according to Ned Beatty, had once said "he always wanted to do a movie where someone walks into a revolving door and somebody else comes out and then you go with that person."

Knowing Altman's penchant for the tragic denouement from her work on *McCabe* and *Thieves,* Tewkesbury said to him half-jokingly, "I suppose someone's going to have to die."

"I suppose."

Back at her home in Los Angeles, she drew up a list of characters. She then constructed a large graph, with the days of the week and the time of day written on the vertical edge and the characters' names written along the horizontal. Taping the graph to the wall, she systematically plotted out where each character would be, whom they would be with, when they would be there, and what they would be doing. She then supplemented her graph with separate yellow pieces of paper for each character, which she could move around like flags on a war map.

Some of the characters would be drawn from her first two visits to Nashville. Wade, ex-con and knight in blue-collar armor to Sueleen Gay, was a twist on James Broadway. Bill and Taffy Danoff, who had a partnership with John Denver, would provide the inspiration for the folksinging group Tom, Bill, and Mary. The role model for the womanizing Tom, often attributed to Warren Beatty, was actually country-rocker Jerry Jeff Walker. "Jerry Jeff was one of the first country guys I saw that really had balls," says Tewkesbury. "And he had a big rep with women."

Their chauffeur, Norman, was a modified take on the bumbling driver who shuttled Tewkesbury and the Danoffs around Nashville. Called Norman Bergmann in the early scripts, his real-life counterpart was the only Jewish person they had encountered during their first visit to the big city. He was usually late and invariably got them lost—in short, he was a regular *shmendrick.* "He was so in with the stars and into meeting famous people it was a nightmare," remembers Tewkesbury. "He ended up throwing up. I felt so sorry for him, I could have died." In the earliest scripts, Norman's chronic cookie-tossing becomes a running gag.

Intriguingly, the first scene that Tewkesbury wrote for *Nashville* was not set in Music City itself, but New York City. The scene, which was never filmed, finds Tom dashing across a traffic-snarled Times Square in the rain and into the offices of his record label to pick up a gold record he has earned with Bill and Mary. There is much jokey bantering between Tom and the secretary, who observes that the singer is not particularly beholden to his two partners. As Tom ruthlessly grabs a cab away from a lady shopper, the scene jumps to Haven Hamilton cutting a

David Arkin as Norman, modeled after a hapless limo driver Joan Tewkesbury met in Nashville. (*Jim Coe*)

record in a Nashville studio. It is this latter scene, juxtaposed with a shot of Hal Phillip Walker's campaign van turning out onto Nashville's lower Broadway, that would be used to introduce the film over the opening titles.

Tewkesbury explains the choice of the original New York City locale: "The whole music industry was still in New York. It was being pulled apart. The country-western thing had suddenly exploded in Nashville, but they still had to come to New York for getting paid, and business deals. Yet it was shifting in a very dramatic way. So we took Bill, Tom, and Mary, and had them coming out of this New York situation to work in Nashville."

The links that would inevitably be drawn between the movie's fictional country stars and real-life singers could be justified, to a point. Black country star Tommy Brown was indeed intended to be a surrogate for Charley Pride, down to the cowboy clothes.

While Barbara Jean and Connie White were universally considered to be thinly veiled caricatures of Loretta Lynn and Tammy Wynette, however, the similarities didn't extend all that far beyond hairstyles. If Barbara Jean's frailty may have owed something to Lynn's medical history, the former's crossover music style could only be attributed to her noncountry interpreter, Ronee Blakley. For all her hospital bills, Lynn is a survivor, and at the time of this writing was going full-throttle with the release of a new recording.

Connie White was conceived as a composite of several up-and-coming artists of the day. A last minute Opry fill-in for an ailing Barbara Jean, she is, according the screenwriter, the "personification of Nashville rivalries" and the prototype of "what Nashville music wanted its women to look like. Tammy Wynette. Dolly. These women are tough, but my God they believe in religion. Dolly is up at four in the morning writing her songs and saying her prayers and she is not bullshitting you about that. There is great heart to these women." When passed through the barbed filter of Altman and actress Karen Black, that openheartedness would be subsumed by a steely competitive edge.

The headiness of the author's newly won independence from her husband, coupled with the promise of her burgeoning movie career, would find a corresponding spirit in the drive and tenacity of her women characters. "If you look at Albuquerque, L.A. Joan, Mary, Opal, they are all facets of the same diamond. They are all girls looking to get out of these hideous little lives that were just coming out of the fifties. It had not been that long when it would have been unheard of for a girl to go out on the road, have a recording career, go with a guy who wasn't married. So this was the first generation of gals who put a knapsack on their back and hit the road."

Albuquerque, a recording-star wannabe perenially on the run from her husband, shared origins with Sueleen Gay in Tewkesbury's experiences as a nightclub dancer. But the writer also admits to using Altman regular Shelley Duvall, whom she got to know on the set of *Thieves Like Us,* as a prototype. "They are girls with ambition, that want to go somewhere, that know where the free meals are. They are very street savvy, and they know how to manipulate to get their needs met. Shelley wanted to get next to the action. Her survival techniques went into Albuquerque."

Duvall's drive to get in on the action would also spur her own character, L.A. Joan. As Tewkesbury wrote her, "She was one of those girls, and there were a lot of them at the time, who were disgruntled at home because they couldn't get close enough to fame. They had older relatives in New York, Los Angeles, Nashville, and would go anywhere with anyone for anything as long as they could to get next to fame."

L.A. Joan and Opal were prime examples of the complicated nexus that would soon emerge between the director, his writer, and their cast. While many of the characters would find their origins in Tewkesbury's travels and travails, they would eventually be transformed by a free-flowing exchange between the director's sensibility and the actor's own personality and history.

Opal, the barnstorming reporter from the British Broadcasting Company, was originally drawn from Tewkesbury's own vision

Shelley Duvall as L.A. Joan arrives at Nashville International Airport. Reflective glare masks a joke adjacent to Duvall: ALL PERSONS LEAVING CONCOURSE ARE SCREENED FOR WEAPONS.

of herself in Nashville: a Californian hippie chick invading foreign waters. That foreignness would be made more concrete after Altman and Tewkesbury attended the Cannes Film Festival in the late spring of 1973 and witnessed Geraldine Chaplin marauded by journalists. The pair were appalled at the audacity of the news hounds, and by what they perceived as an egregious invasion of privacy. (Accustomed to the public glare, Chaplin was entirely unfazed by the assault, later pooh-poohing any assumptions that Opal was intended as her vengeance upon the media. "I like journalists," she insists.)

Altman decided then and there he had found his Opal. Exploiting Chaplin's polyglot upbringing (British dad, Santa Monica birth, Swiss upbringing) she would become a British-sounding journalist of indeterminate origin and dubious credentials. Having been initially conceived as a surrogate for the screenwriter, she had become a stand-in for the director, who saw himself as barging paparazzi-style with his cameras into alien and potentially unreceptive waters.

Chaplin recounts her first instructions. "The original idea was that I was to do an absolute takeoff on Robert Altman in the movie. He said, 'In this movie, you're me. I just want you to follow me around, watch me, and imitate me.'"

For Altman, Opal was a device, a way to open up locked doors and carry the viewer from place to place. "She became a great tool," he explains. "She could always be the reason why 'I' showed up, my camera. She became a surrogate tour guide. I'm showing the audience, through her. She gave me access to the Tommy Brown van, for example, to set up that whole black-contained culture that was operating in a white Southern world."

Another one of Altman's so-called "tour guides," the Tricycle Man, found his prototype not in Nashville but in Jackson, Mississippi. One of the crew members on *Thieves Like Us* was a Hell's Angel with a theatrical wardrobe and a wizardlike aura. "He was short," recalls Tewkesbury, "had a great huge beard, icicle-blue eyes, wore yellow sunglasses and a bugle-beaded hat with a lot of black tulle on it that sort of shone on his head. He scared the shit out of people, but he had a kind of magic. If there was ever anything wrong and this guy drove by, there'd be a kind of sea change."

By the time she finished her graph, Tewkesbury had identified a total of eighteen characters. Over the next two weeks, she navigated them through a Friday-to-Tuesday itinerary in Nashville that climaxed in the requisite death, as ordained by her director. The victim would be buxom, no-talent Sueleen Gay, and she would die by her own hand.

Altman, however, had bigger game up his sleeve for the picture's end. Mulling over her screenplay from his desk at Lion's Gate, he had the notion to add in a political element to the film. "I said, 'This has to be something that matters here. This is what I'm going to do. There has to be a political assassination, but of the wrong person.'

"I thought it shouldn't be a political figure. It should be Barbara Jean. They never go after a woman. It's always been these guys, these politicians. And the minute that hit my mind, it exploded. I said, 'Wow, now I've got something!'"

Altman got an inkling of just how incendiary his whim would prove to be when Polly Platt staged a small-scale mutiny. Platt, who was crawling out of a troubled marriage with director Peter Bogdanovich, had become best buddies with Joan Tewkesbury during *Thieves Like Us*. Platt had asserted herself to useful effect on that film, offering answers to Altman's occasional design questions. He invited her aboard the *Nashville* train as a production designer, and she joined Altman, Tommy Thompson, Tewkesbury, and longtime Altman aide-de-camp Scott Bushnell on a location-scouting mission to the city. She returned with some strong ideas of her own.

Platt hated the assassination addition. "She thought Bob had wrecked the script," claims Tewkesbury. "But that's Polly. She really has opinions and she sticks to them." The Altman version: "She's a very ballsy woman. She was influencing Joan quite a lot at the time. Joan didn't like it either, as far as I can see."

When Platt and Tewkesbury went in to Altman to protest, according to the director, he stood firm. "I said, 'Well, then you're going to have to quit, because this is what I'm going to do.'"

Platt accepted the challenge, and walked off the picture.

Tewkesbury wasn't that bold, but she was frustrated. Having spent the better part of a month researching and mapping out a labyrinthine strategy for her characters, she was exasperated at the prospect of having to accommodate Altman's radically revised mandate.

"Sometimes these things will come to Bob, like that," she says, snapping her fingers. "He'll say, 'Okay, we're gonna do this.' And you're thinking, 'Ohhhhhh, fuck. How are you gonna get there?' Because you're the storyteller who has to lay it out, to give the actors some indication of what they're to do. You're the one that's tracking the logic, and he doesn't give a fuck about logic."

On some level, Altman pleads guilty. Ned Beatty, addressing a seminar of students at the American Film Institute who had just seen *Nashville,* commented that he thought Altman's weakness as a director was his laxness with storytelling. "He wanted to go where things led him. And as an actor I don't know what else to be strict about. If you took Bobby Duvall's performance out of *MASH,* you'd see a mess, a lot of behavior which is totally without sense. And I think Altman needs actors who are rigorous about storytelling."

Unbeknownst to Beatty, the remarks were published in the AFI magazine. Shortly after, he received a call from Altman, who said to the perplexed actor, "You know, you're right."

Tewkesbury decided to counter Altman's cockamamie logic with a provocative solution. She said to him, "Okay, then the nicest guy in the movie has to be the one that pulls the trigger." And that became Kenny.

Kenny Fraiser, a sweet-pussed loner who moves into a Nashville rooming house run by the aged Mr. Green, was initially modeled after, and intended for, Keith Carradine. "Keith was the nice guy," says Tewkesbury. "I used his quiet, weak, genuineness with people to establish how this young man comes into this old man's life." In an early script, Kenny was depicted as a tourist/ drifter from Terre Haute, Indiana, who "believes in everything he has been taught that is right, including God, the president, dirt breeds disease, and you might get the disease if you hang around any girl except your mother."

With a killer and a victim established, Altman knew they needed to invent a presidential candidate: not only to give the film a substantive political grounding but to provide the killer with a proper target so that a "wrong person" could take the bullet.

If they were going to plant a political candidate, they would need a fully conceived political campaign, a third-party spoiler replete with a detailed platform, a campaign truck, and campaign paraphernalia. And Altman knew just the man for the job.

CHAPTER FOUR

HOW TO INVENT A POLITICAL PARTY

*(Wherein Tarzan's Screenwriter Runs for President and an Ice Cream Heir from **Hair** Whistles Dixie)*

"Nobody knows the words. It is impossible to sing. You can't understand it. But Congress in its infinite wisdom gave us 'The Star Spangled Banner,' and I suppose all the lawyers voted for it because a lawyer wrote the words and a judge wrote the tune."
—FROM HAL PHILLIP WALKER'S CAMPAIGN LITERATURE

THE MISSISSIPPI FARM WHERE THOMAS HAL Phillips was born in 1922 was at least three miles away from anywhere and eight miles from somewhere. "Somewhere" was Corinth, a former Confederate hub whose sprawling repository of Civil War dead increased the town's population by half. "Anywhere" was Kossuth, a peaceable gathering of 238 or so folk who somehow managed to keep the cash registers ringing in three groceries, four filling stations, three blacksmiths, and a hotel. It was named for Louis Kossuth (rhymes with *go-shoot*), "the Hungarian Patriot" who emigrated to America in the 1850s to generate support for his cause. No one there seems to remember anymore that the cause was democracy, but he's fondly spoken of all the same.

Thomas's parents, William Thomas and Ollie Fare Phillips, moved their five sons to Kossuth in the early forties. Their mission was to get the family closer to the town's agricultural school, the most prestigious in the county. The Phillipses were poor, but the boys benefited from the erudition of their schoolteacher mother. Despite their youthful intimacy with the secrets of cotton and corn, Thomas Hal developed an aptitude for writing, his brother Rubel a flair for politics, and brother Frank an obsession with trucks. This peculiar splintering of family genes would prove beneficial to Robert Altman several decades later.

The most enduring effect of Thomas Hal Phillips's modest Depression upbringing was to confirm his status in later years as a dyed-in-the-wool Democrat. To the young Tom, Franklin Delano Roosevelt was God. He would later admire, if not exalt, JFK, Jimmy Carter, and, despite the blotch of scandal and impeachment, William Jefferson Clinton. His politics, coupled with his literary bent, certified Thomas Hal as a family anomaly. His brother Rubel founded the Mississippi Republican Party at a time when the notion of Southern Democrat had not yet achieved oxymoronic status. Rubel's slow-starting G.O.P. currently controls the state's legislative offices and has long dominated the Phillips clan voting record.

Thomas Hal Phillips has long since left the Phillips family residence in Kossuth for an apartment in Corinth, where he lives alone. He is a gracious, affable Southern gentleman of seventy-seven who speaks of Robert Altman with gratitude and a measure of awe.

When first introduced to Altman in 1972 through *Long Good-bye* producer Jerry Bick, Phillips was the chairman of the newly formed Mississippi Film Commission. His credentials for the job were a Faulkner–like mishmash of high literary achievements and low screenplay trenchwork. After leaving the Navy at twenty-three, Phillips attended the University of Alabama on the G.I. Bill and earned his masters in writing under Hudson Strode. His thesis was *The Bitterweed Path,* a gracefully turned antebellum novel with a potent homoerotic undertow. Published in 1950, it initiated the first of five novels whose writing would be subsidized by part ownership in his brother Frank's trucking business and Hollywood screenplay assignments on the order of *The Brain Machine* and *Tarzan's Fight for Life.*

Phillips and Altman hit it off like gangbusters, drawn perhaps by their good-humored rebel temperaments. Thanks to Phillips's easy charm and first-name acquaintance with high-level bureaucrats throughout the Deep South, Altman was able to sidestep immigration laws to hire French cinematographer Jean Boffety for *Thieves Like Us.* Phillips's access and insider's knowledge soon became indispensable, and he was made associate producer in tandem with longtime Altman organizer Robert Eggenweiler.

It was Phillips's experience on the mine field of politics that Altman recalled when it was time to plot a campaign for *Nashville.* In 1963, Phillips's brother Rubel ran for governor, enlisting Thomas Hal to write his speeches and stumping literature. Rubel never won, but no matter. Altman never intended his candidate to win either. He would be a spoiler, a third-party candidate. What's more, he would remain unseen throughout the film, until the final political rally. And Phillips would write his speeches, run his campaign, and, what the hell, "be" the candidate.

The inspiration for this mythical third party would grow, in part, out of Altman's theory of assassins: Political killers only go after big game so that they can inherit their fame. "The main reason they do it, the majority of them, is not for the politics, but for the statement. They don't assassinate people who aren't famous. It's almost like they replace them."

And when they switch their target to a singer, as Altman's assassin would do in this case, the celebrity in effect "replaces" the politician.

Enter the Replacement Party. Thomas Hal Phillips, novelist, screenwriter, and red-tape slasher extraordinaire, was now running for president in the phantom persona of Hal Phillip Walker.

The convergence of politics with good old-fashioned showbiz know-how had fueled the diminishing genre of American satirical cinema since before *The Great McGinty*. Now an American filmmaker was suggesting that the line between the two had blurred to the point where performers and politicians had become interchangeable. In the public eye, they were equally capable (or culpable) of embodying our values, courting our reverence, and fielding our contempt.

Whatever the impetus for Altman's political foray, the actual content of Walker's platform would be totally left up to Phillips. "He didn't give many instructions," Phillips recalls. "'Write what you think would be a good speech for a president to make.'"

After months of cajoling from Altman, Phillips finally sat down and pumped out a classic of hog-wild populism, framed by an Old Testament aphorism ("to strain at a gnat and swallow a camel") so favored by Kossuth residents it might as well have been written there. In it, he anticipated with thunderous glee the lawyer-phobia that would soon be sweeping comedy clubs, if not the nation ("A lawyer is trained for two things and two things only. To clarify . . . that's one . . . and to confuse."). He flattered the media. He goaded the affluent. He drop-kicked the generation-splitting issue of mind-altering drugs without committing himself to it. He performed a quintessential smoke-and-mirrors act of appearing to say everything while saying nothing at all.

"I attacked the whole business of Washington," he now asserts. "I believed you should be able to sing your national anthem—nobody but an opera singer can sing it. Then I went and got all the figures on the senators and congressmen and found out that out of five hundred thirty-five congressmen, two hundred eighty-eight were lawyers. And that just seems foolish to me. I also said—I think this was cut out—that as far as the Supreme Court was concerned there should never be a majority from the same profession.

"I thought that anyone who would come out and say that could replace somebody. And ninety-eight percent, if not all of it, was what I believed."

Phillips went into Nashville's Woodland Studios and recorded the speech. The finished rant, at eighteen-and-a-half minutes long, tickled the director to the bone. "Altman got more fun out of my saying that I knew more about money than the rich because I never had any until I was twenty-seven."

"I didn't change anything, to make it funnier, or sharper," Altman insists. After the filming was complete, Altman's sound team would cut and dub Phillips's earnestly conceived diatribe into a series of screwball sound bites that would drone from the speakers of Walker's prowling campaign van. The Walker van is the first and most ubiquitous of Altman's stalkers in *Nashville,* a mostly benign golden-goose trail of hopefuls and hangers-on that also includes Opal, PFC Kelly, Kenny, Albuquerque, and L.A. Joan.

With a candidate and platform in place, the director then teamed Phillips with a professional self-promoter and organizer named Ron Hecht whom Altman had recently met in Denver. Hecht had the requisite moxie to abet and galvanize the courtly Phillips in running the Walker campaign. In lieu of a title, Altman refers to Hecht as the "enabler," or the "instigator" of the campaign.

"He was an obnoxious, pushy asshole," recalls Altman. "People thought he was me because he was a little overweight and had a beard. So he'd pass himself off as me in front of the New York Film Festival and tell everyone about his successful sexual encounters."

Altman assigned Phillips and Hecht a "campaign office" and a budget for buttons, stickers, handouts, and other campaign paraphernalia. They received a shooting schedule that showed where the crew would be filming on any given day. They were then given a van with a public address horn attached to the roof. After they were fully equipped, Altman issued a single command: "I want you to invade my picture."

WITH THE political machinery lubricated, Altman would add four more characters to Tewkesbury's gallery. As was the case with so much of *Nashville*'s populace, their origin is a typically Altmanesque chicken-egg conundrum of which came first, the actor or the character?

As the idea for Hal Phillip Walker began to percolate, according to Tewkesbury, "Bob said, 'Well, we have to have a handler.' I never want to see the Hal Philip Walker character, all I want to see is his handler. And I said, 'Murphy!'"

Michael Murphy had become a staple of the rotating Altman ensemble since the director hired the dimple-cheeked Los Angeles native and Marine Corps veteran to work on *Combat!* when he was

The Hal Phillip Walker Campaign van.

barely out of the University of Arizona theater department. Since then, he was reenlisted for the ill-fated *Nightwatch,* a character-driven astronaut drama called *Countdown* (Altman's first theatrical feature), as well as *Brewster McCloud* and *McCabe & Mrs. Miller.*"

Altman's faith and Tewkesbury's instincts were dead-on. Murphy "was" Walker organizer John Triplette, seducing the Nashville singing elite with a slinky grin to perform in a rally for his candidate. Triplette would be abetted by well-connected Nashville attorney Delbert Reese—the rubelike embodiment of the nation's ills in the world according to Hal Phillip Walker. Triplette was Watergate oiliness tempered by Murphy's hands-in-pocket finesse.

"I knew a guy in college who wound up being one of Nixon's dirty-tricks guys," says Murphy, explaining the impetus for his performance. "He was like an advance man who would go into town and arrange for the train to pull out with the candidate on it. His thing was, Nixon wins, and I'm a big player in Washington. If he loses, then I'm back to selling hospital furniture. So it was all or nothing with this guy.

"Always with me and Bob your character develops as you go along. There was a certain obsequiousness about this guy that we didn't plan. But Bob said, 'You gotta maneuver around these people, you gotta make 'em feel good.' It sort of would begin to happen."

Michael Murphy and Ned Beatty surround Cristina Raines at Nashville airport.

"Michael's character came out of all those guys we were watching on television during the Nixon trials," says Tewkesbury. "[John] Dean comes to mind. He'll do anything to get his candidate taken care of. Lying brilliantly and lying to the point where it was the truth. The most polished out-of-towner in Nashville. He knows the drill, he knows how long to be nice to people, he knows who to juice, he knows when to get out. He is ruthless. Ambition taken up to the level of sophistication. And a lot of money to back it up."

"What Michael brings to it," adds Alan Rudolph, "is the befuddled-ness, the flaw in the character. He's an aristocrat, a pureblood of political hypocrites. Bob casts him so well that as soon as you see him on the screen a lot of the work has already been done."

One of the brass rings of Triplette's star search would be Haven Hamilton, Nashville singing legend and reigning sonofabitch of the Grand Ole Opry. Hamilton, all golden fringes and asbestos underclothing, was concocted to showcase the astringent screen persona of Robert Duvall. An Altman veteran from *Countdown* and *MASH* like Murphy, Duvall had run into the director at a party and expressed his interest in singing country music.

Altman wanted a Hank Snow type for his cast of characters, so Hamilton became *Nashville*'s resident Snow by way of Hoyt Axton. Tewkesbury would add her own personal experiences of Conway Twitty and Tex Ritter from her research trips to Music City. "These men were deeply loyal to Nashville," explains Tewkesbury, "in the way one is loyal to the Rotary Club or Republican Party. They are men who contribute a lot to damaged children, who have drunk too much, done too much, who are the most hypocritical but who are the most honorable men in a funny way."

Altman and Tewkesbury had gleaned enough of the dynastic privilege of the Nashville music society to determine that Haven needed to have a son in the business, to enhance his royal aura. Bud, barely a blip on the radar screen of Tewkesubury's earliest scripts, has returned from Harvard where he was sent to learn how to run his father's business. That Haven sent Bud to the law school and not the business school not only reflected the elder Hamilton's arriviste inclinations but also gave a winking nod to the litigious nature of the high-stakes, bicoastal bureaucracy that was creeping into Nashville as it began to exert more and more influence in the entertainment industry.

Another Hamilton son is alluded to in Tewkesbury's early draft, which speculates that "rumor has it that after [Haven's] other son Wendell was shot in an accident, he became an alcoholic." The draft is chockablock with such grace notes of character background, most of which would never see the screen. From her years in and out of acting programs at USC, Tewkesbury understood the value of subtext to guide an actor's performance.

Barbara Baxley (foreground) as steel magnolia Lady Pearl, mistress and confidante to Haven Hamilton (Henry Gibson, rear).

The late Wendell would surface, but barely, in a prop contrived by the actor who eventually played Haven, Henry Gibson. And if Haven was ever an alcoholic, he was a confirmed milk drinker by the time the cameras rolled.

Lady Pearl, the fourth addition, was based on the owner of a venerable Broadway joint just around the corner from the Ryman Auditorium. Tootsie's Orchid Lounge continues to beckon the tourist at seemingly all hours with its psychedelic lavender exterior and amplified live music. The crusty and convivial Tootsie was usually around to greet the visitors and make them feel as special as the celebrities whose photos covered her walls. Tootsie welcomed everyone but Altman's camera crew, so Lady Pearl would have to set up shop at the Picking Parlor down the block.

As Haven's character evolved, Lady Pearl was soon pulled into his immediate sphere. A steel magnolia of the first order, Pearl had the right stuff to play mistress to Haven, who was otherwise too garrulous and impossible to keep his wife by his side. (Mrs. Hamilton is off, we learn from Bud, in Paris.) As his chief confidante and supporter, she would also provide the corresponding female double for Barnett. Once ardent Democrat Barbara Baxley was cast and began to infuse her own political ideals into her character's, Lady Pearl was also the only person who might dare to challenge Hamilton's implicit America-love-it-or-leave-it politics.

As if two dozen main characters were not enough, Tewkesbury envisioned a twenty-fifth. "All of the other characters never get in touch with each other, or only in a brushing way. It was essential that one person held all the information, and what better person, and a silent one, I might add, than the audience?"

THE AUDIENCE would not remain silent for long. If any single element of *Nashville* could be said to have stirred controversy, it ultimately was not the assassination, but the music. Robert Altman's decision to have his actors write their own songs rather than enlist real country musicians performing their own stuff was either a stroke of genius or a gross miscalculation, depending on whether you poll the movie's admirers or the country musicians of the day.

One of the most significant impacts of Altman's decision is that it made the film less "about" Nashville, 1976, and more of an idea of America, 1976. Joan Tewkesbury's first official screenplay was littered with character-defining song cues for signature tunes (Haven Hamilton sings "The Wabash Cannonball," a jukebox plays "Okie From Muskogee") that centered the film squarely in a particular place and time. Occasionally, the music choices in Tewkesbury's original conception walked a thin line between the erudite and the obvious. In one, the philandering Tom plots a clandestine meeting over the phone with the married Linnea, as Tammy Wynette's "D–I–V–O–R–C–E" plays in the background at his end and Menotti's *The Telephone* sounds from hers.

Along with the calculated inclusion of marijuana smoking and the murder of Stringbean and his wife (reported to us by the ever-inquiring Opal), the early drafts of the screenplay more accurately reflected the shifting tides of Music City that impressed the screenwriter during her research trips to Nashville. All of this, along with the song standards, would go by the wayside. As documented in her original screenplay, the local trauma over the mysterious murders of Stringbean and his wife could have been perceived as ripping off Altman's scatological farce *Brewster McCloud,* in which anxiety over an unsolved murder provides a running plot point. It is not clear, however, how much the decision to minimize the references to drugs and contemporary headlines was prompted by the preemptive release of Daryl Duke's *Payday,* a corrosive but little-seen 1973 film in which Rip Torn plays a third-tier Nashville star given to boozing, drugs, and womanizing. *Payday* was an uncompromising, relentlessly downbeat film, a kind of country-and-western variant of those hubris-heavy gangster flicks about a crimeland kingpin who is ultimately the victim of his cumulative abuses of those most loyal to him. Had *Payday* gotten the attention it deserved, it might have deflected some of the effrontery and indignation accorded *Nashville* by the country music community.

"It became too expensive," insists Altman as he attempts to explain why he avoided the inclusion of bona fide country songs and singers. Of greater consideration than the expense, perhaps, was the dam break of prima donnas that might result by casting country stars. "Everybody's going, Oh, my songs will cost you this and this and I want so and so! I just didn't want to deal with any of that. I didn't want the agents walking around telling me what to do, mainly what the fucking songs would be.

"We had to get songs, but I didn't want them competing. I wanted them to be the same cross section that those songs in Nashville are—that means I didn't want them all to be good songs. Henry's [Gibson] were a little obvious, but they're not all that different than some of those by Hank Snow. The Barbara Jean songs were a little smarter. 'Dues' is not a real good country-western song, but it was Ronee's favorite, she wanted to do it. My point is that making those choices is an arbitrary thing under the best of circumstances, and who is that person who says, 'Oh, we're going to use this'? The Nashville companies, the songwriters, want to use the ones they think are going to sell the most copies. So, I just felt I didn't want them professionally written."

Chief among the pros Altman interviewed, but ultimately passed on, was the man whom Tewkesbury used as her model for Tom, Jerry Jeff Walker of "Mr. Bojangles" fame. "That's a brilliant piece of work. I loved it. But so what? This wasn't about how good the songs were."

Given Altman's seeming resistance to established artists, obscurity could only have helped a baby-faced neophyte named Richard Baskin secure the job as *Nashville*'s musical director—along with a flair for flimflammery that Altman must have admired.

Baskin was only twenty-three when he walked into the Lion's Gate offices fueled by an unstoppable creative energy. A pianist from the age of eight, he sidestepped his father's pioneering ice cream business to try his hand at acting (he is another one of

Nashville's alumni from the earliest casts of *Hair*), directing (films, at USC film school), and composing.

Baskin's talents were all-consuming, according a roommate from his teens and resident *Nashville* assassin, David Hayward.

His obsessiveness was on a par with his chutzpah and drive. "Richard was always working, always trying to get somewhere. He wrote a song that he thought was right for Linda Ronstadt. The Fifth Dimension had a song, 'Surry on Down' [Laura Nyro's 'Stoned Soul Picnic']. So he wrote 'Merry on Down,' which was pretty much the same song. He pursued Ronstadt's manager and got an audience. He didn't take the song, but Richard never doubted what he did. If someone didn't like it, he'd bounce right back and go to the next place."

That resolve was in high gear when Baskin's sister Edie told him her girlfriend Gwen Welles needed some songs for a new Altman movie she was cast in. Welles brought the script to Baskin's Crescent Heights apartment; he looked at it, and told the actress he'd write the songs if she promised to introduce him to the director.

Welles delivered. On his first meeting, Baskin convinced Altman to hire him to coach the tone-deaf Welles for five bucks an hour. ("She really needed help.") On the second meeting, Baskin presented the songs.

"By that time, I decided I should do all the music for the movie. So I pitched him very hard: 'You should hire me to do the whole score and we should

Richard Baskin, *Nashville*'s music director, also played the ubiquitous guitarist Frog. (*Jim Coe*)

do it live.' He looked at me like, Who is this kid? And he said, 'What do you know about country music?' And I said, 'Well, I know all the best players.' It was complete bullshit. I went home and called my friend Curt Allen, who is Rex Allen the cowboy singer. His son, who I had gone to high school with, was living in Nashville at the time.

"I said, 'Quick, you got to tell me who the really good players are in Nashville.' And he gave me the names of all the really good players in Nashville. So when I went back to Bob, I said, 'And these are the people I'd use.' Two or three weeks later, we were on the plane to go make *Nashville*."

Along with writing Sueleen's songs, Baskin would supervise and arrange the rest of the score, as well as cowrite songs with Lily Tomlin, Henry Gibson, and Altman himself. His most under-sung contribution to *Nashville*, however, would be to find Altman's boy-next-door assassin and his girl-next-door victim.

CHAPTER FIVE

DOING THE REPLACEMENT PARTY SHUFFLE

(Wherein Susan Anspach Balks, Robert Duvall Walks, and Barbara Harris Goes Where Bette Midler Fears to Tread)

THE LAST WORDS BARBARA JEAN SINGS before being cut down by Kenny Fraiser's bullets pay tender tribute to the family bosom. Ronee Blakley's "My Idaho Home" is an American idyll, a post-frontier childhood recaptured through a Vaseline-filtered lens. Indeed, if Thomas Hal Phillips could have transposed Hal Phillip Walker's campaign literature into a song lyric, it might just sound like this.

> . . . I still hear Daddy singin' his old Army songs,
> We'd laugh and count horses as we drove along
> We were young then, we were together
> We could bear floods and fire and bad weather
> But now that I'm older, grown up on my own
> I still love mama and daddy best, and
> My Idaho home.

Blakley wrote the song on a plane out of Idaho, where she visited her family after an extended separation. When Blakley shifts into a retro gear, the Idaho home she dredges up from her adolescence shimmers with the sort of sun-dappled nostalgia that could give Barbara Jean a run for her money.

She speaks of the Snake River, huge and mighty, that fed the land surrounding her Nampa birthplace. She describes the Owyhee Mountains and Sawtooth Mountains that stretched upward from opposite sides of the river, and the farm where her grandfather kept pigs and chicks and eighty acres of crops. She remembers playing in the drain ditches with her brother Steven. They would lie on their backs under the sun as the warm water entered the ditches. They would pluck tomatoes and pop them in their mouths.

Blakley's childhood was not all reverie and ripe tomatoes, however. Her parents instilled a firm work ethic. Every morning at six, Blakley would rise and practice the piano for two hours before breakfast. "Being firstborn," she wrote in a poetic résumé in 1972, "I was taught to hunt and fish and walk like an Indian brave over the sugarbeet fields at dawn. I studied ballet, piano, and sewing. I belonged to Girl Scouts, girl's quartet, CYF, and was a cheerleader. I did everything I was supposed to do and everything I wasn't supposed to do."

ACCORDING TO Robert Altman, Barbara Jean would "replace" Hal Phillip Walker in taking his death and his spotlight. The singer and the politician are kindred spirits in another way, seasoned as their creators are by the vigorous imaginations of two farm-country lefties. Ronee Blakley's parents, like those of Thomas Hal Phillips, came from a humble English lineage and scooped their children out of generations of agrarian poverty. Her mother was a member of the Convention of the International Churches of the Disciples of Jesus Christ; her father strayed from generations of farmers and studied to become a civil engineer. If you go to Lebanon, Kansas, you will find an old barn that belonged to his forefathers. And somewhere amid the family relics is the honorable discharge that Ronee's great-great-grandfather earned from the Civil War.

The Blakleys, like the family barn, are survivors. Ronee's parents' house was swept away in a flood. When she was six, Blakley's dress caught fire from a sparkler two days after the Fourth of July. She suffered third-degree burns which scar her to this day. Blakley incorporated the memory into *Nashville* (Barbara Jean has just been released from a burn center at the film's opening) and spoke freely about her childhood trauma at the time of the movie's release. These days, however, the mere mention of the incident makes her grow very aloof and uncomfortable.

There is another Idaho home that Ronee Blakley invokes. It is the town of Caldwell, where she lived from the age of nine. There, prompted by the spirit of inquiry that spilled from the College of Idaho (now Albertson College), she became an outspoken feminist and civil-rights worker in her late teens. Blakley learned Spanish, hoping to be of help to the farm laborers who were sequestered in a special section of the next town. She read St. Thomas Aquinas, and came to love Nietzsche, Baudelaire, Faulkner, and Joyce. Her first published work was a poem used for the frontispiece of the closing defense statement of Angela Davis, and her snaking river of activism would fork off to embrace Greenpeace, Vietnam Veterans Rights, Nine to Five Working Women's Alliance, Idaho Prevention of Child Abuse, Pismo Beach Preservation of Indian Lands, and campaign work for Jerry Brown, Walter Mondale, and Tom Hayden, among others.

Blakley appears to have absorbed her empathy and civic-mindedness through family osmosis. Her mother was active in gay rights and introduced a bill to keep gay preachers from getting kicked out of their churches. She also wrote a dissertation on the impact of investments by multinational corporations in South Africa. In his retirement, Blakley's father negotiates the water rights for the consolidated Indian tribes.

Hence, the Ronee Blakley who was chipping away at a music career in the days prior to *Nashville* was an impassioned and earnest creature. She had already recorded her first album, a soulful collection of poppy-folky-rocky tunes for Warner Brothers, composed a film sound track and hung with the Joni Mitchell-Joan Baez L.A. music set. She was a svelte, raccoon-eyed beauty (physically she would often be likened to Baez) and the object of actor Edward Albert, Jr.'s, affections.

It was at a party thrown by Albert that Blakley met Richard Baskin. The two struggling songwriters became friends in the ensuing months, playing their songs for each another and trading war stories. Once Baskin was tapped to be music director on *Nashville*, one of the first items on his agenda was to sell some of her songs to Altman. One of the next items was to get her into the picture. The only prob-

Raccoon-eyed beauty Ronee Blakley, before her Barbara Jean makeover.

(© *J. William Myers*)

lem was that the shoes he hoped she would step into had already been filled.

A small headline in the April 26, 1974 issue of *Daily Variety* announced SUSAN ANSPACH TO MAKE SINGING DEBUT. The self-styled free-spirited, free-thinking Anspach had come to Altman through her agent, and he was taken by her intelligence and off-center beauty. When the director tapped Anspach to play the banner role of Barbara Jean, she was primed to rescue a career that had lost its way after the early promise of *Five Easy Pieces* and *Play It Again, Sam*.

It never happened. The reasons, depending on whom you believe, were either economical, philosophical, or musical.

Altman recalls, "She was the first person I cast, and I made a deal with her agent to pay her fifteen thousand dollars. As time went on and I saw how many actors we were going to be dealing with, I realized that that would be unrealistic, that we would have to pay everyone on a lower 'favored nations' [equal scale] agreement. When I went back to her to explain, she backed out. I don't blame her, really."

Altman's favored nations solution was a two-tiered salary scale in which name actors would receive $1,000 per week and lesser-knowns would get $750. Even by the standards of 1974, an $8,000 fee for eight weeks on a studio-financed picture was tantamount to acting at gunpoint. No one would have thought less of Anspach had she chosen to scream bloody murder over the pay scale, but she preferred to espouse higher principles. Talking with Arthur Bell in the *Village Voice,* she explained, "I wanted to play the part more like Dolly Parton than Loretta Lynn. You have to understand that I research and study for a part months before the cameras roll. Before *Nashville,* I traveled with Evel Knievel, hung out in country-western bars, and found myself understanding the kind of people Robert Altman was depicting. I felt great love and compassion for them and couldn't mock or spoof them or deal with Altman's condescending attitude."

"Singing was not her thing," says a diplomatic Richard Baskin of Anspach. "She could sing, but it was an actress singing and not a singer singing. And unlike Gwen, who really didn't have to be a singer, this girl had to be good. I didn't know if Ronee could act but I knew that she was special. I had hired Ronee to write songs for the movie, or rather choose songs from her repertoire, because she had so many. More and more I became convinced that Anspach was not going to be able to handle it. And at the exact moment—I watched very carefully—I brought Ronee down to Nashville to meet Bob, with the idea that she should play this part."

"He said, 'Look foxy,'" recalls Blakley, who was in a break from a road tour with Hoyt Axton. "So I selected a dress and brought my brother Steven with me. I was nervous. And then I did something I now find shocking. We were going to play my music early in the morning, which I find difficult to do. So we stopped off and got tequila or beer and took it with me. Altman asked me to play for an hour. And then in came Keith [Carradine] and Scott [Glenn] and everyone was sending out for tequilas and passing the guitar around. It turned into a wonderful party."

The *Nashville* party, of course, was just beginning. As was the vibrant tug of wills that would inform the creative relationship between Robert Altman and his new Barbara Jean. Blakley relates her first conversation with the director at her impromptu morning concert. The subject was John Huston's *Key Largo,* which she had recently seen in Cambridge.

"We were talking about the scene where Claire Trevor descends the stairs while the rest of the assembled party is held under gunpoint by Edward G. Robinson. She wants a drink. She's his moll and he won't let her have one. And he says, 'What ever became of you? You were going to be a big star. Sing me that song you used to sing when I met you and I'll give you a drink.' And she sings the song, and he still won't give her a drink. 'Why not?' 'You were terrible.' And Bogart goes to the bar and pours her a drink.'

"And Altman says, 'It shouldn't have gone that way.' And I said, 'It would. She had lived a life of debauchery and partying and hadn't been performing for ten years. She would sound terrible.' And Altman said, 'Well, that life should make her sound better.' I said, 'No, I thought it had been directed properly.' And he said, 'Well, you make your movie and I'll make mine.'"

THE REPLACEMENT Party may just as well have been coined to describe the complex shuffle of substitutions that went into casting *Nashville,* of which Ronee Blakley's eleventh-hour arrival was the last step. The leaps that Altman would make from his first choices for any given role to his final ones were indicative of a porous approach to making movies that refused to be locked into a single route.

For some, that malleability was perceived as a debit. "Bob was talking to me one night," recalls Michael Murphy. "He said, 'I get this criticism that I'm lazy with my casting.' I think he's very bold with his casting. He's not afraid. In *McCabe*, when Warren [Beatty] wasn't sure if he was going to do it, Bob said, 'Well, we'll make him this Jewish guy in the West. We'll make him a merchant. We'll get Elliott [Gould] to do it.' At one point it was going to be Warren or George C. Scott. Most directors would be terrified. Bob just makes it all work."

"He really is the puppeteer," says Sue Barton, *Nashville*'s elegant unit publicist, who is also seen in the film at various points

Elliott Gould and Altman. The director cast the actor against type in *The Long Goodbye* and recruited him for a cameo in *Nashville*. (*Jim Coe*)

introducing Elliott Gould and Julie Christie to Haven Hamilton and his entourage. "He has a knack for knowing who you are and putting you in situations where that is very apparent. He does see people in a way that no one else does, and he can use that to tremendous advantage for himself. It's always manipulative but it's not always bad."

Perhaps no example proves Murphy and Barton's point more surely than the casting of the imperious Haven Hamilton. When Robert Duvall's agent balked at Altman's niggardly salaries, the director summoned Henry Gibson, an actor of considerably shorter stature (5'4¾") and dewier reputation. Altman wasn't fooled. At a time when the public identified Gibson as the poetry-spouting twerp with the big flower on *Rowan and Martin's Laugh In,* Altman had tapped into the actor's latent George Sanders qualities to play a sinister psychiatrist in *The Long Goodbye.*

Altman also discerned the dark side of nice-guy Keith Carradine when Gary Busey drop-kicked the Lothario role of Tom Frank to pursue a TV pilot. While there were still roles to be cast, Busey was deep enough into the process to have already contributed one song ("Since You've Gone") and to lodge himself in the director's affections as "that asshole."

At the time Busey left, Carradine had been set to play Bill, trio member and hapless husband of Mary, whom Mary cheats on to sleep with their partner Tom. With Busey out, Carradine was hustled into the role of Tom, wherein he was compelled to dredge up reservoirs of smarminess that made him squirm with discomfort from the first day of filming to the last.

While Carradine was also used as a template for the sweet killer Kenny, the role itself was to go to the baby-faced young actor who played Sandy Dennis's captive Romeo in *That Cold Day in the Park,* Michael Burns. But Burns bailed out rather than suffer the indignity of being slugged into the lower, $750-a-week slot. Like Busey, Burns was well into preparations for his *Nashville* assignment when he split. "He had cut his hair and everything," mused Altman.

Once again, the ever-percolating Richard Baskin was poised

in the wings with a pal up his sleeve, ready to spring into action. David Hayward, his housemate from college days, had just moved into a tiny new apartment in L.A. and was priming himself for an austere summer playing a familiar role, the unemployed actor. He'd even sold his car to drum up quick cash, borrowing a Volkswagen from the Nashville-bound Baskin to get around in for the season.

Hayward's lifestyle was realizing the worst fears of his father, a thriving farm-machinery distributor for Ford Tractor and the state of Ohio. Baskin had met the young Hayward years before in an acting class, after the latter had finished a particularly raw acting exercise in which the students imagine their fathers in a chair and talk to them. Baskin was moved: he had lost his own father just months prior. The new friends would team up to write a paternally inspired script called *Ice Cream and Tractors*. Hayward winces at the mere mention.

Settling into his new apartment, Hayward didn't know what hit him when the phone rang and Scott Bushnell greeted him from across the country. She was calling from Nashville. "We lost an actor. Bob wants to meet you. You're flying in tonight."

The next morning in Nashville, Hayward intercepted Altman at the production office. The director eyed him skeptically, saying, "I always thought that Kenny's insecurities would come out of someone shorter." Hayward responded, "Very truthfully, when you've been five-ten and a hundred and sixteen pounds with size-twelve shoes when you're sixteen, it doesn't get much more insecure than that—at least it didn't for me." Altman relaxed, turned to Tommy Thompson, and uttered the seal-the-deal words: "We'll have to cut his hair."

Hayward left the room, elated at his new job and pissed at having to relinquish his hippie identity in order to keep it. As he walked down the hall, he thought, Glasses. I have to wear glasses. Hayward spun around to run the idea past his new director. And as he entered Altman's office, the demon barber of Westwood Avenue looked up at him and said, "Glasses."

THE SURFACE casualness with which Altman hired an unknown for the pivotal role of Barbara Jean's killer epitomized not only his utter faith in his own native instincts but his disdain for auditions. With a few exceptions (which he can count on his fingers plus maybe a couple of toes), Altman has shunned auditions like a Sunday schoolboy cowering before the dark specter of Hades.

"They do such a cursory judgment," he says, invoking the unholy mob of casting agents and directors at an audition. "Twenty people sit in a room and bring in an actor. He reads four lines and they go, 'Oh, he's great!' and I want to say, 'He's not great.' Or they'll say, 'That person is not good,' and I say, 'That person is terrific!' How can you make a judgment like this?

"Also, I don't want to impose my thoughts on what this character should be. I don't want to box the actor in, and afterwards have a performance that's, 'Oh, that's what he told me to do.' So I try to give the least amount of information as possible so they come in and bring me what they have to give."

Altman's laissez faire would pay off in spades for Lily Tomlin, the fortuitous beneficiary of the most unpleasant replacement scenario behind *Nashville*.

The imprint of actress Louise Fletcher on the role of Linnea Reese cannot be underestimated. As *Nashville* began to germinate in the imaginations of Altman and Tewkesbury, Fletcher was creating a solidly unsentimental performance in *Thieves Like Us*,

"Glasses. I have to wear glasses." David Hayward trying on his Kenny Fraiser spectacles for Nashville. (*J. William Myers*)

which was being coproduced by Fletcher's husband, Jerry Bick. Altman was moved by the tight relationship that Fletcher shared with her parents, who were deaf. Gradually, the notion for Linnea and Delbert Reese's deaf son and daughter began to emerge. Even before the script for *Nashville* was fully sorted out, it seemed like a given to Fletcher that her participation in the film was a done deal.

What was not certain was her husband's involvement. Bick and Fletcher had become chummy with Altman and his wife, Kathryn. He fully expected to be part of the *Nashville* equation. What evolved was a situation Altman baldly terms "blackmail."

"He wouldn't let her go unless he was working on the picture. So she told me she couldn't leave their kids to go to Nashville unless he was on it as one of the producers. It seemed like trouble to me. So I didn't cast her. I don't know what he told her. I'm sure she heard a different story."

Fletcher and Altman didn't speak for years, a professional silence that was broken when the director included her as one of many star cameos in *The Player*. If Altman feels any remorse for the situation, it is partly ameliorated by his sense that he was indirectly responsible for Fletcher's Oscar-winning job as Nurse Ratched in *One Flew Over the Cuckoo's Nest*, the film that would also steal the Oscar away from *Nashville*. Altman recalls, "I recommended her. Milos Forman was casting *Cuckoo's Nest;* he called me to ask what I thought of Lily Tomlin. And I said, well, what about Louise Fletcher?"

Lily Tomlin was a stranger to the movie business when she first approached Robert Altman through agent Sam Cohn, who represented both of them. She had become a household fixture as *Laugh-In*'s snorting telephone operator Ernestine in the early seventies, gaining a recognition value that enabled her to do her own television specials. With one foot lodged firmly in the mainstream, she continued to keep the other planted on the fringes where she got her start in the sixties, trying out her more cutting-edge material in small comedy clubs. She wanted an "in" into the movies, and figured the only way she could get it was to create the door herself.

"It was very hard to cross over from television to the movies at that time," she recounts. "I was fairly new, and it was hard for people to get that I *was* Ernestine right away. And then I became so closely identified as that extreme character, stylistically. But it never daunted me. I never *dreamed* that that was so. I thought that was just in the mind of people who 'did things,' not in the minds of real people. But I've always tried to create my own jobs anyway."

The way in, it seemed, was to buy herself a movie. Tomlin was working at a small club in Boston when she received the galleys for a new novel by Cynthia Buchanan called *Maiden*. She fell in love with the central character, and decided with her companion and creative partner, Jane Wagner, to option the film rights. After Buchanan tried her hand at writing the screenplay, Wagner wrote a second. It was that script that Cohn sent to Altman.

Lily Tomlin undergoes the makeover to Linnea Reese by makeup man Tommy Thompson (not to be confused with first assistant director Thompson). (*Jim Coe*)

"The next thing I knew I had a bid to go and be in *Nashville*. When I got the script, I didn't even know what part I was being considered for. But I thought, I could play any one of these parts. Including the boys.

"In the meantime, Altman had read *Maiden* and was very taken with it. The word I was getting was that he was going to produce it and Joan Tewkesbury was going to direct it. So she and Jane began working on another revision of the screenplay, and Columbia paid me all the money I'd invested in it. It was supposed to be the project after *Nashville* for me."

Despite her flip bravado in thinking she could take on any of the roles, Tomlin was thrown when she found out whom Altman wanted her for. "Altman told me I was going to be Linnea. And all I could think was, I'm not right for Linnea. I took the part because I wouldn't think of not taking it. To work with Altman, I was thrilled beyond words. So I went to Nashville and all I could think was, I'm not right for this part. But as I began to watch each of the twenty-four actors, I thought, Gee, everybody's so right. I must be best for Linnea."

Linnea Reese, the sole white singer in a black gospel choir, mother of two deaf children and housewife with a cheatin' heart, would be the first film role for "Ernestine." Had Fletcher stayed with *Nashville*, she would have tilted the balance of the film's ensemble toward Altman veterans. Among the others who had taken the Altman ride prior to *Nashville*, besides Michael Murphy and Henry Gibson, were Bert Remsen (Albuquerque's ever-pursuing husband, Star), Barbara Baxley (Lady Pearl), Timothy Brown (Tommy Brown), Robert Doqui (Wade), David Arkin (Norman), Gwen Welles (Sueleen), Shelley Duvall (L.A. Joan), Keenan Wynn (Mr. Green), and, in cameo bits as their then-superstar selves, Elliott Gould and Julie Christie.

Wynn and Baxley's history with Altman extended back to his television directing years, Wynn in a Desilu series called *Troubleshooters* and Baxley to a similarly short-lived weekly TV series inspired by William Inge's play *Bus Stop*.

Bert Remsen held a special niche as an old Altman drinking buddy and eight-time Altman actor. Just prior to *Nashville*, he played the showiest of his Altman roles as the most jocular of the convicts in *Thieves Like Us*. Remsen had met Altman on the tennis courts in Plummer Park in the early sixties. When Altman found out he was an actor, he threw him into a pilot he was directing with Frank Lovejoy, a *Bus Stop* spinoff called *County General*. (Remsen recalls that making a cameo appearance in that ill-fated pilot was

Danny Kaye. It was Altman's thank-you to the comedian for having cast him as an extra in *The Secret Life of Walter Mitty* when the director was making a hapless attempt to become an actor.)

Altman was devoted to Remsen, tenaciously at times. When Remsen fled acting to become a casting agent, the victim of a crane accident that broke his back and shattered a leg, Altman drummed his reluctant friend back into service to appear in *Brewster McCloud*.

"'I told you, Bob, I quit, I don't want to do it,'" recalls Remsen after Altman insisted he come out of retirement. "I

Bert Remsen as Star. (© *J. William Myers*)

Remsen catches forty winks off camera. (*Jim Coe*)

said, 'I can fly in two actors from New York, two from the coast, tell me what you want.' He said, 'I want you.' And he went to the head of the studio and forced me into doing it. That's how I got back into acting."

Arkin, Brown, and Murphy were the *MASH* contingent. Arkin, an L.A.–born comedy writer with a self-deprecating Oscar Levant–ish wit and a regard for Charles Laughton, put his stamp on Altman's Korean War comedy by writing the voice-overs for the squawk box. A former Baltimore Colt, Timothy Brown sang in nightclubs for eight years when he wasn't on the ball field. He had hung up his shoulder pads to go into show business full-time when his agent sent him to Lion's Gate to talk to Altman. *MASH* was already cast and in production but Altman was so engaged by Brown that he invented the role of camp medic Corporal Judson on the spot.

Shelley Duvall was discovered by Altman cohorts Tommy Thompson and Bert Remsen at a Houston party. (*Jim Coe*)

Shelley Duvall was marking time in the comparatively modest role of L.A. Joan after playing a lead in *Thieves Like Us* as Keith Carradine's lover. "Shelley Duvall may not be an actress, exactly," wrote Pauline Kael of her typically ethereal performance in that film, "but she seems able to be herself on the screen in a way that nobody has ever been before."

Duvall was the least trained of the Altman regulars, and for good reason. She was in her second year of college, nurturing dreams of becoming a research scientist, when Tommy Thompson and Bert Remsen attended a party at her Houston home. They were in town setting up shop for *Brewster McCloud*, which still did not have its female lead. When they arrived, the pair were agog at the gangly hostess with the extraterrestrial gaze who was excitedly hyping her boyfriend's artwork.

Tommy Thompson remembers the much-publicized meeting. "Shelley opened the door. The place smelled of joints, everybody was smoking, and down in the basement they had a den with all these little animals, battery-operated robots and things moving about. I don't know what we were there for, but we were in awe of this goofy girl. We went to Bob and said, 'You gotta meet this girl. We're gonna invite her to a party.' Fine. So she comes in, and he says, 'I thought you guys were putting me on.'"

Duvall, for her own part, thought her party guests were friends of her boyfriend's parents. Shortly after meeting Altman, she got a call from Remsen, who asked her if she wanted to be in a movie. It is a testament to the peculiar charm and self-assurance (some might say self-delusion) of the would-be research scientist that she immediately assumed they wanted her to be in a porno picture.

Another Altman "discovery" of the offbeat kind, Jeff Goldblum, was also the youngest of the Altman vets on the set of *Nashville*. At twenty-one, he had executed a now-you-see-him-now-you-don't walk-on in *California Split*, which was filmed between the cracks of *Thieves Like Us* and *Nashville*. Altman was merely warming up the wide-eyed Goldblum, whom he had come upon performing in the pre–politically incorrect comedy revue *El Grande de Coca-Cola* in the bowels of the New York's Plaza Hotel.

In contrast to Duvall, Goldblum's talents were multifarious and unstoppable. *El Grande de Coca-Cola* showcased his gifts as the starstruck nephew of Pepe Hernandez (played by Ron Silver), a Coca-Cola bottler who produces a show in which the pair pass themselves off as an international parade of stars. In a maniacally hideous send-up of Latino variety-show conventions, Goldblum played the piano (which he does, splendidly), performed a bad magic act (Altman's inspiration, no doubt, for the Tricycle Man), impersonated a tango dancer, barked through a German specialty act, clomped around on his knees in a play about Toulouse-Lautrec, and all in a pretend Spanish lingo by way of Sid Caesar and Imogene Coca.

The new Altman kids, in addition to Lily Tomlin, Ronee Blakley, David Hayward, and Geraldine Chaplin, benefited from either good agents, good friends, or good luck. Most certainly in the latter category was Allen Garfield, a brash bruiser of an actor from Newark, New Jersey, who shared Altman's fondness for gambling. "He was the one," commented Henry Gibson, "who stayed up till five in the morning wiping out crew members who

Altman discovery Jeff Goldblum with Altman veteran Keenan Wynn. (*Jim Coe*)

were getting a hundred and twenty-five bucks a week."

Garfield was busily losing his shirt at the roulette table at the Cannes Film Festival when Altman and Tewkesbury ran into him dressed in a leather jacket and a bowtie. Tewkesbury knew him from acting workshops years back at the Actors Studio, and thought him a natural to play Barbara Jean's manager-husband Barnett. Altman told him, "I have a role for you in my new movie and I want you to wear just what you're wearing."

Altman was concerned that Garfield's agent might balk at the wage scale. Eyeing his opening, Altman loaned Garfield a thousand dollars for an airplane ticket home in exchange for his promise to do *Nashville*. It was a business transaction that, on more than one occasion throughout the filming, Altman would come to regret.

"These teeth, that hair, that face." Golden boy Dave Peel as country music scion Bud Hamilton. (© *J. William Myers*)

THE ROLE of Haven Hamilton's all-American son Buddy was still up for grabs when Henry Gibson's wife, Lois, took a detour into a music store on Santa Monica Boulevard. She was hoping they might know someone who could give her husband a crash lesson in guitar fingering.

"They sent a young man to the house," recalls Gibson. "He came in and started working. Within minutes I looked at Lois and said, 'This has got to be my son!' Those teeth, that hair, that face!" The fellow was named David Peel, an aspiring country singer-songwriter who had done a few turns on the *Daniel Boone* series. He was blonde and dimple-cheeked, exuding a Glen Campbell wholesomeness that made you feel purified to be in his presence. The icing on the cake: Peel was a bona fide native of Nashville, Tennessee. Gibson called Altman, and the boy with the teeth, the hair, and the face was in like Flynn.

A reviewer would later point out that Peel was the only real musician in the film, a claim which, aside from misconstruing the training of such pop professionals as Ronee Blakley and Allan Nicholls, also undercut the actors with musical backgrounds who would not perform in the film. Robert Doqui, who played the man who hoots Tommy Brown off the stage, began his career singing in New York jazz clubs with the likes of Les McCann and Ron Jefferson. Ned Beatty, who also started out as a singer, wrote songs and played a country-and-western singer earlier in the year in the Nashville-set drama *W.W. and the Dixie Dancekings*. And anyone who heard Jeff Goldblum bang the ivories at the former Lucky Sevens on Hollywood's Vine Street (with a combo he started in 1998 with actor Peter Weller) would tell you he could have been another Thelonious Monk, if not Victor Borge, if he only applied himself.

SOME MAY speculate that rare, otherworldly elements are contained in the soil of Illinois, which sent both Karen Black and Barbara Harris to *Nashville*. Black, a dark beauty from Park Ridge, boasts a genius IQ and manipulates the English language in strange, often hilarious ways in interviews or casual conversation. Black dropped out of both high school and Northwestern University but managed to go clear in Scientology, a take-charge belief system that lends a paradoxically spacey edge to her not-always-clear descriptions of acting.

A granddaughter of Chicago Symphony first violinist Arthur Ziegler, Black landed jobs in two off-Broadway revues, one of which she composed the music for, shortly after coming to New York at the age of eighteen. She eventually formed Karpet Music

Company with a performer's manager named Peter Rachtman, with whom she also shared a romantic alliance for a spell.

In the seventies, after the actress hit paydirt with *Five Easy Pieces*, she spent more time on her guitar, picking out new songs with an emphasis on country. Eventually a club act came together. That background was only mentioned in passing when she first went to talk with Altman about possibly appearing in a film he was to shoot in Ireland called *Images*, an imperfect but undervalued meditation on the inner disturbances of a married woman. (Susannah York got the part). When she returned to the Lion's Gate offices a year and a half later, however, Black's musical experience would take center stage.

"He mentioned that he was going to be doing a country-and-western movie where everyone had to write and sing their own songs," says Black. "And I said, 'I sing country-western songs.' He said, 'Why don't you come over tomorrow? we'll have a pianist.' I said, 'I'll sing them now.' So I stood up in front of the fireplace and I sang [Black belts out in a bold, country-laced alto], 'Well, I'd like to go to Memphis but I don't know the way / And I'd like to tell you how I feel but I don't know what day it is / And I'd sure love to see you—'

Karen Black as Connie White. Black landed her role on the spot, singing her own "Memphis" for Altman at his Lion's Gate office. (*Jim Coe*)

"He said, 'You've got the part.'"

Karen Black was now Connie White, last minute fill-in and eternal runner-up to Barbara Jean.

When Barbara Harris phoned Altman about appearing in *Nashville,* the role of the ambitious farmer's wife Albuquerque had already been passed on by both Bette Midler and Bernadette Peters (the mind boggles). "I was out of work," says Harris. "I had run out of money. And I said, 'Do you have anything for me?' He said, 'Maybe something. I do have one part left, but you'll have to come here at your own expense.' So I flew out there, he gave me a script, sent me upstairs, I read the script real fast, said, 'I'll do it,' he said, 'Okay.'"

Prior to that moment, it seemed as if Barbara Harris's career had been a twenty-year audition for the *Nashville* role of a voluptuous showbiz aspirant from the boonies who quietly harbored huge talents. The daughter of a tree surgeon–turned-restaurateur and a piano instructor from Evanston, Illinois, the deceptively shy Harris soon rebounded from inauspicious beginnings (she was rejected for membership by her high school drama club and dropped out of Wright Junior College), hooking up in the mid-fifties with a repertory company operated out of a converted Chinese restaurant by a gaggle of ambitious undergraduates from the University of Chicago. Her manner then, as ever, was tentative and unassuming; when she first agreed to be an apprentice cook and bottle-washer for this student-run Playwrights Theatre Club, neither her acting abilities nor her Broadway-sized voice was readily apparent.

Fourteen years later, when she was the toast of New York in the Bock-Harnick musical *The Apple Tree,* those Chicago beginnings would be recalled by the show's director (and former Playwrights Theatre Club member) Mike Nichols. "We were painting and building [the theater] when a young girl wandered in because she lived on the block. She asked what we were doing. 'We're going to have a theater,' we said. 'Do you want to be in it?' She replied okay. For months she handled the mimeographing machine and then she began to act. While we were working in

Chicago, Barbara used to kid around by doing imitations of the people in the show. One day she sang because she was imitating a girl who sang, and we all said, 'Wow! Listen to the big voice coming out of that little peanut.' She just happened to sing. She never knew she could because she had never tried."

When the fire department forced the fledgling group to shutter, its members regrouped and formed the Compass Players, named for the University of Chicago coffeehouse that gave them a stage. The Compass gang toyed with the notion of ad-lib revue, a largely unexplored format that would soon put Chicago on the map as an innovative force in theater, paving the ground for the emergence of the Steppenwolf and Wooly Mammoth companies two decades later. Among its members, besides Harris and

Bert Remsen and Barbara Harris relax in-between takes. (*Jim Coe*)

Nichols, were Elaine May, Shelley Berman, and Paul Sills, who would marry Harris in 1956 and go on in the sixties to reformulate the improvisational legacy of his mother, drama coach Viola Spolin, on Broadway in *Story Theater.* The first year of their marriage, a twenty-one-year-old Harris accompanied her husband to Europe, where he was pursuing a Fulbright scholarship to study theater. While there they observed the Berliner Ensemble and the Bristol University Old Vic, with whom she played Miranda in *The Tempest.*

Soon after Harris and Sills returned home, the Compass Players disbanded and regrouped one more time, emerging this time in a converted Chinese laundry. In another year and a half, the Second City would open on Broadway, with Harris as its peripatetic diva. Over the course of its giddy, if uneven, two hours, this moon-faced sprite Harris exchanged a dazzling gamut of masks that included Jackie Kennedy, an Italian movie heroine, an Arabian vixen, a whorehouse madam, a secretary, and a repressed waif losing her inhibitions in a modern art museum. The show ran all of ten weeks, long enough to catch the eye of director-choreographer Jerome Robbins, who was on the prowl for the female lead in a new absurdist comedy by a twenty-five-year-old novice named Arthur Kopit.

In her bubbly turn as the Lolita-like baby-sitter, Harris would all but walk off with *Oh Dad, Poor Dad, Mama's Hung You in the Closet and I'm Feeling So Sad.* Harris's transitions from saucy to demure as Kopit's Rosalie only reconfirmed what was gleaned from her Second City debut: Here was a limpid comic actress who could morph personalities in the blink of an eye. That was precisely the sort of quick-change versatility Richard Rodgers and Alan Jay Lerner were looking for as they brainstormed a new musical about a chain-smoker with extrasensory perception who leaps precipitously between her identity as a hapless New York schlepper and that of a former life, in which she was a poised English aristocrat. At the time, it bore the whimsical title *I Pulled a Daisy.* When an audition confirmed that Harris could sing (she

performed a folk song and an aria from Menotti's *The Telephone*)
she was signed to take the title role in the still-unwritten show.

Harris was retained by contract during the protracted gesta-
tion of the show, a nettlesome process during which Rodgers was
replaced by Burton Lane, male lead Louis Jourdan was dropped
in favor of John Cullum, and the title enjoyed a felicitous makeover. If the reviews for *On a Clear Day You Can See Forever* were disappointing, Harris's captivating Daisy Gamble made her a star,
albeit a reluctant one. Since being relentlessly grilled and then
reductively sound-bited by a *Time* magazine interviewer during
her *Oh Dad, Poor Dad* run, Harris distrusted the publicity mill and
exasperated journalists with her frugal responses. Her distaste for
the whole star trip would also not sit well, predictably enough,
with the star machine of Hollywood. After Harris allegedly put
Paramount Pictures through hoops to deliver her a first-class air-
line ticket via a Greenwich Village watering hole where she hung
out (and which she purportedly never picked up), studio officials
spread word that she was non compos mentis. Harris vehe-
mently denied the Paramount story, quite credibly claiming that
she would never pay for her own plane ticket to Los Angeles.

Any rumors regarding Harris's state of mind in 1965 were
drowned out by the double coup of her triumph in *On a Clear Day*
and her endearing snowflake of a performance as Sandra the social worker in the film version of *A Thousand Clowns*. The greatest
revelation was that that kooky gal from Second City could sing.
Like Judy Holliday, to whom she was occasionally compared,
Harris's belting alto had a raw, broken-glass edge that exposed
the nerve endings beneath a fluttery comic presence. In *On a
Clear Day,* her unfussy, respectful command of both wistful and
wacky modes was such that when Barbra Streisand inherited her
role in the film version, a writer reviewing the sound-track
recording was prompted to sigh, "Barbara Harris is no Barbra
Streisand, but then Barbra Streisand is no Barbara Harris."

In theory, Harris's improvisational background should have
made her a perfect candidate for the collaborative modus

operandi of the Kansas City director. But Altman would not cotton easily to the brilliant and querulous actress, whose independent working style and penchant for speaking her mind with an occasionally disorienting forthrightness were quietly earning her a reputation as quirky and hypersensitive. During the tortured birthing of Arthur Miller's *The Creation of the World and Other Business,* Harris caught director Harold Clurman off guard when he tried to present a scene-by-scene strategy to the actors and she responded, "If you tell me what to do, I won't do it." Clurman was eventually replaced by the playwright, who found Harris's improvisational approach uncongenial to disciplined ensemble work. Four weeks into rehearsal, he accepted the actress's resignation (and also fired costar Hal Holbrook). "Although her reactions are spontaneous to the extreme," said a reporter in *Newsweek,* trying to get a handle on her working style, "her reactions are carefully worked out in rehearsal, sometimes so privately that her fellow workers don't always know what she's doing." To compound matters, in Harris's opinion, Altman perceived the Chicago émigré as representing a species beyond the pale—"a New York actor"—i.e., an overly reflective, theater-nurtured narcissist who has been corrupted by the Method or otherwise brainwashed with the distracting analytical checklists of an Uta Hagen or a Stella Adler. And on a certain level, she was dead on. The breathless velocity of his work in television had engendered in the director an affinity for actors who were quick studies: short on process, long on instinct, unfettered by methodologies and systems. In a way, Harris would prove to be too cerebral. Too inner-directed. And too insecure.

SINCE ROBERT Altman is never averse to letting an actor drag personal baggage into his roles, one can only imagine the gratification he must have felt in filling out Keith Carradine's romantically embattled singing trio of Tom, Bill, and Mary with Keith Carradine's old friend, Allan Nicholls, and Keith Carradine's lover, Cristina Raines.

Allan Nicholls, like every other nominally experienced musical actor who was not unemployed in the late sixties, had starred in *Hair*. The affable Montreal-born performer played Berger to Carradine's Claude in the Broadway company. The two became fast friends, jamming together between shows. "He looked like the person who was always inside of me," Nicholls said, explaining their compatability, "the tall, straight-haired, and fair-haired guy instead of the medium, stocky, and curly-haired guy I was."

Once Carradine was shuttled into the role of Tom, a Bill had to be located pronto. Carradine dropped Nicholls's name to Altman. At that point, Nicholls's sole film credit was playing in his rock band, B.J. and the Playboys, in a cheap Canadian exploitation flick called *Playgirl Killer*. But he had made the rounds of rock musicals from the smash *Jesus Christ Superstar* to the flop *Dude* and knew his way around the guitar. Abetting Nicholls's cause on the sideline was *Hair* alumnus Richard Baskin, who was making himself increasingly valuable as a casting agent for *Nashville*.

"I was vacationing in Miami," Nicholls recalls. "Keith tracked me down there. I flew out to Los Angeles from my vacation, Keith met me at the airport, drove me to Lion's Gate, we walked into Bob's office. 'Allan, this is Bob; Bob this is Allan.' 'Want to be in our movie?' 'Sure.' In three minutes I was upstairs signing a contract with Scotty Bushnell."

The seesaw role of Mary had originally been inspired by Taffy Danoff, the female third of the trio that once included John Denver and her husband, Bill. Altman kept Danoff on the back burner for the role until he tested her for a part in *California Split* that would eventually go to Ann Prentiss. "It didn't work out," explained Altman tersely. Months later, Joan Tewkesbury would be left to bear the news to Danoff that Altman had farmed out the *Nashville* role that she, like Louise Fletcher, expected she owned by birthright.

The new Mary was Cristina Raines, a darkly stunning model manqué who detoured into the film business after her boss, Eileen Ford, bullied her into going to an audition. There, she met Keith Carradine, embarking upon a roller-coaster relationship that continued on and off for nine years. It happened to be on when *Nashville* was being cast, but Carradine, off in Europe making a picture, was not a factor in this instance. Raines had been pulled into Altman's Westwood kaffeeklatsch after she and Carradine were cast in a nonstarter called *Grasslands* with Scott Glenn and Gary Busey. And as she idled one afternoon at Lion's Gate, Altman asked her if she wanted to be in *Nashville*. So what if she couldn't sing, he figured. The camera adored her. The intimacy with her acting partners was built in. The rest would follow.

Raines and Carradine's hang-out buddy Scott Glenn had first come to know Altman through Joan Tewkesbury. Like Garfield, they had been colleagues at the Actors Studio. The first wind he had gotten of *Nashville* was when Tewkesbury came to visit him and his wife, Carol, at their Topanga Canyon home one day. "She said, 'I just finished writing my patchwork quilt,'" Glenn remembers. "'There's a part in it which I really thought of you for, but I don't know if you can do it or not because Bob really casts these things on his own. But I'll mention you to him.'"

One late afternoon, Glenn was hanging out at Lion's Gate. "I had really long hair at the time, a big Fu Manchu mustache. I looked like a Hell's Angel. We were sitting around talking about football when Bob comes out.

"And he said, 'Who do you like for tonight's game?'

"'The Pittsburgh Steelers.'

"'Why?'

"'I'm from Pittsburgh.'

"'What are you doing this summer, Scott?'

"'Well, I don't know.'

"'Well, how'd you like to come to Nashville and play around with us this summer?'

"'How do you mean?'

"'What do you mean how do you mean? You know, be in this movie with us.'

"'I'd love to.'

"'Okay, okay. Consider it done. Cut off all that hair. You're going to be in the Army.'"

CHAPTER SIX

BASIC TRAINING

(Wherein Jeff Goldblum Cycles in Place, Shelley Duvall Goes Shopping, and Ronee Blakley Porks Out with Loretta Lynn)

ROBERT ALTMAN LOVES ACTORS. "IT'S THE one job on the set that I can't do as well or better than anyone else," he once told Scott Glenn. "I can cook, I can cater, I can run the camera, I can light. But what you guys do I couldn't do at all."

And he doesn't want to know how they do it, either.

Michael Murphy remembers preparing for *The Caine Mutiny Court Martial,* Altman's 1988 television version of the play taken from Herman Wouk's novel.

"He's not rehearsing any of this. And there's this big, long scene. The dialogue is a bit on the overblown side, especially in front of a camera. We're all struggling with it. I was struggling with my character. So I get ahold of the original novel. And I'm reading the novel. And something clicked. I thought, I've got it! He'd enlisted in the Navy, he was the head of the court. He had worked his way up through the ranks and now he's the top-ranked officer in the court. Now I know what this guy's about!

"So I went to Bob and said, 'Bob! I've figured it out! I've read the novel!' And he said, *'What are you tellin' me for?'* "

His message to the actor is loud and clear. Here's your role. Have a good time. If you feel the need to go off and read novels, scour microfilm, take fencing lessons in order to play a prince, or sleep on a subway grating before you can be a pauper, may you live and be well. Just show up for work and do what actors do. Whatever that is.

So, when Scott Glenn was told he was going to be in the Army and needed a haircut, he quietly flew down to Fort Campbell in Kentucky.

Glenn had served three years in the Marines in the early sixties, and left with a string of connections in the Army's 101st division. Arriving at Fort Campbell, he phoned one up.

"Hey, killer, what're you doing?"

"I'm an actor."

"You're kidding me. You're an actor?"

"Yeah, blah blah blah."

"Yeah, sure we can get you on the base."

"Can I meet your C.O.?"

"Scott, meet Captain so-and-so."

"Hey, listen, Captain, I'm going to be playing a paratrooper."

"Do you know anything about the military?"

"I was in the Marines."

"A marine playing a paratrooper? What do you know about jumping?"

"I was airborne."

"Oh, you've already jumped."

"Where's the PX?"

Glenn was in. He beelined to the PX, told them he was reporting back for duty, and got his haircut.

The next two weeks would be spent on and off the base, doing physical workouts with the enlistees, hanging out in bars with the officers, scoping out the uniforms. There was no subterfuge or pretense. He wore civilian clothes and told his hosts that he was going to be portraying them in a film. Tell me how you want to be seen by the world, he would say to them.

"I just wanted to come from Fort Campbell to Nashville and not from L.A. to Nashville," he explains. "I wasn't looking to hear war stories. That wasn't something I needed to know. I just wanted to pick up terms that were specifically Army terms as op-

Former marine Scott Glenn (right) hung out at Fort Campbell army base to prepare
for his virtually nonverbal role as PFC Glenn Kelly.

posed to Marine Corps terms. In the Marines everything you
learn is essentially like Navy terms: not right and left, but star-
board and port. You're never in a room with a ceiling, it's always
an overhead. Rooms never have walls, but bulkheads."

Glenn would not actually utilize any of this knowledge in front
of the camera. Research informs an actor's performance more often than not in posture and attitude. The PFC Kelly that would
emerge from Glenn's Fort Campbell stay would assume the mask
of a grave sentry who has witnessed untold sorrows, perhaps in
Vietnam, perhaps at home with a mother who worshiped Barbara Jean.

Unlike the Marine-groomed Glenn, Gwen Welles had no ba-
sics prior to her basic training. She grew up in the fashion world,

the daughter of designer Rebecca Welles and niece of Gus Tassell, a designer of conservative men's clothes who took over Norell's after the death of Norman Norell. "When we were young my sister and I used to be the best-dressed girls in school," she told fashion columnist Eugenia Sheppard. During three years living in France with her onetime lover, director Roger Vadim, she became fluent in French.

She would have to drop all of that panache to play the self-deluding Sueleen Gay, counter waitress and tone-deaf singer. The latter task was not a huge leap—Welles could not sing a lick, as Delbert Reese says of Sueleen during the climactic "smoker" strip scene. Welles launched into singing lessons for three months, coached by her new chums Richard Baskin and Ronee Blakley. ("So she could sing badly, with conviction," says David Hayward.) When she proudly boasted of her progress to Altman and Tewkesbury, they looked at each other dubiously and said, "Oh God, don't. Just do what you do."

She would have more success in her three-day employment as a soda fountain waitress at the Nashville airport. Many of her fellow cast members came for lunch one day and threw their per diems at her for tips. When her temporary stint was finished, she offered her earnings to the other waitresses. They refused, with a warm Southern wink. "You earned them, Sueleen. You keep those tips, hear?"

Singing lessons proved anathema to Timothy Brown as he contemplated how to approach Tommy Brown, his Charley Pride–ish namesake. Instead, he would play Conway Twitty and George Jones tapes in the car and sing along as he rolled down the freeways. Brown knew his way around a song, having worked nightclubs on and off for eight years when he wasn't on the playing field. If anything, he felt a need to untrain himself.

"Ironically, I didn't want to work on my voice for some odd reason. I thought that it would sound more country if I couldn't sing that good. I was wrong, of course."

Learning how to become a traveling musician was also a non-issue for Allan Nicholls, who had roamed his native Canada with a group called B.J. and the Playboys. Once Altman signed him up to play Bill, he spent the next three weeks rehearsing songs with his new singing partners, Keith Carradine and Cristina Raines.

"We treated ourselves as a trio. We worked on the song Gary [Busey] had written for the movie, 'Since You've Gone'; we worked on 'Rose's Cafe' [one of Nicholls's tunes] and a couple of Keith's."

Adding to the sense of group intimacy, Nicholls stayed in the loft space that his screen wife, Raines, shared with her on and off-screen lover, Carradine. "Staying there was a test of everyone's ingenuity," recalls Nicholls. "It was a great funky house in Laurel Canyon, but it was like one big room and I was in the guest bed over in the corner. Their bed was over by the window. I'm sure they waited for me to go to sleep every night. I never heard them."

For Raines, the role of Mary was a test of courage. She never imagined she could ever sing, and the prospect terrified her. "I was extremely shy. I said to Bob, 'I will take off my clothes and run down the street naked before I will sing! Don't do this to me!' I don't think I could have done it without Keith and Allan. Allan was particularly supportive."

By the time Raines got to Nashville, she projected the brio and confidence of Mama Cass. "She had this incredible voice, which she finally got in touch with," says Nicholls.

Most of the *Nashville* recruits were pursuing lessons of one sort or another. Classes have a phototropic allure for actors. They're more than just something to do in the lulls between jobs. They're a way to keep alert, fit, identified as an actor. The attitude becomes, "This is what I do. I train, therefore I am."

When Altman asked Jeff Goldblum if he knew any sleight of hand, he decided to enhance his thrift-shop hocus-pocus from *El Grande de Coca-Cola* with a crash course in magic. He quickly learned how to perform improbable acts with salt shakers and scarves. "I took daily lessons," Goldblum recounts, "and when I got down there, I showed him my whole bag of tricks. He said, 'Oh, those are all great. I don't know when and where you'll use them, but bring them to the set every time.'

Jeff Goldblum as Tricycle Man shows off his legerdemain with magic.

"I wasn't a good magician and he didn't try and make it look like I was. I was exactly what I was, and when I do that salt thing, you kind of see what I'm doing. Which is ambiguous and fine."

While Goldblum was taking magic lessons, he realized he was going to have to learn to ride a motorcycle as well. Altman had told him that he was going to be the Motorcycle Man.

"I looked in the yellow pages and got a driving school to teach me. Vito was my teacher. We went all around Manhattan on this motorcycle. And the first time, I went down to Fourteenth Street, I meet Vito. He says, 'Okay, it costs this much, give me the money, I'm going to put you on a simulator.' It was a kind of stationary motorcycle. He said, 'Get on that.' I got on. He said, 'You need a helmet, give me another couple of bucks, I'll give you a helmet.'

"So he gave me a helmet and I'm on the simulator. And I'm not doing anything, I'm just kind of riding this thing. And now he leaves. I'm there by myself. And after a while I started getting nervous. He wasn't coming back. 'Vito! Vito!' I started calling out into the street. 'Get Vito! *Get Vito!*'"

Vito returned, eventually. Goldblum took his motorcycle test, and a few days later the results came back. He had flunked. "So in fact, I didn't have a license to drive a motorcycle. But I didn't have to anyway."

Goldblum had been slightly misinformed: He was not the Motorcycle Man, but the Tricycle Man. When he arrived in Nashville, he was presented an elongated, three-wheeled *Easy Rider* monster with a stick shift. "I wanted to get as much practice as I could, so I drove it to and from the set. Till I sort of mismanaged my fuel tank one day and it ran out of gas on the highway going to the location. Somebody from the teamsters came and got me, and said, 'Don't let him ride that thing anymore!'"

The actors were learning that the Nashville teamsters did not look kindly upon anyone who appeared to be co-opting their responsibilities, one of which included transporting the actors to and from the set. Goldblum apologized meekly, deferring to the union member and returning to the set with his tail between his legs.

Goldblum was not the only actor to have a run-in with the local teamsters. David Hayward spent the first few weeks in Nashville driving around town in Kenny's car, dressing and acting in character to get people's reactions. One day he drove by the set in costume and stopped for lunch, when he was accosted.

"I got put up against the wall by about a three-hundred-pound teamster, who said, 'You workin' today, boy?'

"'No.'

"'You're not workin, huh? You in your costume, you got your car. You're not at work?'

"'No, I do it for research.'

"'Don't give me that bullshit.'

Jeff Goldblum testing his tricycle on Nashville streets and in the film.

" 'Look, I'm not workin' today. You can watch me. I'm not workin'.'

" 'You drive yourself to work, you put one of my boys out of work. One of my boys out of work, I come lookin' for you!' "

As if Barbara Jean's assassin needed another lesson in menace, American-style, Hayward studied case histories of people who had committed murders in recent years. He zeroed in on Arthur Bremer, the mysterious and none-too-swift young man who shot and paralyzed George Wallace in Laurel, Maryland, on May 15, 1972.

As he pored over Bremer's story, what came together was a profile of utter normalcy. "I tracked down a couple of people from names in the newspaper, friends who had known him. They all said, 'Quiet. Nice guy, though. A little strange. No, I didn't date him. Not a bad guy. Not spooky or anything. Nice guy.' So that was the strongest link."

Lily Tomlin studied sign language every day for three months. Once she arrived in Nashville, she invested much of her off-camera time becoming acquainted with the two local hearing-impaired children who had been cast as Linnea's kids, Jimmy Calvert and Donna Denton.

Tomlin's other task was to drill herself daily with Linnea's chorus, the Fisk Jubilee Choir ("to just try and be the least bit proficient"). The choir hit it off with the gregarious actress, who had been raised in a black neighborhood in Detroit.

A stickler for personality detail, Tomlin also canvassed a few upstanding white Nashville matrons about Linnea's avocation. "Because Linnea, being a Baptist, married to a guy like Del, who was an attorney, you know, very middle-class—I said to them, 'What would your reaction be to someone like Linnea, being the only white woman singing in a black choir?' And I had some really startling reactions.

"One of them, I hesitate to say, was something like, 'Well, I can see how she would identify with people who were disenfranchised, because of her children. And I would accept her singing in a black choir and going to a black church. But if she didn't have those children, I would just think she was a nigger lover.' "

As Wade "the Velvet Spade," ex-con and self-styled protector of Sueleen Gay, Robert Doqui's marching orders from Altman were brief: "Find him." For a grounded, churchgoing family man such as Doqui, it was a search. And what he found was someone a lot feistier than Joan Tewkesbury had envisioned when she first tailored him from James Broadway, the smooth talker who bought her a drink at the Exit/In.

Having grown up black in Stillwater, Oklahoma, in the thirties and forties, Doqui knew what he was setting himself up for when he decided to do a full-frontal assault on Nashville's saloons.

"I started drinking rum and hanging out in bars. I'd go into the country-western bars and I'd be the only black spot in there.

Robert Doqui haunted Nashville bars to prepare for his role as Wade, shown here with Barbara Harris's Albuquerque.

Just *to see how it felt.* Because Wade was that kind of guy. A guy like that is not afraid. From growing up in the Midwest, I knew when people had stepped off the sidewalk to let white people walk by. But as Wade I decided I would never let him step off the sidewalk. I'd say, 'No, I've been to prison. You can't fuck with me!' He knew the rules, he knew the penalties. He knew from prison if you screw up, if you overstep your bounds, you get your ass kicked."

A consummate character actor, Doqui slips into Wade's woozy, rummed-up delivery as he describes his "research" visits. "And I'd be sittin' at the bar, just downin' this stuff, trying to get a sense of the place and to see what would happen, how people would respond. I just minded my own business. I wouldn't even look at the bartenders, because one of the things I know, sometimes if a black face is in a place he's not supposed to be, the eye contact says, 'I'm not serving you.' So I'd do this [Doqui thrusts his hand forward with an imaginary five-dollar bill, his head tilted sideways, and says assertively], 'Gimme a drink.' So you're not dealing with me. You're dealing with a presence. And they gave me a drink."

Ronee Blakley threw herself into the Nashville trenches by way of the Bridal Suite at the Ankle Motel, where she was staying during her Hoyt Axton gig in Nashville. She had passed her tequila-soaked audition for Barbara Jean with flying colors, but still hadn't gotten word from Altman whether or not she had the role. Still, there was work to be done. Blakley's backup work with Roy Acuff notwithstanding, she identified herself as an L.A. singer-songwriter with Stanford refinements and Juilliard polish. If she was any country, she was California country rock with a punkish undertow.

Blakley immediately phoned the Palomino Club in Los Angeles to find out how to hook up with the managers of the country stars who were in Nashville at the time. The annual International Country Music Fan Fair showcasing Nashville's A-list singers was in full gear at the Tennessee State Fairgrounds. Blakley hoped to bag Dolly or Loretta or Tammy for a rush tutorial in how to be a country diva.

Parton, as it turned out, was performing at the Grand Ole Opry the same night that Blakley was backing up Hoyt Axton. Parton was charmed by Axton's partner, and sang "Jolene" at her request.

Blakley finally hit the jackpot when she got a call from Loretta Lynn's manager, David Steckner.

"He said, 'Come join us for dinner. There's a hog roast for Loretta.' And I said, 'Okay, well, thank you. What time and where?'

"'Seven o'clock.'

"'Will you be coming to pick me up or shall I meet you there?'

"'We'll pick you up . . . What is the Palomino Club going to do without you?'

"'The Palomino, without me?'

"'Isn't this Bonnie?'

"'This is Ronee.'

"'This isn't Bonnie Blakely, the girl who books the Palomino?'

"'No, this is Ronee Blakley and I work with Hoyt Axton and I'm up for a movie part.'

"'Well, come anyway.'"

Blakley was the belle of the hog roast. She plunked herself next to the coal miner's daughter at dinner and over the next few days hovered in her dressing room, chatting, observing, and meeting with both Lynn's husband and her biographer. She hung backstage as Lynn performed, gaped as Lynn submitted to being photographed for three hours ("an eternity of Instamatics," recalls Blakley) and learned how to imitate Lynn's earthier side. Before long, Blakley could call, "Hey, *Conway!* Yur the ugliest thing I ever seen," at the drop of a hat.

Henry Gibson, on the other hand, avoided studying the Acuffs and the Snows whom Haven Hamilton was patterned after. If there were any models, he later conceded, they were Henry Kissinger (for the power) and Bob Hope (for the longevity). Where Gibson felt he could use some spit and polish was standing in front of an audience. So, he took a job at the Sacramento Music Circus opposite his former *Laugh In* colleague Jo Anne Worley in a production of the musical comedy *Once Upon a Mattress*.

"The characters couldn't be more disparate, could they, Haven Hamilton and sweet, gentle little Prince Dauntless?" laughs Gibson. "But I felt one of the most important preparations I could make for Haven was to appear in live performances so I could have the command, the presence, the ease Haven Hamilton had to have walking out and performing on the Grand Ole Opry stage."

As Gibson endured nine performances a week in the sweltering Sacramento heat, he carefully plotted out Hamilton's look. He suggested to Altman that Haven sport a "bizarre kind of hair, not so outrageous that you were offended by it, but you knew damn well it wasn't real." Gibson then recruited one of Hollywood's premier hair and makeup men, Siegfried "Ziggy" Geike. "I asked him to make a wig with an obvious flaw in it. It blew his mind. Like asking Matisse to do less than a masterpiece: Could you screw this one up for me?"

Haven's clothes would also have to be top of the line. Gibson's dresser would be Nudies in the Valley, the outfitter of choice for country stars in Hollywood. "Expensive as hell, the embroidery alone. Everything he wore had to fit perfectly. This man didn't have an ounce of fat on him, he was so vain. He may have lost his hair but goddamn he calculated how he looked. Just as he calculated what was going on and what he would say to people before he said it and what they meant by what they said."

Henry Gibson enters the makeup trailer and emerges as the vainglorious Haven Hamilton. (*Jim Coe*)

Armed with small fistfuls of petty cash, the *Nashville* cast spent the month of June scouring shops for costumes. Shelley Duvall plundered thrift shops, emerging with a traffic-stopping closet of platform shoes, halter tops, thigh-length shorts, striped socks, and pocketbooks. David Hayward had his father buy him a Future Farmers of America jacket. Keenan Wynn poked through Nashville junk shops, looking for just the right musty furnishings for Mr. Green's guest house. Geraldine Chaplin invaded London's Kensington Market, making off with flower-print hippie smocks, beads, a frumpy black hat with a white sash, and, gilding the lily out of her own pocket, a very expensive pair of French leather cowboy boots.

They came, they saw, they costumed. And all under the watchful scrutiny of *Nashville*'s wardrobe patrol, Scott Bushnell.

Like many of the influential players in the *Nashville* saga, Scott "Scotty" Bushnell jumped aboard the Altman wagon on *Thieves Like Us*. The pair had met while the director was casting for *MASH* in San Francisco, where she toiled at the American Theater Ensemble alongside her husband, artistic director William Bushnell. Over the coming years, she would make herself the single most essential soldier in the Altman camp. And the most controversial.

Scotty Bushnell was a thin, dark, alternately guarded and amiable woman who chain-smoked and spoke with a lisp. Hired onto *Thieves Like Us* as an all-purpose administrative and wardrobe assistant (her billing on *Thieves* is "assistant visual consultant"), Bushnell quickly demonstrated her theater-honed savvy for matching costume with decor. On *California Split*, Altman began consulting her on casting choices, and with *Nashville*, her costuming responsibilities solidified. She graduated to "associate producer," a privileged position she would maintain until *Kansas City*, when, stricken with an aneurysm, she dropped off Altman's radar screen for good.

Perhaps no other individual had more to do with unifying the show business flamboyance of *Nashville*'s costumes with the Old Glory color strategy of its decor. "Scotty Bushnell had great taste," remarks Henry Gibson. "She was so skillful in color-coding the characters. It was all subliminally working throughout the picture."

Bushnell attacked her duties with the vigilance of a stern headmistress. Sue Barton remembers pulling out an outfit to wear for one of her three appearances in the film. "I put on a red shirt and she made me change it. She didn't want all the eyes coming to me." Barbara Harris recalls one of her scene entrances, riding in on the back of Jeff Goldblum's bike. "I wanted to get on the bike with one outfit and get off the bike with another outift. I thought that would be good. And Scotty had a fit. But she was the one who had to make sense out of it."

As Bushnell assumed more and more responsibilities with each film, she consolidated her power as an arbiter and gatekeeper to Altman's favor. The opinion on Scott Bushnell tends to split in two directions. To the actors, she played the felicitous role of the welcoming contract bearer and sympathetic hand holder. For others, she was a combination Iago and Carlotta O'Neill, keeping unwanted influences away from her beloved boss or manipulating him in subtle ways against them.

"I think Scotty was more the woman behind Bob than anyone else," says Geraldine Chaplin. "He needed her approval for everything. Absolutely everything. Everyone was in awe of Scotty. She reminded me of my mother with my father. All she would have to do is just hint to Bob: 'Oh, so-and-so looks rather tired today. I wonder if he's not been—' And that would be it. Out! So, if you were in Scotty's good books, that meant you'd be okay with Bob. And if Scotty took a dislike to you . . ."

"She was the end of Altman as we all knew him," says Kelly Marshall Fine, the production coordinator. "People started dropping out. Tommy [Thompson], Egg [enweiler], we were all lifers till she came along. But she did work very, very hard."

Altman, for his own part, was oblivious. "She was one of those squirrels. She didn't share information. She was unpleasant, but never around me."

"Evil," says Tommy Thompson, who, years after severing ties

with Altman as a result of Bushnell's alliance with Altman, flew from Los Angeles to the director's apartment in New York to explain the source of the estrangement. "We'd always say, 'Scotty Bushnell, cover your drink when you say the name.' She had a mysterious hold over him. You'd come in a room and say, 'Hi, I'm Jan Stuart, I'm doing a book on *Nashville,* and I'd like to come talk to you in a couple of weeks.' Altman'd say, 'Sure, that'd be interesting,' and after you left, she'd say, 'I wonder what he's really doing. Do you think he was looking for something else?' And he'd say, 'No.' But it would be planted. And in a couple of weeks you couldn't get in the door.

"She was a control freak. And she got rid of everyone who was around him. Everyone. There wasn't a soul left but Scotty."

AT THE end of June, the cast and crew began to stream into Nashville. They arrived by car, they arrived by plane, they arrived by caravan.

Allan Nicholls drove down from Montreal.

Keith Carradine motored cross-country from Los Angeles in his Toyota Land Cruiser, taking his cat and his aging dog Sundance for company. (Cristina Raines, who didn't want to go the highway route, hopped a plane instead.)

Ned Beatty, living a self-styled "old hippie life" in the Santa Monica Mountains, hitched a camper to the back of a Chevy truck and trekked overland with his wife Bulenia (who was suffering from postpartum depression), their two-week-old baby, their three-year-old son, and a brutally homesick fourteen-year-old whom they employed as their au pair girl.

Geraldine Chaplin flew in from England, but not before Thomas Hal Phillips was summoned by Altman to pull strings with his old family friend Senator James O. Eastland of Mississippi so she could clear customs to work in the States.

Perhaps the most formidable arrival was made by the film's director of photography, Paul Lohmann, who, accompanied by his wife, Karen, and two children, pulled into town in a forty-foot motor home. (One of his children, a baby boy at the time, is the companion of Altman's granddaughter.) Lohmann, a contemporary of Altman's, was a tall, blustery figure. Despite a bad eye, he had driven tanks, raced motorcycles, and flown planes in his prime before Zen-ing out with his GMC trailer. He was usually in reach of a cigar, except when he was whipping up a movable feast from his kitchen for his family and fellow cast and crew members.

Except for Lohmann and Ned Beatty, whose entourage was so large he was given a large rented house for the duration, the cast and crew were corralled on the edge of town in either a modest lodging of suites called the Jack Spence Motor Hotel on Murfreesboro Road or a freshly minted townhouse complex called the Haystack Apartments. The Haystacks were so new that the grass had yet to poke its way out of the surrounding mud. Suite 107 of the Jack Spence would also serve as the *Nashville* production office. On the main floor, a conference hall was hastily converted into a screening room for dailies, complete with full bar.

Scott Bushnell divvied up the housing, relegating the production crew and single cast members to the monastic Jack Spence rooms. Actors arriving with spouses or live-in lovers (or in the case of Allan Nicholls, actors who were friends of actors with live-in lovers) got the apartments, which were tarted up in advance by Bushnell and Robert Eggenweiler with Kmart plants, kitchenware, and TV sets.

The one holdout, at least for the first few days, was Lily Tomlin. Prizing her privacy and as yet unversed in the communal esprit de corps of her director, Tomlin took an apartment in a hotel. "I think the lesbianism made her feel a little different," explains Sue Barton, "and she was a bigger star in her own right."

What struck others as reclusiveness was, for Tomlin, merely a question of aesthetics. With only one answer. She couldn't bear the thought of having to choose between a small motel room and a treeless apartment complex with acrylic carpeting and heavy repro Mediterannean furniture. But Altman would have none of that. "Bob said to me, 'You go back and live in the regular hous-

Director of photography Paul Lohmann (right).

Matthew Altman, adopted son of Kathryn and Robert Altman, during the filming of *Nashville*.

ing!'" recalls Tomlin. 'We don't want anybody, you know, being different.'"

Anyone, that is, except for the director. Altman, his wife Kathryn, and their adopted son Matthew sublet a grand stone ranchhouse on the edge of Nashville from one of the local musicians. No one can remember anymore where the house is, but everyone can remember the swimming pool and the Eden-like forest surrounding.

"We're all equal," says Geraldine Chaplin with an ironic laugh, "except *he* stays in this enormous, beautiful palace. So he can get to invite everyone over and no one will say no."

On Saturday, the sixth of July, with four days left before the first shoot, Altman invited everyone over for a preproduction meeting and holiday weekend barbecue. The only ones who would be obliged to say no were Henry Gibson, who was winding down his run in *Once Upon a Mattress*, and Karen Black, who would be flying in and out for only a week and a half of shooting.

When everyone was assembled, the director welcomed his cast and crew. "There's food and drink," he said with a papa bear smile. "Meeting's over. You can throw away your scripts. You won't need them."

Everyone cooed with delight. Everyone, that is, with the notable exception of Joan Tewkesbury. Aw, *man!* she thought with a silent groan as her heart performed a backflip.

CHAPTER SEVEN

ACTION

(Wherein Altman Hijacks Nashville Airport and Breaks Some Sound Barriers)

"Altman throws it up in the air, and he
photographs where it lands."
—KAREN BLACK

"GIVE ME A GROUP OF PEOPLE and put us on a desert island," Robert Altman is fond of saying, "and we'll make a movie."

The exotic land that Altman invaded in the summer of 1974
didn't quite qualify as an island. The Cumberland River scoops
around Nashville to the east, north and west, leaving it wide
open to incursions of every variety from the Deep South. But for
the twenty-four actors, thirty-five crew members, and sundry
spouses, lovers, and children who settled in to make a movie, it
was as torrid as any island outpost in the Tropic of Cancer.

There was little relief from the Tennessee sun that summer,
and it would come when it was least wanted. The filming of
Nashville began under the threat of rain and finished forty-six
days later under the threat of rain. Shooting in rough chrono-
logical order, Altman had scheduled epic outdoor scenes for
those first and final days: you can plainly see the puddles at the
Metro Airport opening and the dark clouds over the Parthenon
finale.

Storm warnings from above were accompanied by political
rumblings from the north. In July of 1974, the Supreme Court
was hearing oral arguments in the Watergate trial, *U.S. v. Nixon*.
Before the month was out, burglars Bernard L. Barker and Vir-

Nashville shooting schedule as drawn up by assistant director Alan Rudolph.

gilio R. Martinez would be found guilty of breaking into Democratic Headquarters along with Kissinger aide and finance counsel G. Gordon Liddy. John Connally was indicted on two counts of accepting an illegal payment, one count of conspiracy to commit perjury and obstruct justice, and two counts of making a false declaration before a grand jury. The House Judiciary Committee adopted impeachment resolutions charging President Nixon with obstruction of justice, misuse of power, violating his oath of office, and failure to comply with House subpoenas.

"The tension was so thick," recalls Henry Gibson. "The atmosphere in the country was totally focused on Watergate. [H. R.] Haldeman was indicted the day before we started the shooting. Earl Warren died. The focus was on the Supreme Court. Plus, there was tremendous violence. I think on the day of July fifth they indicted the man who stormed into a church and assassinated Martin Luther King's mother. No one remembers that. This is four days before the picture begins. The progression was inescapable.

"The fifth day of the picture, I guess it was the fifteenth, the big news that evening was that a newscaster in Sarasota ended the program by saying, 'And in accordance with our policy of bringing you the latest in violence, blood, and guts, we're going to do something that's never been attempted before on television. We're going to bring you a live suicide.' She took out a gun and blasted herself in the head. These are all very spooky things. And they obviously had an influence on us."

Anyone prone to fatalism might choose to put an ominous spin on such beginnings and endings. But it was in the bendable nature of Robert Altman to ignore portents, shrug off hurdles, and somehow make them work for him.

So, when Geraldine Chaplin nervously announced to her director that she was three months' pregnant (by her companion, director Carlos Saura), he replied, nonplussed, "Oh, that's fine. Opal would be pregnant anyway. Any gals who work with me, they always get pregnant. Susannah York, she was trying for years to have a baby, then she did *Images,* and there she was, suddenly, pregnant." Altman also managed to keep his cool on his next film, *Buffalo Bill and the Indians,* when Chaplin broke her shooting arm learning how to ride a horse for her role as Annie Oakley. Rather than recast, he wrote the injury into the script.

Similarly, when Allan Nicholls learned the day of Altman's preshoot barbecue that his father was gravely ill, he didn't want to sully the festivities by telling Altman that he might have to leave the film even before it began. Nicholls found surprise absolution from his personal crisis on the first day of shoot. It was Wednesday, July 10, and the *Nashville* crew had taken over a section of Metro Airport to film Barbara Jean's return to Nashville from a burn clinic in Baltimore. (The recording-studio scene, which actually begins the film over the credits, crosscutting with

A pregnant Geraldine Chaplin relaxes off camera (*Jim Coe*)

shots of Hal Phillip Walker's campaign truck, would be filmed out of sequence weeks later.)

Nicholls knew that Altman had his hands full. The opening-day shoot was a "logistical nightmare," according to a.d. Tommy Thompson. Altman was setting up virtually his entire roster of characters (minus Kenny and Albuquerque, who would arrive in Nashville, respectively, by car and by truck in the following scene) in a chaotic overture of movement, sound bites, and music.

One camera was stationed in the airport soda fountain, to introduce Sueleen, Wade, Mr. Green, Tricycle Man, and Delbert Reese. Another was planted around the inside gates, to catch the arrival of L.A. Joan, John Triplette, Tom, Bill, and Mary. (A record poster introduces us to Connie White—Altman didn't want to bring Karen Black in till the Opry sequence was filmed, hoping to avoid paying the actress a full two-month salary for a

couple of weeks' work.) Outside, cameras were alternating between Channel Two newscaster Bill Jenkins (playing himself)
and the entrance of Barbara Jean, Barnett, Haven, Bud, and
Lady Pearl. Adding to the hubbub, Altman had hired a flotilla of
pearly-toothed local beauties to play Hal Phillip Walker's ubiquitous campaign workers. The locally spawned Tennessee Twirlers
were geared up to wreak synchronized havoc with batons and ri-
fles while Franklin High School music director Wayne Simpson
was coaching the school's band through a Sousa-like arrangement of Barbara Jean's "One, I Love You."

"Bob was there setting up," recalls Nicholls. "He saw me, and
in the midst of everything, he called me over and pulled me
aside. And he said, 'Look, I know what's happening with your father. Just treat it as if it's happening to me. Don't worry. You're
going to be in this film.'"

Altman's response to Nicholls's family dilemma exemplified a
patriarchal streak that resided in odd concert with his pricklier
inclinations. The tension between the two tendencies, abetted by
a broad-brimmed white hat and an unbridled zest for women
and scotch, lent Altman the air of a celluloid Papa Hemingway.
"Tough love," as Keith Carradine termed it. "He'd say things
like, 'Just remember, you don't owe me anything.' Or, 'I'll give
you one piece of advice: Don't take advice.'"

Michael Murphy is less equivocating regarding Altman's
brand of paternalism. "When the big events happen in your life,
like when you think you're going to die or your mother's going
to die, you want to discuss it with Bob. Because Bob's got the
handle on it. Dad tellin' you not to worry. He knows how to hand
it to you logically in that Kansas City kind of way. And why he's
so good with actors is he can do it [snaps his fingers] in a sentence. Don't worry, you're not going to die. He can tell you that
about a scene or when you're mother's got cancer. He can sum it
up for you quickly."

Altman's sixty-second parenting is part and parcel of a get-in-
get-out m.o. he developed during his television days. "Bob works
like a bandit," says *Nashville* production sound mixer Jim Webb.

And faced with the daunting logistics, cast size, and seven-week shoot schedule of *Nashville,* Altman felt his cinematographer from *California Split* seemed the man for the job.

"Paul was an odd case," says Alan Rudolph, who observed the Altman–Lohmann collaborations on the earlier film, *California Split,* and the movie that followed *Nashville, Buffalo Bill and the Indians.* "He had a Germanic streak and a sensitive side in him. There wasn't a self-importance about him. He was very much set in his ways, but perfect for Bob. A fast cameraman. He liked to hurry and sit down: quick and easy and no fuss about it. Bob didn't want artistic or artificial touches. Any artificiality was part of the theatrical side of what we were doing."

Altman was never one for spending much time on camera set-ups: It is rare that you go out of an Altman film humming the composition. Rather, he essayed in *Nashville* to shoot events in a documentary fashion, employing what he calls "escape hatches": open-ended routes that enabled him to bleed two independently constructed scenes together fluidly, as with the bridging of the Exit/In and political-smoker sequences in the second half.

For the look of the film, Altman and Lohmann decided to emulate the cheery, clashing sheen of tourist attractions on a plastic cafeteria placemat. Patriotic reds, whites, and blues would be emphasized whenever possible, with the help of Scott Bushnell's costume supervision. "Since we were dealing with so many people off the streets, masses of people, we had no control over color," explained Altman. "These crowds would show up and we couldn't just say, 'Don't let anyone wear purple tomorrow.' So we went for the bright look of the placemats that say 'Nashville,' 'the Parthenon,' 'Opryland,' 'the Ryman Auditorium.'"

In an effort to lend performances the cinema verité aspect of people being discovered in the midst of an action, actors were not always made aware of when a camera was going to be trained on them. Their only instruction: Stay in character at every moment.

For many, it was a disconcerting freedom. Scott Glenn remembers an actor accosting Altman before the airport scene was shot. "He said, 'Well, am I in a close-up or two-shot here?' And

Bob said, 'Well, what makes you think you're on camera at all?' And they said, 'What do you mean?' And Bob said, 'When I say action, just live your life. I'll either see you or I won't.'"

But there was nothing accidental about what the actors would be doing once the man said "Action." Each of the actors had carefully worked out their lines and activities for the scene in the days prior, taking their cues from a skeletal shooting script that Altman enlisted Alan Rudolph to distill from Tewkesbury's screenplay. The text that Rudolph cobbled together was purely functional, a goosing tool for the actors; little of the dialogue in it appears in the movie. Rudolph still credits Tewkesbury with the meat and soul of *Nashville*'s characters. "Joan would go in and find the language, the nuance of a character. But her script was a hundred and forty pages, and Bob always thought a script should be a blueprint." But Rudolph was merely an assistant architect: If actors wanted to make last-minute adjustments, they had to run them by chief planners Altman and Tewkesbury for discussion and approval.

In such an environment, it was easy for a character's ego to take over the actor. Henry Gibson, for example, assumed Haven Hamilton's identity from the moment Altman instructed him to drive Dave Peel (Buddy) and Barbara Baxley (Lady Pearl) out onto the landing field in his white Jeep. "Goddammit, I'm having the kid drive!' says Gibson, recreating his immediate impulse as he and Haven merged for the first time. "I have to stand up here and play to the crowd. They didn't come to see me drive!" So, Peel got behind the wheel and chauffeured Gibson and Baxley in.

The other white-plumed diva in the crowd, Barbara Jean, got the better of Ronee Blakley, who remembered Altman's instructions to her on the first day of shooting. "Just don't contradict me on the set," he told her, perhaps recalling their little *Key Largo* tussle. "If you disagree about something, we'll discuss it later. But time is very precious on the set."

As Blakley psyched herself up to make a royal descent from a private jet to a welcoming throng, Altman's admonition quickly went up in smoke. "The very first thing I was to do was to get off the airplane and make a little welcoming speech, which I wrote. I remember sitting in the plane, which was unbelievably hot, and everyone was sweating like mad and wondering why I wasn't sweating. I remember just concentrating, trying to be totally still.

"And as I was standing at the lectern, Bob came up to me and said, 'Okay, you're going to go out there and faint. And I want you to do this sign so that Allen Garfield will know that you're going to faint. And then I want you to go like this. [She mimes him demonstrating a move.] And I said, 'No, Bob, my knees would go first.' So there it was, my very first direction, and I had contradicted him."

Processing the needs and whims of willful actors was a piece of cake for Altman after spending the better part of the recent

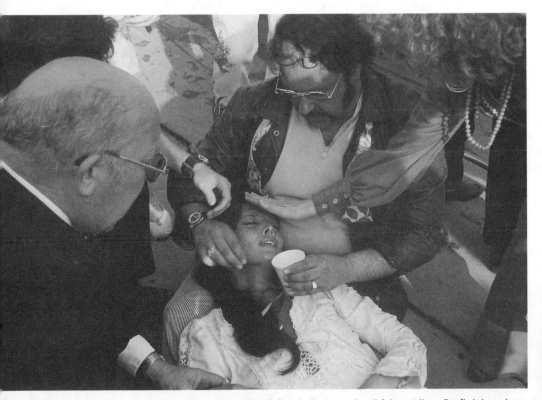

ee Blakley, as Barbara Jean, after executing a carefully choreographed faint. Allen Garfield, as her husband, Barnett, comforts her (right).

weeks wrestling with his perennial bête noire: the technician's unions. Altman had a habit of hiring local talent whenever feasible; for someone who was always working on a dime it was always a budget-conscious way to go. It also never hurt public relations with the local community. The crew for *Nashville*, by Altman's estimates, was about 50 percent local. In order to reach those numbers, however, Altman had to weather not only the bullying of the local teamsters, whose demands threatened to close down production before it started, but the bellyaching of Hollywood unions, who insisted that a local hairdresser he wanted to hire didn't have enough hours to qualify for the job.

But the worst, for now, was past: *Nashville* was off and running. "Everybody was charged up," recalls Alan Rudolph. Nobody more so, perhaps, than the marching band Altman had found to give the airport scene its galumphing brass cheer.

THE FRANKLIN High School Band was hired on in part because it was one of the few local bands that rehearsed during the summer. The town of Franklin is a well-to-do enclave that sits twelve miles south of Nashville and which has grown in proportion with the economic boom of its big-brother city. The band was all of sixty musicians strong at the time, and had not yet grown into the huge touring enterprise it is today.

Like many of the young *Nashville* cast and crew, Franklin music director Wayne Simpson was in his mid-twenties when Lion's Gate asked to showcase his marching band in *Nashville*. After meeting with Richard Baskin at the Jack Spence office, he agreed to arrange and rehearse two Barbara Jean numbers for the band in exchange for a small fee and donation to the music organization. He wasn't very film-savvy, but the project seemed honorable. Besides all the big stars involved, he'd heard they had hired the prestigious Fisk Jubilee Singers, booked the Ryman Auditorium for filming (no easy feat, a Nashvillian knew), and he had been promised that the film would have a PG rating.

Whatever vaunted expectations Simpson may have had about

the *Nashville* operation began to wither when he sat down to work with the film's young, longhaired music director. "I was expecting a Henry Mancini and I got Richard Baskin," Simpson says with a laugh. "I was surprised that he didn't seem to know much. I think he was in a little over his head. I had to tell him what the chords were, and write the lead sheets. The piano we were working with was an old upright. I was wondering how they got it into the room. I thought, Is this some kind of joke?"

Simpson rehearsed the band two hours daily for a month, a regimen that would be acknowledged by Lady Pearl in the film. No amount of practice, however, could prepare the band for the number of takes Altman would require of them in the ninety-degree heat ("Thirty-two," Simpson estimates, inflating for effect). Before the Franklin band's two-day shoot was through, two musicians passed out.

Altman took it all in stride. The "logistical nightmare" of trafficking the airport sequence seemed to have a galvanizing effect on him. He had marshaled crowds before in *MASH, Brewster McCloud,* and *McCabe & Mrs. Miller,* and felt utterly in his element. "He seemed to thrive on being the benign general behind this campaign to create something transcendent," says Keith Carradine. General Altman also knew that he was surrounded by expert troops who could take charge of the details, freeing him up to concentrate on his actors. Tommy Thompson, Bob Eggenweiler, Scott Bushnell, and Thomas Hal Phillips finessed the airport crowds and Barbara Jean fans, while Alan Rudolph choreographed the Tennessee Twirlers with the band. "It was the kind of thing I had always done well before," says Altman with an aw-shucks humility, "keeping a lot of balls in the air and improvising my way through a situation. I felt that I was at least ept with it."

One of the chief skills that Altman had become terrifically "ept" at over the years was shanghaiing dozens of nonactors into doing crowd scenes and walk-ons. It was typical of Altman's constant upstream swim against the Hollywood system to shun professional extras.

The airport. Altman stages a
car ballet in the parking lot.
(*Jim Coe*)

Scott Glenn as PFC Kelly watches as crowds storm Barbara Jean at the airport.

"Bob hates extras!" explains Geraldine Chaplin. "'Those damn extras!' Every film I've ever worked on with him you would always have to walk through the picket line of union extras. [He thinks] they don't know how to work. So he just gets people off the street."

"I don't know why there is such a big *chazerei* over this," says Altman, who hired two busloads of recovering addicts from Synanon to play gamblers in *California Suite* and a small army of American draft dodgers dwelling in the hills outside Vancouver to play the mining-town residents in *McCabe & Mrs. Miller.* "If you've written a line for them, you've got to pay them this. And then the residuals. These restrictions send me back to the time when I was doing all those television shows. I started writing characters in and giving them a line just so I could have an extra who could talk. That was one of the basic things in *MASH.* I had to go through the script and give every one of those characters names. And I'd give them one line in the script so I could use them as actors in improvisations."

Altman first came to blows with Allen Garfield over the irritating fine print involved in hiring on union extras. Staying with Garfield at the time was his wife-to-be, an attractive, waifish young woman with reddish hair named Carol McGinnis. When Garfield cajoled his director into putting McGinnis in front of the camera, Altman agreed that she could be part of Barnett's entourage. At the airport she is seen escorting Barbara Jean off the plane and rushing to her side when she faints.

"The night we watched the dailies of the airport scene," recalls Henry Gibson, "[Garfield] went crazy with pleasure because he had never seen her before on-screen, this woman he thought was so beautiful." In her next scene, as she helps settle the ailing Barbara Jean into her bed at the Vanderbilt Medical Center, Garfield started giving her lines. "Then he insisted that she be given billing and a salary! And they had the ugliest fight about this."

"Finally we gave up," said Altman. "We just put her under contract as a bit player. Then, when he went home for some kind of break, she went with him. And when he came back he didn't bring her back. She just suddenly disappeared. They had a fight or something."

In the coming seven weeks, Altman would enlist a legion of doctors, nurses, Shriners, and Chamber of Commerce folk to play themselves. Anyone who was hanging out on the set was invariably hustled before the cameras, including production assistants, soundmen, and hapless visitors.

Alan Rudolph, second assistant director, created scenarios for *Nashville* extras to play.

In order to heighten a sense of documentary reality, Alan Rudolph created on-the-spot scenarios for these instant actors, many of whom would be glimpsed on screen for a nanosecond, if at all. Working by the seat of his pants like a director of silent two-reelers (or an Altman acolyte), Rudolph coached his amateur charges into a makeshift character for whom which they could either improvise small talk or remain mute, with a purpose. Visiting journalist Harry Haun was researching a piece on *Nashville* for the *Los Angeles Times* when he was thrown into a scene in which Sueleen Gay sings "Let Me Be the One" to an unreceptive crowd at Deemen's Den. Ushering him into a seat down front, Rudolph briefed him. "Okay, now, you're a field man working for ABC/Paramount. Your boss is down in Nashville from New York and you want to impress him by taking him and his wife to this little dive on lower Broadway. And you're telling him all about this great singer he's going to hear . . ."

Haun sat down next to the fictional boss and the missus, getting into character. As Gwen Welles ascended the stage and proceeded to croak wretchedly through her song, Haun realized that his position at ABC/Paramount was on the line. His entire body crumpled in dismay. "If you look closely," says Haun with discernible pride, "you can see my elbow go limp in silhouette."

Rudolph's painstaking work with even the most marginal players was neither simply an aesthetic choice nor a director's ruse to keep his second assistant director off the streets. It exemplified the ego-shattering ensemble ethos that shot through all of *Nashville*, a movie in which the country bourgeoisie and upper crust rub shoulders. (It did not pass Henry Gibson's notice that *Nashville* began shooting on Proust's birthday.) In Rudolph's words, "It was giving audiences equal exposure to people who are supposed to be stars and people who are supposed to be anonymous. And that usually doesn't happen in films."

IT WAS undeniably admirable of Altman to want to level the playing field between king and spear carrier. But how can one possibly sort out the babble in a movie that has twenty-four main spear carriers competing with hundreds of Nashville centurions?

That was a question that had haunted Altman back in 1970 when he made *McCabe & Mrs. Miller* for Warner Brothers. Canadian sound editor John V. Gusselle had neither the experience nor the equipment to make Altman's experiment in overlapping speech decipherable. When the movie had its first press screenings in June of 1971, the multiple conversations on screen were all but drowned out by the testy chorus of "What did he say?" from the attending critics. Warners nervously rushed the film over to Richard Portman, a sound mixer working at Goldwyn who had a reputation as a dialogue king. Despite Portman's eleventh-hour surgery and a life-giving review by Pauline Kael, audiences continued to complain about the muddiness of the sound track.

The solution arrived via a young documentary whiz named

Jim Webb. A USC film grad who had made a name in the industry doing multitrack sound for the music documentaries *Joe Cocker: Mad Dogs and Englishmen* and *Elvis on Tour,* Webb had learned a thing or two about sound working on golf shows in which he hooked individual radio mikes onto four and five participants at a time. The technique itself was not new. The innovation that Webb was toying with was to split the chat picked up on the mikes onto individual sound tracks, enabling him in effect to browse the tracks and pick out the good stuff for the final cut. "There wasn't anyone in Hollywood who knew how to do that," testifies Richard Portman, a self-styled hippie freak whose work on *McCabe* would launch him onto the Altman team for the duration of the seventies.

Webb came to Altman through a recommendation from Paul Lohmann. Altman liked the flexibility that multitrack afforded of being able to sift through the sound in the editing room. He asked Webb if it was possible to use multitrack on dialogue the way he had used it on music and golf matches. "Well, sure," Webb answered, "but you're going to have so much sound that the only really sane thing to do is to put radio mikes on everybody, and that way you'll have some control over it."

With the help of sound engineer Jac Cashin, another USC whiz kid, Altman built the equipment for the Lion's Gate eight-track sound system. It was not immediately clear which of the two movies he had in the works, *Nashville* or *California Split,* would inaugurate the new machinery. Given its epic scale and musical demands, *Nashville* seemed the likely candidate.

In Webb's opinion, it was fortunate *California Split* came first. A gambling saga that rotated around essentially just two actors, George Segal and Elliott Gould, *California Split* would provide a more practical laboratory in which to tool around with the new sound system. The way Webb figured it, he could perform damage control by containing the two stars onto three tracks, left, center, and middle, the way he had with the live music in his concert movies. It would also help him minimize the potential for

Sound mixer Jim Webb mans the 8-track sound cart. Webb's innovations in multitrack sound were first employed in Altman's *California Split.*

phasing, the whooshing hum that can occur when sound crosses between two or more mikes in close proximity.

Among the techniques that Webb would discover on *California Split* was the "sound zoom," in which the sound volume adjusts to reflect the movement of the camera. "There were three desks in a room, and George Segal and Elliott Gould have to sell their insurance to raise quick cash. Segal is sitting at the last desk, [there's] a conversation going on at the second desk, and something going on in Spanish at the first desk. Three distinct things, so I miked each desk. Later on watching the dailies, I notice the camera starts at the first desk—that's the first track— the camera zooms to the second desk—the second track—and onto to George's conversation at the third. So I went back and literally did a 'sound zoom' at the same time and speed as the camera."

Using related techniques, Altman would be able to shift the sound emphasis from one area of a room in which a number of conversations are occurring to another area. "We found out at the Picking Parlor in *Nashville,* where you have Henry Gibson talking at a table and then it goes over to Bob Doqui yelling across the room at Timothy Brown, that while you can't isolate what everybody is saying (because there is always a leakage between mikes) what you can do is tip the balance of the scene one way or another."

Pushing the limits of eight-track on *Nashville,* Altman had his soundmen attach body mikes to six or seven of his actors at a time. Finding the right spot on the actor's person occasionally required a little ingenuity. Since a woman's mike would hook onto her brassiere, the minimally attired Shelley Duvall had to wear a transmitter between her shoulder blades. If there were more than seven actors speaking in a scene, some crafty sharing was the order of the day. "In the big scenes I had to talk into Keith's shoulder," recalls Allan Nicholls.

Not all of the sound would be processed by body mikes. In the airport scene, for example, an old-fashioned overhead boom captured the Franklin High School Band and ambient noise while television reporter Bill Jenkins announced Barbara Jean's arrival into a live hand mike.

Hal Phillip Walker's ever-nattering sound truck would actually "invade" a scene silently (driven not by Thomas Hal Phillips, but one of the Walker girls). Walker's platform bites, recorded in one breathless speech in a studio, were edited and dubbed into a scene later. The deployment of Walker's campaign speech as a recurring sound fixture throughout *Nashville* was the consummation of a technique that Altman had carried over from the comical public-address system announcements in *MASH* into the recurrent radio bulletins in *Brewster McCloud* and the omnipresent radio shows in *Thieves Like Us*: using mediated chatter as both a running character and an aural glue that binds the visual elements of the film.

One of Webb's more enduring sound innovations was the system he created for phone conversations, most notably the ones in which we see and hear Lily Tomlin being propositioned in real time by an off-screen Keith Carradine. "I tried patching in phone calls in *California Split,* but I hadn't yet figured out that what I really needed to do was to get rid of the on-camera voice over the phone to make it work. By *Nashville,* I figured out what I had done wrong.

"I ran battery-operated phones. And we took the speaker transmitter out of [Tomlin's] on-camera phone. When you do that, Carradine [who is in another room "offstage"] can't hear her. So you give him earphones, so now he is hearing Tomlin live through the microphone that is replacing the transmitter. And then he can talk right back live into the transmitter in his off-camera phone, and what he is saying is going into Tomlin's ear. It's the perfect system because you can do it in real time and sound isn't leaking into anything."

The mutual bravado of Altman and his chief soundman usually blinded them to the scary reality that they were making it all up as they went along. The sheer newness of what they were up to surfaced weeks into the filming, as they tried to figure out how to shoot Henry Gibson taping "200 Years" in the recording studio. "We had dialogue going on inside the studio and inside the glass control rooms. I had no idea if there was any perspective. I said, 'Bob, are we doing this right?' He said, 'Yeah, yeah, that's fine, that's right, we're doing this right.' So I got all these mikes going and about ten minutes later he came up to me and said, 'We doing this right?'"

At the dailies in the evening and in the postshoot period in the editing room, Altman would comb over a scene repeatedly, listening in turn to each of the tracks to sift through what the different mikes were picking up. It was a painstaking process that would test the mettle of his soundmen. Webb recalls, "I'd go up to Bob and say, 'What do you want to hear at dailies tonight?' Because we ran them three tracks at a time, dividing them into two three-tracks and a left over seventh if we needed it. The eighth was in sync. And he'd go, 'I want to hear these three.' So I'd write

Ned Beatty, as Delbert Reese, overhears his wife Linnea on an extension phone.
A microphone placed where the phone sits allowed the cast (and audience) to
eavesdrop on phone calls.

down A,B,C, and then 1, 2, 3 for the alternates. And then I had
to sit there in dailies at night and redo the whole thing, put back
together what I had split apart during the day. And you think,
God, I hope I remember what I did so it doesn't sound weird or
I miss somebody."

Of all the oversights in the 1975 Oscar nominations, none is
more inept than the failure of the film Academy to acknowledge
the eight-person team behind *Nashville*'s audacious and complex
sound. "We felt that there was a lot of jealousy or something,"
says Richard Portman, who would win an Oscar three years later
for his Best Sound on *The Deer Hunter.* "No one had ever done
this before. The editing procedures were brand-new, as was the

technology. We just dreamt it up off the top of our heads. To this day, they're going more and more to multitrack on production recording, but they aren't even close to what we were doing in that day."

For his part, Jim Webb is not convinced that multitrack ever caught on as a device for dramatic film. "You're working with seven times the information. Unfortunately, today it's about speed. They cut schedules, everything, back. Money is everything. People today don't want more, they want faster. Multitrack is not faster, it's more inventive, it's more interesting, it's richer. But nobody wants to spend the time and the money."

Jim Webb took his phone speaker system developed for *Nashville* and worked it to the hilt the year following in Alan J. Pakula's *All the President's Men.* He got his Oscar, at last.

MONDAY, JULY 15, the entire cast, but for Karen Black, was assembled on a closed-off section of Interstate 65 to film a highway accident scene. The thermometer hit a new high for this, the fifth day of shooting, and the reflecting heat from the Tarmac threatened to melt the actors like a wax candle. They would be there for the next three days.

Given the complexity of the scene they were to shoot, preparations had been relatively cool. A freeway pileup would bring traffic to a halt, spilling all of the characters who had just left the airport onto the road for a series of defining encounters, each of which help to solidify the various dramatis personae. A lot of cars had to collide, a lot of actors had to bump up against one another. The scene would inevitably be compared to the apocalyptic traffic jam in Jean-Luc Godard's *Weekend,* but it was less of an homage than an unpleasant reality of Joan Tewkesbury's second visit to Nashville.

First, Altman needed a road. "This is where graft and corruption surface in Nashville," says Jim Webb, alluding to the old-boy network that cut through the government red tape. Sections of the Silliman-Evans Bridge off Interstate 65 had recently fallen

Alan Rudolph (center left) and Altman ready
  the traffic accident. (*Jac Cashin*)

Alan Rudolph, Altman, and Tommy Thompson. (*Jim Coe*)

Altman takes five under a
  way overpass. (*Jim C*

Opal crashes Tommy Brown's van. Timothy Brown (center left, pointing) and Geraldine Chaplin (center right).

off into the Cumberland River, requiring a two-mile stretch of the divided six-lane highway to be closed off to traffic in one direction while repairs were done. It was an answered prayer, since ongoing city traffic in the other direction could offer the scene a measure of verity at minimal cost.

How do you book a closed highway in Nashville? Call in Thomas Hal Phillips, the set's resident Houdini with a knack for opening up the

Albuquerque and Kenny confer after the accident.

The accident pileup. Haven Hamilton's jeep is at the left. (*Jim Coe*)

most tightly sealed of government doors. Phillips phoned up his brother Frank, the trucking magnate. "He hauled a lot of people in and out of Nashville," explains Phillips with obvious pride. "He was also very, very close friends with the governor." Frank made some calls, Thomas Hal went to see the people he called, and Altman got a piece of the interstate for as long as he needed it.

With stuntmen in tow, Tommy Thompson headed over to the freeway to hatch up an accident strategy. The plan: A couch would slip off the back of a car, which would continue on oblivious to the chain of havoc it was unleashing. A car conveying a speedboat would then swerve to the left to avoid hitting the couch, and the next car in line would spin around in an attempt to avoid the boat. Three more cars would bang into each other in

Haven Hamilton and entourage: Henry Gibson,
Barbara Baxley, Dave Peel.

quick succession, and then the *Nashville* folks could pull up slowly behind them once the wreckage had been safely effected.

The accident went off without a hitch, first take, freeing the camera crew to hop around the pileup like bees collecting pollen as they caught the actors playing out their individual scenarios. (A makeup truck was parked along the side of the interstate set for the women and Henry Gibson, who, in addition to hair adjustment, required pencil lines to look older than his thirty-eight years.) Most of the actors had spent their free day before improvising and polishing dialogue for the scene. Tewkesbury's script, and the shooting script Rudolph culled from it, contained only a horrified "Oh my God!" from Norman (David Arkin), followed by Bill (Allan Nicholls) imploring him not puke. (Both Norman's and Mary's lines are cut from the finished scene.) Instead,

Nicholls, roasting under a polyester shirt from within Bill and Mary's limo, bartered with a stranger for a turtle-shaped ottoman. Given the fraying state of Bill's relationship with Mary, it would be his surrogate source of comfort to have and to hold for the rest of the film.

The first time we see the sweet drifter Kenny (David Hayward), he is attempting without luck to restart his stalled-out car. In a bit of business whose prophetic nature does not register the first time one sees *Nashville,* a hose explodes after Kenny lifts up the front hood. Exasperated, he pulls his violin case from the backseat and heads off into town by foot. Over the course of the film, the case will be opened to reveal his violin and later, in a sinister allusion to the old gangster movie cliché, a gun.

Tewkesbury had originally written the prop in as a guitar case, upon which Kenny had pasted "one of those street-artist sketches of himself that looks more like somebody else than Kenny." Days before the freeway shoot, David Hayward was roaming Opryland Amusement Park with Kenny's violin case as part of his on-the-town-in-character training. Passing a portrait artist, Hayward decided to have a caricature done for the case. Without identifying himself or the intended purpose of the sketch, Hayward sat patiently while the artist scribbled away. Finally, the artist ripped the finished work off the pad and handed it to the actor with a proud grin. The caricature had Hayward pulling a machine gun out of the violin case. He paid the artist, and stalked off to find another portrait artist.

The camera also discovers Michael Murphy and Ned Beatty paired together in a car, as campaign handler John Triplette explains his theory of the "grassroots appeal" of country singers—as opposed to those "crazy" movie stars—to country-star attorney and liaison Delbert Reese. Murphy and Beatty brainstormed closely throughout the film on the odd alliance between the characters. "We were playing one of the stronger through lines in the piece," explained Beatty, who utters the prescient line, "This is going to be a big mess," as he saunters over to ask Kenny to move his car.

Beatty says that he and Murphy were working out their scenes with the anticipation that their candidate, Hal Phillip Walker, and not Barbara Jean, would be shot. "Triplette was using me as an end to the people in country music. We spent a lot of time with Tewkesbury, trying to find this thread through to the end when this bullet is fired at a candidate you've never seen."

Tewkesbury explained these seemingly confused expectations. "What you had to do with each of the actors was work on their own truth, for their characters. Their truth was that they were protecting their client, no matter what. But Bob said from the moment I handed in my first script that it was going to be Barbara Jean. How you arrive at that is a very twisted journey."

Altman's basic directions to Beatty and Murphy before training the camera on them carried over to everyone: "You guys talk all you want and when I get bored with you I'll cut away from you." Altman never got bored with Geraldine Chaplin, whose over-the-top inventions for Opal expanded with each passing scene, much to the eventual chagrin of many critics. It is interesting to note that of all the *Nashville* women, Chaplin struck Henry Gibson as exuding the greatest sense of security and self-confidence from day one.

Nothing could have been further from the truth. The prospect of flying without the net of a script terrified the daughter of Charles Chaplin and Oona O'Neill. And her fears reached their acme with her first filmed scene, interviewing Linnea Reese (Lily Tomlin) about her family in the front seat of Linnea's tan woody.

"That's when I thought I was going be fired," says Chaplin. "That's when I thought, Okay, now it's all going to come out that I'm not that kind of actress. I can't do it. I'd never been to any acting school where they'd done any kind of improvisation. And of course you're not improvising [with Altman]. You just think you are.

"He gave me one cue. He said, 'When Lily says she has two deaf children, just say, "That is so awful!" Instead of being interested, be so sorry for her, so horrified. Make it real, because then it will appear to be very false and very fake.'

"And that's how I started it. 'How *awful* it must be!' And Lily says, 'No, it's not awful, they're wonderful.' And he starts laughing and says, 'Yes, come on, do that. That's so funny.' So in fact you would do exactly what he wanted to but you'd think that you were inventing it." But for two memorable soliloquies on the subject of school buses and auto graveyards, Chaplin credits the lion's share of Opal's best lines to Altman.

Chaplin's initial queasiness over improvising was heightened by the prospect of having to film her first scene opposite Lily Tomlin. "I was so in awe of her. She is such a classy and brainy and funny and extraordinary woman. I thought, Oh, God, my first scene has to be with her. I think I could have dealt with just about anyone else."

Albuquerque (Barbara Harris) discusses flyswatters with her husband, Star (Bert Remsen). Harris asked to have her scenes reshot after seeing the dailies.

Barbara Harris would also arrive with a truckload of apprehensions, but unlike Chaplin's, they would haunt her for the duration of the shoot. Significantly, the improvisationally trained Harris was not parroting her director's suggestions. The pearls of dialogue she came up with were self-generated.

In her first appearance as Albuquerque, sitting in the cab of her husband Star's (Bert Remsen) red pickup, Harris delivers a wondrously off-kilter, Second City–style improv.

ALBUQUERQUE: . . . And ya see what happens, he made a million dollars on a flyswatter, because it had a red dot in the center.
STAR: Flyswatter?
ALBUQUERQUE: Yes, that's right. Red dot. He was sitting in the buffet and he was eatin' and he saw a woman and she was swattin' flies, and she, he said, 'Well, what makes the difference between, y'know, flyswatters?' Because it has to do with the industrial revolution.

One would love to hear what else Harris had up her sleeves before and after Altman got "bored" and cut away. Harris had tossed around ideas with her friend, the late cartoonist-writer-songwriter Shel Silverstein, who had written songs for the country-music flick *Payday* and with whom she cowrote a number for *Nashville* (which was eventually cut). She shared thoughts with Silverstein about women like Albuquerque who are always running away from their husbands. But the final impulse for her dizzy line of attack came from her director. "He'd always say, 'Harris, you gotta be crazy. Really crazy.'"

It was Altman's method of getting maximum mileage out of a character he felt was the least credible of Tewkesbury's gallery and an actress who had her own share of eccentricities with which to contend. Among the most irksome, Harris had a habit of disappearing, not unlike her character.

"We could not find her from the first day she was to shoot," recalls Joan Tewkesbury. "It was about fear. It was almost an out-of-body detachment. At the time, Bob and I were beside ourselves. Who the fuck can we recast? 'Cause we had waited and shot around her and everything possible. And then she pulls up in a cab two hours late?"

"At one point she wanted to leave the shoot; I remember putting myself in front of the door and saying, 'You can't leave, you're not leaving!'" claims Richard Baskin, adding, "She was very afraid of her singing stuff in the film, which is very interesting, because she was so experienced."

"I think Barbara became that flaky, flighty character," says Tommy Thompson. "She would wander off, or not understand. It would drive him crazy."

Looking back, Harris doesn't deny her fears. Many of them were focused on her director, who she said fired her several times over the course of the picture. "Me and Barbara Baxley. He'd say, 'Oh, you New York actors! You're fired.' He was very scary. I stayed away as much as possible. You had to know him, and I didn't know him. He wasn't predictable. And that's fine. It's just sometimes when people aren't predictable and they ask for the unpredictable and you get punished for the unpredictability that they asked for, it's a bit confusing."

Keith Carradine empathized with Harris's anxieties, locating a hazard zone in Altman's laissez-faire policy toward his actors. "If you had the moxie, he'd say, 'Okay, show me what you got.' You could get stroked, or you could get shafted. There was an invitation to bring everything you could to the party. But it was at your own peril."

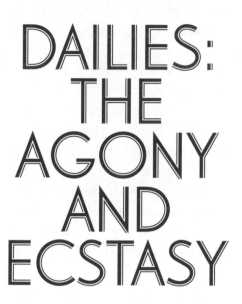

CHAPTER EIGHT

DAILIES: THE AGONY AND ECSTASY

(Wherein Allen Garfield Misbehaves and David Arkin Goes Postal)

A FAMILY SNAPSHOT FOR THE MANTELPIECE.

Mother listens raptly while her son tells a story of how he passed his swimming test at school that day. The boy is partially deaf, so he uses a combination of signing and speech, miming a deep dive with his hands and exclaiming proudly how the kids and teachers called him "goldfish." The boy returns his mother's smile, revealing braces on his teeth that have the effect of heightening his youthful exuberance. A crucifix dangling below his chest is thrown into glowing relief by his dark T-shirt. Father chuckles absentmindedly at his son's high spirits. His arms cradle the shoulder of the boy's younger sister (also hearing impaired, also smiling), who is waiting to set the table for dinner.

The at-home scene that Lily Tomlin and Ned Beatty share with their screen children is about as close to a Kodak moment as the jaundiced *Nashville* (or any Robert Altman movie) ever comes. After the high-pitched succession of political pitches, seductions, and diva turns that have preceded this scene, there is something especially comforting about the family iconography at play here. We bask in the warmth exchanged by Tomlin and the boy, James Dan Calvert, noting all the while that there is something slightly askew with the picture. As Delbert Reese, Beatty projects discomfort with his son's performance and seems impatient for him to get on with it. Delbert's daughter, played by Donna Denton, is not entirely at ease with dad's arm around her shoulder. In the next room their dinner guest, campaign manager John Triplette, is on the phone arranging a girlie act for a political fund-raiser. And in just a few minutes, Tomlin will be interrupted from dinner by a phone call from a near-stranger with adulterous intent.

Altman lights up at the mention of the scene. It is one of two resplendently sentimental incidents in the film (along with Mr. Green's reaction to the sudden news of his wife's death), a surefire repudiation to any suspicions that Altman's oeuvre lacks heart. The scene shines with the authenticity of a director who thrives within the family hearth—he dotes on four sons and two daughters from three marriages, including an adopted son—and without. Upon the release of *Nashville,* he simultaneously acknowledged to *The Washington Post* his commitment to his long-time wife Kathryn and his unquenchable thirst for other women.

The shining focus of the Reeses' dinner-table gathering is unquestionably James Dan Calvert, beaming insouciantly as young Jimmy. Calvert was a student at the Tennessee School for the Deaf in Knoxville when Altman and company canvassed the League for the Hard of Hearing for two children. Completely deaf in his right ear, which was missing a nerve at birth, he compensated through his left with the boost of a hearing aid.

Calvert's father, a National Guard member and farm laborer, ducked out of the picture shortly after learning his son was deaf. Young James lived alone with his mother, a drug technician whom Tomlin and Beatty each recall with great effusiveness.

"She was a wonderful woman," says Tomlin. "Very simple, very supportive of the boy. I based a lot of my relationship with the kids just from observing, hearing her talk and knowing that she was completely okay with it."

Tomlin thought James was perfect when she saw him at an audition: bright, vivacious, demonstrative. Both of his screen parents responded in kind. "He loved to be touched and hugged," recalls his surrogate dad Beatty, whose own paternal affection in the scene is undercut by Delbert's awkward refusal to accommodate his children's deafness by learning to sign. "And he loved to hit me. He was strong. This was my 'connect' with Del. I have for some reason in my three marriages been the toucher, the hugger. And I left the other things to Lily."

Lily Tomlin demonstrated potent maternal instincts throughout the filming of *Nashville*, lavishing quality time on Scott Glenn's kids and commiserating with the Tennessee Twirlers on the tribulations of being a drum majorette. She was most concerned that the young actors playing Linnea's children not be exploited. "I was worried about the kids being picked up and thrust into the limelight, and then suddenly we leave town."

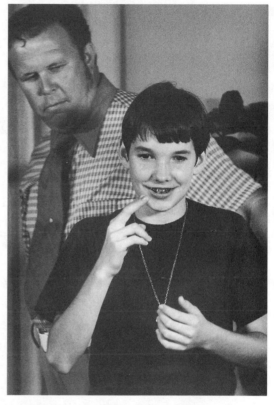

Delbert Reese (Ned Beatty, rear) looks on as son Jimmy (James Ray Calvert) relates a school anecdote through signing. The model for the Reese children were the deaf parents of Louise Fletcher, originally considered to play Linnea Reese.

Calvert soon came to regard Tomlin as an idealized second mother. Even his own mother, according to Calvert, was not as conscientious about signing as Tomlin. "The day I was to get married," he recalls, "my mother came up to me when I was fixing breakfast and she was crying. She said she wished she had learned all of sign language to communicate with me, but it was too late. The movie really teaches that communicating in sign language between mothers and children in these situations is very important."

The anecdote that Calvert tells his family in *Nashville* was plucked out of his own experience of learning how to swim at the Boys Club in Nashville. Altman always encouraged his actors to dip into their own lives, and *Nashville* is littered with self-referential throwaways. When Star tells Kenny how he reminds him of a guy he knew in the Navy, Remsen is obliquely hearkening back to his naval days in World War II when he sustained shrapnel and burn injuries over the course of eight invasions. When Tom nudges one-night stand Opal out of a dream and she says, "For a moment I thought I was in Israel," it is a glib nod to Chaplin's recent stay on a kibbutz.

Altman could manipulate knowledge of his actors' lives in diabolical ways. Filming an early scene at the Old Time Picking Parlor in which Kenny sets himself down at a table next to Bill and Mary, David Hayward shuddered with surprise to hear Cristina Raines say to Allan Nicholls, "He looks like Howdy Doody." Raines, who had apparently been fed the line in rehearsal by Altman, would be disturbed to discover years later that Hayward's grade-school chums used to taunt him with that name.

Altman explains his propensity for drawing upon actors' backgrounds in developing his characters: "When an actor is looking for something to talk about and they have something in their own lives, I say, talk about that. It pushes them into using themselves as research rather than trying to make up a character. It comes out with the smell of truth about it. It's a shortcut device for me, rather than having some writer just writing a history and then making the actor fit into it. And I still find that very valid."

As did James Dan Calvert, who turned in one of the more natural and pleasing cameos in *Nashville*. Calvert still treasures the two autographed Lily Tomlin comedy albums the actress gave him in 1974, even though he can no longer listen to them. Five years later, he woke up one morning to discover that the hearing in his left ear had mysteriously disappeared, never to return.

WHEN THE cast of *Nashville* speaks of the nightly ritual of watching the dailies, many of them recall the awe and amusement they felt watching a troubled Ned Beatty tell Lily Tomlin that he was going to hard-boil himself a couple of eggs. Beatty's turn as attorney-to-the-stars Delbert Reese is one of the unsung joys of *Nashville,* a credibly understated portrait of a hapless family man and a fitfully unctuous industry insider.

If Beatty's performance has a particular ring of authenticity, it may be because he grew up in Delbert country. The son of a heavy-equipment salesman, Beatty was raised in Louisville, Kentucky, which he describes as a "Nashville without the music." His initial model for Delbert was his mother's brother William. "Nice-looking guy," says Beatty, describing his Uncle Billy. "Married a rich girl from a little mining town, Harlan, Kentucky, got set up in a business, and sort of lived his life quietly out. He sort of went along to get along."

Before gaining screen prominence as one of the victimized outdoorsmen in *Deliverance,* Beatty spent seven years honing his technique in the hothouse environment of Washington, D.C.'s Arena Stage. Under Zelda Fichandler, the company was a doctrinaire pioneer of multiculturalism ("we almost invariably had one Arab actor"). Beatty accepted his niche as "the company redneck," a loutish role that gave him the latitude to speak his mind with impunity. When Fichandler announced to the ensemble that she was going to integrate the company the following season with 15 percent black actors, Beatty stunned everyone to silence by saying, "It's wonderful that black actors should get a chance, but how many people can you hire that can function at the level we've been functioning?"

Ned Beatty's native outspokenness had saved his butt just

prior to making *Nashville,* when he survived an ugly eviction tussle with the help of a little good-old-boy intimidation. "I have a bad habit: If I think somebody is leaning on me, I try to get them on the phone or look them in the face and explain to them that I'm from Kentucky and we don't hire lawyers. We just hurt people." The landlord backed off.

For all the bluff, Beatty is a big teddy bear of a guy, good-natured and polite. Still, no one was about to question his absence from the viewing of the dailies at the end of the day. Going to dailies, a ritual usually reserved for the director, screenwriter, producers and technical crew, was de rigueur for the cast on an Altman set. Everyone went to dailies. Watching the rushes from the day's filming was the big family wind-down, the way to monitor your performance and the progress of your fellow actors. Altman regards attendance at dailies as important for morale. "The actors become infatuated with the project. They become a team, pulling for one another and not competing."

Altman never strong-armed anyone into attending dailies, but he had a convincing way of making you feel like a meathead if you didn't. When Scott Glenn asked him at the outset, "What if I don't feel like coming to dailies?" he responded, "Well, Scott, if you're not emotionally mature enough to handle them, don't show up."

Not that it was necessarily a grind. For many, dailies was the party after the party of filming. Altman always had a full bar set up in the screening room at the Jack Spence Motor Hotel, with plenty of Cutty Sark in reserve for himself. As the lights went down, the room filled up with a biker's perfume of Budweisers, Cheez Doodles, and marijuana.

"I had no drinking restrictions then," admits Altman, who gave up his punishing love affair with scotch in the early nineties. Altman's alcohol consumption could have unpleasant consequences for the crew. "He was capable of tongue lashings," says Sue Barton, "more so on *California Split,* where we sat in a little room, than *Nashville.* He always did that, get ahold of somebody and murder them. Not as much with the actors. You were always thinking, When is it going to be my turn? There's always been with Bob an air of dangerousness; you're never quite sure of where you stand."

Even fired up by scotch, Altman seemed to show more respect for the frailty of his actors. After watching herself in the freeway pileup, Barbara Harris was overcome with distress. "Barbara sat down front and suddenly she got up and ran out the back door," says Altman. "Within ten minutes I got a message that she wanted me to come to her room. I went to her house, and she said, 'Okay, don't get excited about this. I'm going to pay for this. But we have to reshoot everything.' I said, 'Barbara, first off, everything you did was terrific. I loved what we got from you. I don't want to change any of it. And there is no way that anyone

Altman checks in with Barbara Harris before her scene at the freeway pileup. (*Jim Coe*)

can pay to set up that situation again. We had ten different stories going on shooting in hundred-and-ten-degree heat.' What she asked was impossible."

Just before dailies one evening, Allan Garfield sent Altman a request that they be pushed back to later. He finally arrived after missing several scenes, saying he'd been in a poker game. Pushing Altman to the limit of his patience, he told him he wanted to leave the set for a few days to go back to L.A. Words were exchanged, and Garfield stormed out, cursing at Altman over the mortified heads of fellow cast members.

"That was almost a knock-down-drag-out," recalls William Myers, a Nashville graphic artist who observed the fracas. "Allen said, 'Nobody can take direction from a goddamn drunk! Always smoking pot! Never gives a clear direction!' And Altman said, 'You'll never work in this town again!'

"And he didn't," Myers adds with a sly wink. "Garfield never worked in Nashville again."

"I placated him and bit my tongue all through the picture," claims Altman, who otherwise has high praise for Garfield's characterization of Barnett. "I wanted to kill him through the whole thing. He was just a jerk."

Garfield returned Altman's affection by sporting a necktie that Francis Ford Coppola had given him on *The Conversation* and commenting for all to hear, "That's not how Coppola would have done it."

LOIS GIBSON was worried. Her husband Henry had been off in Nashville for over three weeks. They had stayed in touch by phone every day. Everything had been fine. Suddenly, she noticed a change in his voice, something remote, off-putting, discernibly not Henry. They had been married a long time, so she knew his moods sideways and back. What she was hearing now was bizarre. Threatening. Was there someone else in his life? Was their marriage in jeopardy?

She summoned their oldest son Johnny, they piled into her convertible and together they drove nonstop across the country. When they arrived in Nashville, her fears were quickly allayed. The change she discerned was real, but it was self-inflicted and it was curable. Her husband had *become* Haven Hamilton.

"Henry was Method-ing all over the place," says Cristina Raines, trying to describe the obsessiveness with which the actor had submerged himself into his character. "I was thinking a great deal like him," confirmed Gibson, who would studiously avoid visiting the set of a scene he wasn't in so as not to break the level of reality he had created for himself.

Gibson's exacting attention to Hamilton's attitude, speech, hair, and clothing extended as far as his choice of props. After

"Henry was Method-ing all over the place." Henry Gibson,
as Haven Hamilton, records "200 Years."

Barbara Jean faints and goes into the hospital, Gibson decided
that his peacock-vain character had to have the biggest flower
display sitting in her room. With the help of prop man Bob Anderson, Gibson conceived a giant horseshoe of white flowers with
a prominent HH radiating from the ribbon. Less prominent, but
no less megalomaniacal, is a metal plate that adorns the hallway
wall outside Barbara Jean's hospital room. Taking his cue from
Tewkesbury's notion that Hamilton once had a second son who
was killed in a shooting accident, Gibson ordered an engraved
plate made up to read, THIS WARD IS DEDICATED IN HONOR OF
TEDDY HAMILTON. The camera never gets close enough to make
out the wording, but it was mounted all the same with the bless-
ings of Tommy Thompson.

Gibson's most audacious bid for the soul of Haven Hamilton
would crop up in the raceway scene, as Haven and Lady Pearl

picnic on the bleachers with black country singer Tommy Brown. (The blue freezer case they use came cross-country with Gibson's anxious wife.) Yes, that's right, you did see Haven hand Tommy a hunk of watermelon. "I deliberately packed that container. That was a very racist statement. Earlier, when Bob Doqui says to Tommy Brown that he is the whitest nigger in town and Haven says, 'I won't have that kind of talk in public,' that's my public face. I may say other things quietly."

(He may and he does. As Tommy Brown walks off the Grand Ole Opry stage and makes a crack to Haven about how dead the audience is, Haven mutters from the side of his mouth, "He's lucky to be alive.")

Robert Doqui's total immersion in the character of Wade deliberately seeped into his off-camera relations with his fellow actors. In order to understand Wade, Doqui often gave his friends a hard time, friends like his tennis buddy Timothy Brown. "I had to discover what my relationship with each of the characters was. I had to know whether or not I liked Tommy Brown. I didn't. I thought he was passing. I kind of felt he looked down on a guy like me. [Again, Doqui slips effortlessly into his drunk-Wade drawl.] Here's conch head me and here is Tommy Brown singing his song and looking really suave. He didn't have any respect for me, and I let everybody know I didn't have any respect for him.

"I made life kind of tough for Geraldine. We were friends, but I would always try to find Wade in everything. So I kept needling her and getting on her nerves. It was antagonistic. But it worked for me because the way Bob works you have to be in the moment all the time."

In a couple of significant instances, the line that separated actors from their willful characters would blur to the point of alienating fellow actors. "Allen Garfield *was* Barnett," says Michael Murphy, who was so thrown by the transparent belligerency of Garfield's explosion at John Triplette during their face-off at the Parthenon that he fumfered his lines. Garfield's confrontational style was nurtured in his early days as a journalist. More recently, it was evoked in Garfield's bullish (if not self-congratulatory) *Los*

Angeles Times letter attacking the decision to award his friend Elia Kazan an honorary Oscar.

The other instance was a little more surprising. Ned Beatty recalls an early cast meeting with his usual pull-no-punches esprit. "Bob gets us all together in this room. We're all ready to start the movie. And he said, 'Look, I want you to have fun with this. There is only one thing we have to remember. Every character in this movie loves one character. Every one of these characters loves Barbara Jean.' Well, within a short time Ronee Blakley was the only actor in the film who was universally disliked. Allen Garfield kind of got the second vote to Ronee."

Beatty's claim would appear to be colored by his own perceptions: Both Blakley and Garfield had acolytes and well-wishers to spare. (Geraldine Chaplin's firebrand radicalism made her a kindred spirit for Blakley.) But Blakley's particular style of independence could rub some the wrong way, especially at a time when actresses with fervent opinions were even less welcome than they are now.

"Ronee was in left field most of the time," says Tommy Thompson. "She was making her own movie. You never quite knew where Ronee was going to be. She'd have these inspirations and rewrite this and do that, and Bob would say, 'What the hell is this?' And he would get her straightened around. But it was time-consuming. You never knew from night to morning what she'd done the night before to change her whole attitude. For him to keep it consistent was a challenge."

Beatty identifies Blakley's Achilles' heel in the difference between an actor's and a singer's temperament. "Bob was interested in seeing, if you put twenty-four actors together and then make any one of them better than any one else, how they would go at each other. Well, that's not what happened. You don't go at each other. You're working together, and when you improvise together you had damn well better be open—all the things that lead away from some kind of protectionism or one-upmanship. And she wasn't in on that. And I think it's because she came from a musician's world where singers are out in front."

Joan Tewkesbury concurred with Beatty's analysis, if not his conclusion. "Ronee brought the balls of a songwriter. She had more of an edge than Susan Anspach would have had, because she had no reputation to live up to. She had nothing to do but show up for work. And throw anything she wanted up on the wall."

Blakley's songwriter *cojones* came at a price, according to Beatty. "It almost seems to follow some rule that when you have a cohesive unit, an outsider is created for you, or you create one. There has to be someone or something from the outside. Look at how we work as nations. There is a certain belief that we don't function well unless we have an enemy as a target."

The potential for misfit status was strong in a shooting situation where so many of the actors and crew had bonded in previous films. In the process of trying to effect a democratic social order on his set, Altman inadvertently created a fraternal subculture that seemed to comment obliquely on the world of insiders and outsiders that made up *Nashville*. Besides Ronee Blakley, Barbara Harris and Lily Tomlin either perceived themselves or were perceived by others to be floating on a separate island from the rest of the Altman team at various points in the filming. "In general it was just tougher on the women," observes Henry Gibson of the mid-seventies culture of the south. "They couldn't just five of them get into a car and go have a pizza while they're waiting for the dailies. In the midst of making a movie that [depicts] a male-dominated world, they had to deal with all these cultural prohibitions themselves."

Altman, with the help of his wife Kathryn, tried to nip any feelings of alienation in the bud by rotating his attention among different groupings of actors at dinner in the evening. There were times, however, when an actor's doubts and insecurities were too deeply rooted to weed out.

David Arkin had every reason to feel at home on an Altman picture. A quick-witted actor and writer, he had worked with the director twice before, as Staff Sergeant Vollmer in *MASH* and as Harry in *The Long Goodbye*. He was facile with the art of improvisation from his early days with a comedy troupe called the Ses-

David Arkin: Darkness resided close to the surface. (*Jim Coe*)

sions, when he landed TV appearances with Johnny Carson, Joey Bishop, and Steve Allen.

In Arkin's case, the darkness that fuels a comedian's humor resided closer to the surface than most. He wallowed in great, tragic novels, identified with Charles Laughton, and viewed the world with the acerbity of Oscar Levant. One sweltering July evening, Arkin showed up at the *Nashville* poker circle dressed in a shirt, a sweater, and a sports jacket. When asked by his fellow players what he thought he was doing, Arkin replied drily, "It's just a general contempt for the elements."

Arkin tended to wear his neuroses on his multiple sleeves. He could not have been happy to see his initially showy character role as Norman the chauffeur whittled down to a few sweet but forgettable cameos. Arkin had been developing his bemused, monkey-in-the-middle character from the dyspeptic schnook of Tewkesbury's screenplay into a showbiz aspirant. Taking his cue from all of the actors who were writing their own songs and monologues, he asked Altman if he could write a stand-up routine for Norman. The routine he performed at the Picking Parlor, by all accounts, was dreadful: Henny Youngman by way of Sueleen Gay. As with the deadpan lounge-act send-ups of Andy Kaufman, it was hard to tell whether Arkin intended the awfulness or not. The scene, which would have been his showiest moment in the film, was cut.

Like his character, Arkin's would-be performing career was faltering. For all of his comic savvy, Arkin couldn't get arrested as an actor outside of Lion's Gate (four out of his eight screen credits are Altman movies). And his personal and career demons were aggravated whenever anyone would mistakenly call him Alan, a salt-in-the-wound reminder of another improvisationally trained Arkin whose film career had taken off. This mistake would happen with great frequency. In fact, to this day, his *Nashville* costars often refer to him, without thinking, as Alan.

One evening, Arkin was out having dinner at an upscale diner with his girlfriend, Altman, and a couple of the actors. Also present was Harry Haun, the visiting journalist for the *Los Angeles Times*. Without thinking, Haun said, "Alan, could you pass me the salt?" It was the final straw. His eyes glowered with a "slowly-I-turned" wrath. Arkin lunged across the table, tackled Haun to the floor, and choked him around the collar, screaming, *"My father's name is George! His name is not Alan! I'm not Alan Arkin! Don't you know the difference between Alan and David? I'm David Arkin, I'm not Alan Arkin!"*

Altman, ashen-faced and aghast, pulled Arkin off the stunned journalist. Haun was asked not to return to the set, and was later told by way of reassurance that the actor had been taking Valium.

The pharmaceuticals did not dull either Arkin's resentment or his talent for irony. The next day, he appeared on the set sporting a make-your-own-T-shirt popular at the time. It read, MY NAME IS DAVID ARKIN, IT IS NOT ALAN ARKIN. I HAVE NO RELATIONSHIP TO ALAN ARKIN. In the next few days, T-shirts started popping up around the set. I'M ALLAN NICHOLLS. I'M NOT ALAN ARKIN AND I'M NOT DAVID ARKIN. I'M ALLEN GARFIELD, I'M A FRIEND OF DAVID ARKIN'S. I'M KEITH CARRADINE. I'M A FRIEND OF ALLAN NICHOLLS.

CHAPTER NINE

SUMMER AND SMOKE

*(Wherein the Jack Spence Motor Hotel Mob
Steals a Crystal Decanter and Jeff
Goldblum Makes Goo-Goo Eyes
at Shelley Duvall)*

"Robert Altman is a very moral man"
—BARBARA HARRIS

BURIED BENEATH THE FLOTSAM AND JETÉS of Altman's mercurial output are two curiosities that even the most slavishly devoted aren't likely to have seen. *The Party* and *Pot au Feu* are a pair of brief, mischievous home-movie stunts that Altman tossed out in the mid-sixties. Minutes in length and utterly seductive in their Cracker Barrel cheesiness, they provide more clues to the kick-ass-and-boogie work environment that Altman evolved with *Nashville* than all of his other movies put together.

Shot in 1964 with three cameras tracking the unrehearsed events, *The Party* follows the attempts of a nerdy guy (*Whirlybirds* veteran Robert Fortier, who later appeared in *3 Women* and *A Wedding*) to score at a swinging poolside party. The party was real, the guests were real, the drinks were real (although Altman, for a change, chose not to indulge). Everyone was to go about their business and let Fortier make an ass of himself around them. Bedecked in a ketchup-red jacket, this tirelessly gauche fellow shimmies frantically to Herb Alpert music while sexy gals dressed like shimmering dance-parlor balls shake their booties in tight close-ups. He's a bad Jerry Lewis routine, inadvertently flipping olives into a woman's cleavage and sending the ladies scurrying with laughter at the gracelessness of his come-ons. Fortier's clod gets into the swim at long last when a stray punch from a nearby brawl tosses him into the pool. Six feet below, a woman in full party regalia smokes a cigarette and chats on the phone while a bartender in deep-diver goggles mixes drinks. Even under water, the party goes on.

Pot au Feu, which Altman made for about $1,000 over a series of weekends in 1966, is a hilarious ode to the joys of pot smoking *à la français.* A frumpy housewife in curlers and nightdress makes a concerted but inelegant effort at rolling a joint while, over the sound track, a French television cooking show hostess instructs us in how to make a classic pot au feu. The housewife's bungled attempts are intercut with a *Wonderful World of Disney*–like cavalcade of shots depicting a variety of folk passing joints in everyday settings: in the Laundromat, under the hair dryer, on exercise machines, on a Ferris wheel (Altman is seen in one of the several cameos, grabbing a toke in between moves of a chess game). Kitschy French music over the sound track inflates the Gallic jest to the max (Altman felt the film would be too inconsequential without it), as do the credits, which acknowledge the codirection of "Robert Vieux-homme" and the producing work of "Robert Oeufenweiler." Among the friends and family members whom Altman shanghaied for the project were his mother and father. Perhaps the ultimate inside joke is the opening title, "Georges Litto vous présente *Pot au Feu,*" intended to provide mock restitution to Altman's former agent, who was always grumbling that he never got credit for anything.

There is hardly a soul on the set of *Nashville* who doesn't recall the making of the film in party terms. Altman worked hard and partied with the resolve of a soldier on a twenty-four-hour leave. Dailies, birthdays, arrivals, departures, beginning of shoot, wrap, Saturday night, Sunday afternoons: Every occasion, it seemed, was an excuse for the director to break out the Cutty Sark and the happy weed in the company of his colleagues.

No other off-time event is recalled with as much relish as the Sunday barbecues at the Altmans'. The big log-and-stone home that Altman sublet for his family on the outer edge of Nashville was a pastoral fantasy shaded by a thicket of tall trees. A brook fed into a stone pool, then flowed down the hill from the other end. Flowers below. Birds above. Porches to the side. Robert Altman in the back, flipping steaks over a charcoal grill. Ronee Blakley seated on one of the porches, plucking out a song on an acoustic guitar. Peace. Love. Happiness. "Pure, unadulterated Bergman," as Opal would exclaim in one of her typically dilettantish remarks, referring to the Swedish director's outdoorsy early period. The robust Scandinavian woodland ambience extended to the air-conditioning, which was regrettably nonexistent.

"*Nashville* really was the beginning of what would become a working style," says Kathryn Altman, referring to the rotating regimen of evening dinner parties and barbecues that her husband presided over like everyone's favorite hedonist uncle. Altman seemed to understand that these events could impact his film in ways that transcended their immediate therapeutic benefits. Actors bonded, spirits were uncorked, flirtations happened. And when no one was looking, let alone thinking, great ideas would bubble to the surface that might end up in tomorrow's shoot.

It was perhaps inevitable that one of the bright ideas to emerge from those parties was actually to film one of those parties, with everyone in character, of course. The Altmans' organically lavish summer residence seemed just the sort of spread that screamed Haven Hamilton. And a pre–Opry-show party at Haven's setting would be just the place to stir the embers of Thomas Hal Phillips's overtures into show business.

As luck would have it, Elliott Gould was blowing through town in between promo stops for *California Split*. Gould had attended a pre-*Nashville* party that Altman had given at his home in Malibu for West Coast cast members, so it was fitting that he should end up in the film, buzzing in and out as the Big Hollywood Star visiting a Nashville party. (An "extraterrestrial identity," as Gould termed his walk-on.) And in 1974 he was very much a player, riding the wave of seventies fame that began with *MASH* and continued on with Paul Mazursky's *Bob & Carol & Ted & Alice*. As John Triplette reminds us, he also had once been married to "that girl who sang 'People.'"

The plan was simple. Gould would arrive in a black limousine chauffeured by a fawning Norman and accompanied by *Nashville*'s actual unit publicist, Sue Barton. A onetime model who was first

A crowd surrounds celebrity guest Elliott Gould at Haven Hamilton's home (left to right: Henry Gibson, press liaison Sue Barton, Gould, Geraldine Chaplin, Ned Beatty).

recruited by Altman to take over the publicity for *California Split*, Barton boasted a glamorous résumé of her own, having spent years on the arm of a guy who also romanced the girl who sang "People," Omar Sharif. Gould and Barton would be body-miked to catch their conversation inside the limo as it pulled up at Haven's, and Gould's big-star entrance would be anticipated by an unofficial cortege of party crashers consisting of Tricycle Man, Opal, and Albuquerque.

Gould's guarded superstar presence ("There are a lot of cameras here," we hear him say nervously to Barton from inside the car) provides a sly, real-life complement to the calculated royalty of Haven Hamilton at the same time as it points up the chasm that divides the worlds of Hollywood and Nashville. Attorney-to-the-country-stars Delbert Reese doesn't have a clue that he is meeting a movie star ("I just shook the man's hand like he was somebody on the street," says Delbert in one of his more beguiling moments.) And, like so many of the *Nashville* actors who blew into town with marginal knowledge of the country-music field, Gould has never heard of this Haven Hamilton.

That doesn't stop Haven from aligning himself in the galaxy with Gould, as he uses the Hollywood star to reassert the primacy of country greats such as himself. "I don't know who you are or what you're doing here," says Haven pompously to Opal as she ambushes her way into his meeting with Gould, "but I will not tolerate rudeness in the presence of a star—two stars." It's anyone's guess as to which star he was adding on in that afterthought.

Opal's rebuff by Haven is particularly sweet, given how she had just drop-kicked Haven's son in the middle of a song in order to muscle up to Elliott Gould. We have only to hear one bar of Dave Peel singing "The Heart of a Gentle Woman" to judge that this sweet-pussed boy may have more musical talent in his Harvard Law–grad pinkie than his father from head to toe. And indeed, Opal is seduced by Peel's crooning for the briefest of moments. The transformation that slowly spreads across Geraldine Chaplin's face as Opal is distracted from Buddy's spell by the

Bud Hamilton (Dave Peel) casting a short-lived spell on Opal
(Geraldine Chaplin), roving reporter for the BBC.

sighting of Elliott Gould is a mimetic feat worthy of the Chaplin name.

The lingering presence of an old Southern class system in Nashville as purveyed by Haven Hamilton is doubly reinforced by the servile role of the token black at the party, Wade, dishing up the buffet lunch, and the brusque pleasantness with which Connie White waves off trailer trash like Albuquerque in the subsequent scene backstage at the Opry. The absurdity of this Nashville version of the British class system reverberates with ironic force later on at the Exit/In, when the lowly (to Haven) Opal chops off the head of a lowlier (to Opal) Norman, saying in her best Kensington accent, "Norman, please, I make it a point never to gossip with servants."

While Haven Hamilton was sniffing out Elliott Gould, Lily Tomlin was at another end of the yard inventing a quintessentially Lily Tomlin routine. A local woman who had been hired to cast extras had recruited her mother for the party scene, and she was quickly thrown together with Tomlin as a party foil for Linnea. Tomlin was yakking it up with this prim Nashville matron when Ned Beatty happened by.

"As I approached them, I realized what Lily was doing. One of the wonderful things that Southern women are constantly given over to is somebody's health problems. And I thought, Oh, God, Lily's right on to it, she is so on the money. So I went over to Bob and said, 'I don't know whether you're planning on shooting this, but you've really got to try and hear what Lily is saying to this church lady.'"

What Beatty overheard was a graphically detailed monologue about hospitals in which Linnea describes a ward filled with former motorcyclists who are now paralyzed from the waist down. She then goes on to relate how a small "lick on the head" suffered by her aunt had turned into something horrible. In truth, Tomlin was riffing off an incident that had just occurred in which her mother's sister from Paducah, Eva, had struck her head getting into a car and ended up in Vanderbilt Hospital.

"And somehow the blood began to drain behind her eyeball," says Linnea with Southern gothic relish. "You know, and the pressure just caused the eye to bulge out. And it was all red and looked just awful. Everybody thought she was going to lose her eye. We still don't know how it's gonna come out."

Aunt Eva, Tomlin was relieved to learn, came out just fine.

THE CAST of *Nashville* was taking over the town. "It was like we belonged to this country club called *Nashville*," says Hayward, "and they couldn't take our membership away." Robert Doqui was chatting about acting with students at Fisk University. Allan Nicholls was grooving to the gospel music at a local Baptist church. Cristina Raines and Keith Carradine

Lily Tomlin, as Linnea Reese, riffs about hospital tragedies to a Nashville matron. Her stories were patterned after an aunt's true-life experience.

were cooing at one another over the baking-powder biscuits at the Loveless Cafe. The single guys tried to snare dates. David Hayward frequented the roller coaster at Opryland and nursed a crush on Barbara Harris. Allen Garfield played the ladies' man when his girlfriend left town. Recalls Hayward, "Allen Garfield would come on very strong to girls, and I watched a lot of them walk away from him. So I would just wait for Allen to hit on somebody, and she would walk away, and I'd go over and apologize for him and ask her if she was okay. And try to be her savior. That worked a couple of times."

Jeff Goldblum carried a torch for Shelley Duvall, to no avail. Hayward recalls the moony-eyed Goldblum: "Jeff said, 'I don't know what's wrong, but I look at Shelley, and I look at her fetchingly, and she doesn't seem to respond.' Jeff was so ethereal. You can imagine how Jeff could put on a look like that and scare somebody. I'd say, 'Gee, Jeff, I don't know what it could be.'"

Despite the occasional lovelorn heart, Altman's theory of bonding by partying was working like gangbusters. One night the cast invaded the Exit/In and staged an impromptu performance for one another (and a crowd of startled regulars), doing material that was decidedly against the grain of their characters. Lily Tomlin had the crowd in hysterics as she tried out some new cutting-edge routines, working from notes scribbled on bits of paper. Aspiring country singer Dave Peel sang from his repertoire, as did Ronee Blakley. *Nashville* band partners and romantic antagonists Keith Carradine and Allan Nicholls performed duets and solos. David Arkin did comedy. Henry Gibson mixed humor and song.

On occasion, their freewheeling spontaneity was met with bemusement. Jeff Goldblum recalls a gathering of *Nashville* folk having dinner at a club and listening to a singer perform when Ronee Blakley began to sing along. Con brio. "It wasn't rude but it was very startling and powerful, singing in this full-out, free way, in this beautiful voice even more gorgeously than the person onstage. The performer reacted in a graceful way, trying to make something nice out of it, like in a Greek restaurant when they start throwing the crockery down before the right time and you go, oh, I don't know if we're doing that yet."

Even in the thick of Nashville life, the cast and crew remained cloistered and insular, often unaware of whom it was they were rubbing up against. One night, a large contingent of fifteen or so cast and crew members went out to dinner. At the restaurant, they spotted sitting across the room a local piano player who had been hired by Richard Baskin to play in Barbara Jean's band. They waved at him, smiled, and resumed their meal. As the time approached to settle the bill, the waiter informed the large party that it had been taken care of. When they asked who they should thank, the waiter pointed to the piano player. The *Nashville* group were embarrassed: They wouldn't think of letting one of the pickup musicians cover such a lavish tab. When they protested, their host insisted. When they protested again, he said, "Don't worry, I own the block." Who knew that the musician, David Briggs, was Elvis's piano player and had enough gold records to melt down and keep them all in sixteen-ounce sirloins for life?

Altman played hooky from the group one night to do a boy's night out on Printers Alley, a narrow stretch of clubs in downtown Nashville where one was more likely to find a good bump-and-grind in the mid-seventies than a good band. Keith Carradine got the report. "Bob regaled us the next day with tales of some strip club he went to, filled with the more graphic aspects of the performances. He said there was one girl who could actually go [Carradine cups and manipulates his fingers to simulate a talking vagina], 'It's a Ford!'"

The scene of the most nefarious leisure-time activity was not a sleazy strip club but the town's most piss-elegant restaurant. Julian's was the town's reigning expense-account drain, a tony boîte situated in a Victorian mansion near Centennial Park. For the young and relatively unsophisticated cast of *Nashville,* Julian's cacophony of red-flocked wallpaper and crystal chandelier was the limit. "At that point, T.G.I.F.'s was pretty impressive to me," admits Allan Nicholls. "Wow, a salad bar!"

Since the cast didn't have much else to do with their per diems, the occasional splurge at Julian's appealed to the group's Altman-nurtured appreciation for decadence. After a few visits, however, the forty-dollar-a-pop tab began to tap their rebellious juices. Henry Gibson recalls, "That was a lot of money in 1974. You were paying for the ambience, the fine china and perfect silver. And we were so bummish at the end of the day in our work clothes. The stuff was so overpriced and the food wasn't that good. So, the first kleptomaniac in the group, can't remember who, decided, let's clip an ashtray. The next week we went back and, h-m-m-m, maybe a little bud vase. So they took a bud vase."

The next visit brought the big heist. The mastermind was Allan Nicholls. His accomplices were Keith Carradine, Henry Gibson, Michael Murphy, David Hayward, and David Arkin.

Nicholls also implicates Jeff Goldblum and Julie Christie (who was blowing through town to visit Altman and friends from *McCabe & Mrs. Miller.*) Their target: a crystal wine decanter.

The thing was huge. "It stood about this high off the floor," recalls Keith Carradine, lifting his arm three feet from the ground. "It would have been real hard to decant anything into or out of it. It wasn't cut crystal, but poured glass made to look like crystal. We had had a lot of wine during the meal and by the end of dinner we were feeling pretty happy. So Nicholls decided we should have this thing."

The group decided as a body to create a distraction. "I started singing," says Henry Gibson, launching into "As Time Goes By" to demonstrate. "So we're all singing, and paying the bill, and we're passing the decanter from person to person."

The decanter reached Nicholls. Carradine resumes, "He took his coat and draped it over the decanter and carried it by the very top of it with his jacket hanging over it. It just looked like this guy carrying a jacket over his arm. And we all sort of crowded around him, singing and laughing. They never suspected a thing."

There was one tense moment at the eleventh hour, as anyone who has seen the classic heist films *Topkapi* or *Rififi* knows there has to be. When the group got their trophy out to the parking lot, Carradine realized he had left his car keys back at their table. He dashed in, expecting the jig to be up. The keys were sitting at the table, which had not yet been cleaned off. He smiled innocently at the maître d' as he dangled his car keys, and fled out the door.

Over the ensuing years, the great crystal decanter from Julian's was passed between each of the thieves. Everyone agrees that Keith Carradine was the last to have it. The decanter is believed to be sitting in a basement in Telluride.

THE PARTY fervor that consumed and conjoined most of the cast on the *Nashville* set could be alienating for those, like Barbara Harris, who did not wish to indulge in the stimulant of the moment. For others, like Gwen Welles, it was the ultimate challenge. Welles was certainly no prude. She was a free spirit with her own orthodoxy of life. In one of the more crunchy-granola statements ever to leaven a press release, she told a benumbed Paramount publicist in 1973: "I don't think fantasies hurt us, if you're together. I prefer to live alone rather than to get into partnerships with men. I won't ever lock myself into a particular time in place. I try to keep my balance. I like people who have a different level of consciousness. We're all here for such an infinitesimal amount of time and we take it all so seriously. Our relation to time and space is nothing. Nothingness. The void fascinates me. You stop thinking and you're really into void. I love the void."

Despite Welles's high-handed claims about men, she had lived with (and acted for) the French maître of female sensuality, Roger

Gwen Welles and Robert Altman. Welles had appeared previously in Altman's *California Split*. (*Jim Coe*)

Vadim, for three years, posed nude for *Playboy*, and at the time of *Nashville* was embarking upon a long-term relationship with record producer Richard Perry. She championed yoga, meditation, vegetarianism, and organic beauty treatments with an evangelical conviction. She possessed ravishing, God-given (and, according to friends, Laszlo-enhanced) skin. And she was a recovering heroin addict. More than one *Nashville* amigo recalls accompanying Welles to Alcoholics Anonymous meetings.

For all of her etherealness, Welles was beginning to get her excesses under control. There were others on the set, however, who couldn't stop the party, much as they may have wanted. The cast's veteran members, Barbara Baxley and Keenan Wynn, were inveterate alcoholics. "I remember Barbara Baxley when she was young and beautiful and together," says Barbara Harris. "But here she just stayed alone and drank. Heavily. I remember her bursting into tears because she had drunk her earnings away. Oh God, how sad."

Wynn's habit was such that Altman was compelled to shoot the actor's scenes in the morning, before his hands began to tremble from withdrawal. "He got the D.T.'s right in the middle of a scene," recalls Bert Remsen. "We had to give him a jug, and Jesus, he could drink it. He got so bad they had to send for his wife. She came and straightened him out."

Aside from Wynn's wife, Sharley, Altman also had to recruit one of the actor's nephews to wet-nurse him, since he had a way of disappearing in search of a thirst quencher. In one instance, recalls Remsen, he had to be rescued from a redneck bar by one of the stuntmen. "They were going to kill him because he had jumped on somebody or something."

"We had a sequence on where to find him," says production coordinator Kelly Marshall Fine. "If he didn't show up on the set, there were three places that we sent the driver to look. We knew he'd be at one of them."

One afternoon around three, Alan Rudolph received a frantic call on behalf of Wynn from a restaurant. "They said I was the only one he would talk to. Lubie's Coffee Shop, waitresses in gingham outfits, three and a half days there were maybe three customers. And when I got there Keenan was hunched over the counter with a beer, growling, and the waitresses were all huddled over on one side of the dining room, waiting for someone to take him away. Every day was an event like that."

The sober side of Keenan Wynn was a lovable, overgrown rascal of a man who loved to show off to the girls by cannonballing off a diving board into a lake. "As Bob said, 'Keenan doesn't do knitting very well,'" says Scott Glenn, who shared Wynn's passion for motorcycling. "He wasn't the kind of guy that on downtime you expected him to sit around a room and read Wordsworth.

"Keenan had a knack for trouble, and I seemed to be with him a lot of those times. We hung out with these Hell's Angels who worked for Bob, Angel and Eddie. We were all bikers of one ilk or another, and we were consorts in deviltry. Once, a bunch of us went out into a boat that Keenan and I had rented. We got really wasted, and I ran the boat into a sandbar. At one point, I remember Keenan had a little trouble with a blinking sign across the street from where he was staying, and he took care of it with a large-caliber firearm.

"At another point, we were out at the fairgrounds and we left Keenan with this car with two guitars in the back, and said, 'Keenan, watch out for these guitars, and don't let anybody mess with them.' I guess he was a little drunk when some cops walked up to him and wanted to look in the cars, and he sort of physically wouldn't let them. Geraldine came running back and saved him from them."

Chaplin, who was one of a trio of *Nashville* actors who was descended from acting dynasties, had her own special rapport with Wynn. "We had a lot of empathy because of 'my father,' 'your father.' We would sort of bug everyone because we had these famous fathers, and so we knew more than anyone else. I'd never heard of his father, but I pretended I had."

Even without knowing the mad-hatter comedian Ed Wynn, Chaplin understood implicitly the burden of growing up in the shadow of a legendary comic father. Unlike Charles Chaplin, who abetted his daughter's ambitions to be a dancer, Ed Wynn voiced hopes of passing the baton to his son from the moment he interrupted a vaudeville routine at the Winter Garden Theater in 1916 to show off the baby Francis Xavier Aloysius James Jeremiah Keenan Wynn to the audience. Before Keenan became a contract player at MGM in the forties, the elder Wynn was hovering on the sidelines with advice on how to shtick up even the most serious roles. "That's terrible," Ed Wynn once told his son after rehearsing a scene. "Fling open the door like this, and when you come into the room trip over the sill like this and fall, and then they'll know you're Ed Wynn's son."

PFC Kelly (Scott Glenn) regales Mr. Green (Keenan Wynn) about Barbara Jean, moments after Green has learned of his wife's death. Wynn's off-camera drinking did not deter from his giving a gorgeously fragile performance.

Adding to the pressures and resentments that came with having a famous father were the stresses attendant upon his mother's psychic deterioration. Keenan adored his actress mother, Hilda Keenan, a beautiful, gentle woman who ultimately lost her battle with mental illness. Finally, though, it was his grandfather who would launch the young man on his path toward addiction. Frank Keenan—silent film star, vaudevillian, Shakespearean actor, and alcoholic—took Keenan Wynn on his first drunk.

Wynn's long day's journey into *Nashville* may have contributed to the gorgeous fragility of his performance. His character, Mr. Green, was drawn from Joan Tewkesbury's impression of an elderly and tender man whom she had encountered in Nashville with a wife who was in the hospital. He was typical of the long-time city residents who let rooms in their houses, usually to musicians. Wynn was all of fifty-eight when *Nashville* was filmed, but the effects of booze, combined with his new clean-shaven look, pushed his suffering to the fore.

"When he shaved his mustache for the role, he aged fifteen years," recalls Henry Gibson. "It had always been like a screen, or a curtain. With the removal of that, the vulnerability that came through, I felt absolutely that he was going to die during the making of the film. He really was the most sympathetic man, and the camera caught that."

Whatever may have been churning inside Wynn when the camera caught him, as Mr. Green, receiving the news of his wife's death, the actor's tearful dissolve is one of the most potent moments in the entire film. And nowhere in the performance can you see Ed Wynn's son.

CHAPTER TEN

INVADING THE GRAND OLE OPRY

(Wherein Roy Acuff Retreats, Karen Black Advances, and Richard Nixon Surrenders)

THE STAGE ENTRANCE OF THE GRAND Ole Opry is flanked by flower beds whose carefully orchestrated flow of colors gives off a perky, almost unnatural glow, like the opening titles of a Rock Hudson–Doris Day comedy. The effect of this floral burst of cheer is tempered somewhat by the obvious calculation behind it, reminding one of the manicured banks of flowers outside a hospital for retired war veterans.

The medical-center theme continues to the reception desk, where one is screened by a pleasant, well-dressed matron who checks your name off the list of approved visitors and smiles you on. There is no imposing, uniformed guard of the sort who checks the backstage traffic flow in the Opry segment of *Nashville*. Perhaps management was more diligent about security when the cavernous new Opry House opened in March 1974, just months prior to the invasion of Altman and company. Today, anyone who can put on that don't-mess-with-me-I-belong-here face can strut past the often distracted receptionist without being assaulted by so much as a "Can I help you, folks?"

The dressing room hallways are wide, cold, and starkly lit: You half expect to spot the nurses' station or a post-op patient rolling his I.V. rack on a postdinner constitutional when you turn a corner. Instead, the corridors are abuzz with musicians wearing spurs and spangles, ambling in and out of open dressing-room doors or being Polaroided with an arm around an excited visitor. It's the ultimate theme park, a walk-through celebrity habitat where you're allowed to get out of your car and chat up the lion kings. Everyone seems chummy, knowable, *possible*. There's not a trace of that perfunctory, keep-your-cheap-painted-fingernails-

Albuquerque (Barbara Harris) prevails upon Connie White (Karen Black) in the backstage corridors of the Grand Ole Opry.

off-the-star chill that Connie White throws poor Albuquerque as she tries to slip past the guards.

An outsider feels grateful for the cordiality, yet concerned for the celebrity tenants at the same time: A Nashville Mark Chapman could have a sniper's picnic here. And yet the minute you think that, you feel ashamed for being so cynical, as if you're trying to soil this down-home institution with your citified, loss-of-American-innocence agenda. After all, access—the ability not just to identify with musicians but hang with them as well—is a hallmark of country music. The backstage scene at the Opry is merely a more controlled, exclusive version of Nashville's annual Fan Fair at the Tennessee Fair Grounds, where country fans stand in line for hours just for the chance to nuzzle up to their favorite stars.

Roy Acuff was the hovering backstage royalty when Altman took over the Grand Ole Opry House for three days in early August to shoot his own *Nashville* Opry show. Acuff had been a pivotal Opry mover since stepping up to the lead-performer spot in 1939, only one year after the fiddler-singer and his Smoky Mountain Boys blew in from Knoxville with "Wabash Cannonball." In partnership with country song composer Fred Rose, Acuff would build a music publishing empire during the forties and fifties, solidifying the throne he inhabited in 1974 as an Opry figurehead and banner bearer for Nashville family values.

Like Haven Hamilton, Acuff maintained a balance between a general wariness of outsiders and a host's sense of responsibility toward his moviemaking guests. Stepping before the vast local crowd that had assembled to participate in the filming of the Opry sequence of *Nashville,* he gave a warm welcome to the cast and crew, and cajoled the audience into giving them their all. At the same time, the unstintingly courteous Acuff observed the *Nashville* incursion from a respectful, if not forbidding, arm's length. Somehow it became known that his big-star dressing room, the first one off the stage-left hallway, was off limits to the Hollywood visitors.

Picking up the mixed messages, actor Timothy Brown kept his distance from Acuff throughout the rehearsal and setup that preceded shooting the Opry sequence. Brown certainly knew of Acuff. He had revered the legendary Opry star from his boyhood in a children's home in Indiana, where he taught himself the Top Fifty country songs as a hobby. But Brown also knew that he was more than just a Hollywood outsider in these parts. Charley Pride notwithstanding, a black face was a rare sight at the Grand Ole Opry, on or off the stage.

Brown understood he had been hired to be the movie's resident Pride, but he was damned if he was going to do the carbon copy version. The white cowboy outfit might have been worn by Pride, but Brown's animated singing posture, honed from years on the football field and nightclubs, was a definite departure. "I wanted to have my own identity with it," says Brown, "show them that, hey, I could do any kind of movement. My comfort zone is my body. Of course it had to be controlled with that audience, so that they didn't perceive it as rock and roll or blues. You had to keep it straight."

Of all the actors who perform numbers in *Nashville,* Brown would be the only one not asked to write his own songs, an oversight which fills him with dismay to this day. Altman's explanation was that the actor was brought onto the film too late into the process. Brown was given two songs: "Bluebird," an ineffectual hand-clapper written by Ronee Blakley, and "The Day I Looked Jesus in the Eye," a gospel-tinged collaboration by Richard Baskin and Altman. He performed both numbers for the Opry scene, playing to a capacity crowd (who'd been lured there by newspaper ads promising a chance to be in a movie starring *Laugh-In*'s Lily Tomlin and Henry Gibson), but the Jesus number was dropped from the final cut.

Like many of *Nashville*'s less visible cast members, Brown was painfully aware that a disproportionate amount of his work ended up on the cutting-room floor, most noticeably in his truncated traffic-jam encounter with Geraldine Chaplin. At the end of a private screening Brown attended with buddies Robert Duvall and Elliott Gould, the two actors turned to him and said, "Christ, what did you do to Bob?" Brown certainly didn't know, and his paranoia was inflamed by Altman himself, who appeared to be avoiding him at the screening. Eventually, Brown went up to the director to see if there was any problem. Altman's cryptic response is branded in his memory: "Well, now you know who makes you or breaks you in this business."

Brown consoles himself with a recollection of an encounter with the elusive Roy Acuff. After the actor finished his two numbers before the Opry crowd, Acuff pulled him aside and said, "Son, you want to make a whole lot of money? You should go into country music. What you did out there is just what they wanted Charley Pride to do."

Timothy Brown's affable cover of "Bluebird" kicked off a five-song concert sequence remarkable not only for capturing the peculiar rituals of an Opry performance—the changing of the singers' entourages on the stage benches, the mid-performance commercials, the blinding explosion of flashbulbs aimed at popular performers—but for the reverence with which Altman filmed a song in its entirety. While no other American director since John Huston has jumped genres with as much confidence and spirit as Altman, Altman has always fancied himself as a maker of musicals; his purist's approach to filming a number is evident as well in his later films *Short Cuts, Kansas City, A Perfect Couple* and the Harry Nilsson–scored *Popeye*.

Any doubts one may harbor that *Nashville* is a musical should be dispelled with the song-driven Opry House sequence. Altman and Tewkesbury maintained that the Nashville of the seventies resembled the Hollywood of the forties, a place where young people of talent and ambition got off the bus with little but a month's rent and dreams of stardom. Appropriately, the movie they fashioned from the city hearkened back to Hollywood musicals of that wartime decade, fusing elements particular to both MGM and Twentieth Century Fox. The MGM recipe tended to soften a high-gloss showbiz surface with heavy dollops of Americana (*Meet Me in St. Louis, The Harvey Girls*) while the Fox formula relied upon a kind of tourist-authority urbanity (*Moon over Miami, Down Argentine Way*). In the unalloyed Fox style, a song would be delivered on a nightclub stage in its entirety, cleanly photographed and punctuated by the applause of an audience glimpsed at the edges of the frame.

In the case of *Nashville,* Altman was culling his audience from the ranks of Nashville citizenry, shooting the performances live with the help of five roving cameras and a sixteen-track Fanta recording system typical of the remote truck setups used for concert films at the time. (The eight-track system used throughout most of the film was deemed not versatile enough to handle both the onstage performance and offstage dialogue demands of the concert sequences.) While Altman remained faithful to his actors during their singing efforts, the promiscuous multiple cameras and sound tracks enable us to key into several Opry House events occurring simultaneously in real time: Albuquerque ambushing Connie White at the stage door while Haven Hamilton sings onstage; Connie White fluffing up her dress offstage as she waits for her cue to go on; PFC Kelly slipping up the aisle as it is announced that his beloved Barbara Jean will not be performing.

THE CAPACITY crowd of 4,400 that Altman's production staff were able to pull together for the all-day filming was a typical Opry hodgepodge, meaning that they were tough customers who responded with generous enthusiasm. But they did it selectively. When Richard Baskin came out onstage to rehearse the actors, he was puzzled by the palpable lack of energy he felt emanating from the house. Lily Tomlin was summoned to seduce the restless crowd between camera setups. The comedienne put aside her more subversive (read: feminist) material for another day, choosing instead to haul the crowd-pleasing Ernestine and Edith Ann out of the *Laugh-In* trunk.

By the time Henry Gibson came out to do his Haven Hamilton shtick, the Opry crowd was cooking. Even after a month of appearing in *Once Upon a Mattress* in Pasadena, however, the prospect of the Opry audience had Gibson on edge. The musicians that Baskin had hired to back him up were the crème de la crème; in

Go get a Goo Goo...it's good!

WSM GRAND OLE OPRY 6 5

Haven Hamilton (Henry Gibson) entertains the Grand Ole Opry crowd, comprised of Nashville locals. Gibson's *Laugh-In* costar Lily Tomlin entertained the audiences between takes.

fact, most of them came from that original list that he had drawn up to impress Altman. But of all the *Nashville* actors who were called upon to sing, Gibson had the flimsiest musical pedigree, and he knew it. As a result, the apprehension would cause the actor to go up on his own lyrics in front of the crowd. He vamped for what seemed to be an eternity until the words of the song (called, appropriately enough, "Keep a' Goin'") came back to him.

What Gibson lacked in musicianship, he made up for in irony. In writing lyrics for the vainglorious and sentimental Haven Hamilton, Gibson had license to schlock it up that was given to no other character. Explaining the arch pose of Hamilton's songs, Richard Baskin insists that at no time was he trying to mock or parody the genre of country music, nor did he need to. "Much of country-western music is a parody of itself. The truly great music, if you go back twenty years, is kind of saccharine and trite. I wasn't trying to make fun of it. I sometimes had fun with it."

The songs that Baskin, Gibson, and Richard Reicheg cowrote for Haven are a delicious postmodern balancing act of sendup and the real McCoy. Reicheg's lyric for "For the Sake of the Children" is a droning ode to marital fidelity that appeals to the daytime soap watcher in us at the same time as it defies us to keep a straight face.

> Unpack your bags
> And try not to cry.
> I can't leave my wife
> There's three reasons why.
> There's Jimmy and Kathy
> And sweet Lorelei,
> For the sake of the children
> We must say goodbye.
> 'Cause Jimmy's been wishing
> That I'd take him fishing
> His little league pitching
> Is something to see.
> Kathy's thirteen now,
> She's my little queen now
> And I've gotta see
> Who her beau's gonna be.

In defending Altman's choice to have actors write their own songs, the critic from *Time Out* (London) said, "The song and its presentation compels us to examine Hamilton's own insidiously avuncular and pseudo-naive public facade . . . This sort of critique, which extends to most of the film's country stars, would have been impossible if Altman had used name C&W artists."

The protracted history of "Keep a' Goin'," an inspirational ode to mucking through the bad times, is itself a lesson in stick-to-itiveness. The lyric first made its appearance on an episode of

The Dick Van Dyke Show, in which Gibson was required to do a faux-naive recitation of the sort that would typify his nerd-poet persona on *Laugh-In.*

> If you strike a thorn on a rose
> Keep a' goin'!
> If it hails or if it snows,
> Keep a' goin'!
> Ain't no use to sit an' whine,
> 'Cause the fish ain't on your line,
> Bait your hook an' keep a' tryin'
> Keep a' goin'.
>
> When the weather kills your crop,
> Keep a' goin'
> It takes work to reach the top . . .

Et cetera and so on.

Gibson resurrected the ditty in 1973, when Altman invited him and several other actors over to Lion's Gate to record the voices for the commercials, announcements, and shows to be heard over the radio throughout *Thieves Like Us.*

The third time was the charm. Richard Baskin married Gibson's dweeby poem to a plucky musical setting inspired by a used-car ad. "I wanted it to be like that Cal Worthington ad," explains Baskin. "'If you buy a car or a truck, go see Cal.'" Baskin's country makeover of "Keep a' Goin'" stirred the resistant Opry audience into a participatory spirit. Gibson triumphed over his initial nervousness, effectively capturing the crowd with the sheer force of Haven Hamilton's charisma. Altman proudly noted that, as Hamilton announced that Barbara Jean was recuperating from her airport collapse and asked the audience to "send some letters and best wishes and prayers to her, Vanderbilt Hospital, Nashville, Tennessee 27322," a woman in the crowd took out a pen and wrote down the address.

The year after *Nashville* was released, Henry Gibson would be officially baptized into the fires of a successful songwriter's life when a Washington, D.C., woman filed a lawsuit against him for stealing "Keep a' Goin'" from her. "It was something she had learned as a kid in school," recalls Gibson, "and convinced herself after reciting it all her life that she had written it. She wanted to sue Paramount, ABC, Jerry Weintraub, Robert Altman, and me. So we had to go through this whole legal procedure where I brought out the book it was first written in, showed the excerpt from the TV show, showed the progression where my lyric changed, showed the copyright material, and how I would never have met her. The poor woman was deluded."

"200 Years," the jingoistic paean that launches *Nashville*, was not written and filmed until the first week of August. It would endure as the film's most emblematic song. Both Baskin and Gibson take credit for coming up with the theme. The Baskin version: "The bicentennial thing was sweeping the country, and I said we have to have a bicentennial song." The Gibson version: "I had the very notion. I knew the bicentennial was approaching. And I knew that this guy was his own self-appointed patriot and that he had to cash in and make a comment. And so, almost at once came the notion: We must be doing something right to last two hundred years. Boom. But I had different versions in my head, with different historical references."

Gibson's final version, rendered with an earnest "Spirit of '76" drum roll courtesy of Baskin, was such a canny blend of self-congratulation and populist pandering that high school groups and community organizations fell over each other for the rights to perform it.

> My mother's people came by ship and fought at Bunker Hill.
> My daddy lost a leg in France, I have his medals still.
> My brother served with Patton, I saw action in Algiers,
> Oh, we must be doing something right to last two hundred years. . . .

> I've lived through two depressions and seven dust-bowl droughts.
> Floods, locusts, and tornadoes, but I don't have any doubts.

We're all a part of history, why Old Glory waves to show,
How far we've come along till now, how far we've got to go.

It's been hard work but every time we get into a fix,
Let's think of what our children face in two-ought-seven-six,
It's up to us to pave the way with our blood and sweat and tears,
For we must be doing something right to last two hundred years.

Political manager John Triplette displays exceptional percep-
tiveness when he uses the lure of public office to soften the will of
the asbestos-skinned Haven Hamilton. Gibson's lyrics reveal a
shameless manipulation of personal valor and patriotic commitment that could have been yanked right out of Thomas Hal
Phillips's campaign literature for Hal Phillip Walker. In Altman's
vision of America, the line that separates the easy sentiments of
candidates from those of country tunesmiths is barely discernible. With little retooling, the hard-sell platform of "200
Years" could land Haven Hamilton in the governor's seat faster
than one could say Ronald Reagan.

"I WANT you to study real hard," says Connie
White to children seated in the first rows of the Opry House, "because just remember any one of you can grow up to be the president."

Karen Black didn't have much time to come up with that line,
let alone polish her Opry House act. "Other commitments" kept
her in Los Angeles up to the middle of *Nashville*'s filming, making her the only actor who was not on location throughout.
When Richard Baskin picked her up at the Nashville Airport in
early August, he informed her that the next day she would be
singing in front of five thousand people.

"Of all the performers, Karen was the most interesting,"
Baskin later told a music critic writing for *The New York Times*.
"Ronee Blakley was the only professional singer, and Barbara
Harris was outstanding. But Karen really knocked us out . . .

With only two hours' rehearsal, she stepped before the cameras and sang her two songs, live, with no overdubs."

Following on the heels of Gibson's strutting tour de force, Black's assured and witty appearance as Barbara Jean's Opry replacement represented yet another triumph of actor's immersion over stage fright. "I was really quite frightened in those days to sing in front of great crowds," she admits. "My character wasn't. In character, I was not afraid to sing. Out of character, I would have been terrified."

Black's fears began and ended there. Arriving a month after the rest of the cast had cemented ties didn't seem to faze the actress, who was cheered by the opium-den ambiance she came upon. "[I] go out to Bob's place and everybody's smoking dope. Even though I don't smoke I thought it was amusing. Everybody's wrecked and Bob's cooking for everybody. Then he decided we should sing, so we did. And this incredible blues guitarist came up with all these blues chords, and we just sang every blues song that was ever written. All night long."

In many ways, Black's delayed arrival seemed appropriate for her hard-edged character, who blows in at the last minute. "It really worked on her behalf," says Henry Gibson. "She wasn't there every night at dailies and [Connie] wasn't there in the Nashville circles. There was a great virtue to Karen coming in the way she did, a little like the Wicked Witch of the West."

A more accurate movie analogy for the actress behind Connie White might be Eve Black, the seductive hidden personality of Eve White played by Joanne Woodward in the film *The Three Faces of Eve*. In her two-week splash in Nashville, Karen Black left an enduring stamp as a provocateur, springing come-ons left and right that left more than one male in attendance slack-jawed. Alan Rudolph remembers being called a poet. Allan Nicholls recalls her making a big point about her cellulite and fat thighs at the lunch table outside the Grand Ole Opry.

"A loon," describes publicist Sue Barton. "She just began flirting outrageously and carrying on with everyone. Because most of the wives were there, it was very uncomfortable."

Connie White (Karen Black) waits to go on at the Grand Old Opry.
Black's seductive off-camera style bemused some cast members.

Ned Beatty hearkens back to another lunchtime conversation, when Black was wearing a low-cut gown. "At one point, she caught my eyes and said, 'You're looking at my breasts.' I said, 'I'm sorry.' 'You're looking at my breasts.' I was flummoxed. I had nothing to say."

Karen Black's naughty charms did work their spell on one of the session players backing her up, a fiddler who was engaged to be married. "He developed a crush on me," said Black. "And he came to see me at the hotel when we were offstage. But he had come to find Connie White. I'd taken off my three blonde wigs and I had jeans on. I could see his face falling when he found Karen there."

Fortunately for *Nashville*, the blunt, in-your-face style of Karen Black spilled over into Connie White to hilarious effect. Black invented one of the movie's funniest throwaways for the scene in which a chaotically coiffed Julie Christie, playing herself, is presented to a table at the King of the Road club that includes White, Haven Hamilton, Delbert Reese, and John Triplette. "Come on, Haven," she protests jealously to the fawning Hamilton, "she can't even comb her hair."

"When Allen Garfield came in with the orchids to give me, it went click, I had my character," explained Black, referring to the moment in the same scene in which White snubs Barnett's gift of flowers on behalf of her rival, Barbara Jean. "I knew that she was really shallow and false. But I never thought I would say such a thing to Julie Christie. It was never rehearsed. When they cut, the whole room was laughing."

Julie Christie's walk-on was another Altman whim. Christie was visiting the set, ostensibly to hang with Altman and pals from *McCabe & Mrs. Miller* (which included Shelley Duvall, production assistant Maysie Hoy, Keith Carradine, and Bert Remsen). According to some, the real incentive was Michael Murphy, a former neighbor. "She adored Michael," said Henry Gibson, who was mystified at Murphy's cool distance from the actress during her stay.

Christie was mortified when Altman cajoled her into stepping into the King of the Road club scene as a visiting movie star, à la Elliott Gould. She was allergic to improvisation, having scraped through a freely conceived *McCabe & Mrs. Miller* on the tailcoat of her friend Alfreida Benge, who wrote most of her dialogue. (Benge would also write a lot of Christie's lines for Alan Rudolph's *Afterglow*.) "I had no idea I was going to be put through this complete agony," says Christie. "I should have said no, but it's difficult to do with Bob. You feel like such a wet blanket."

Christie was thrown in a chair for an instant movie-star makeover, then instructed simply to be herself as Sue Barton introduced her to the motley assortment of *Nashville* personages. "I didn't know who myself was. I do remember thinking if I'm going to be myself, how odd it was that I was being made up and having my hair done."

When the scene was finished, Karen Black turned to Christie

and said, "I'm so very interested as to why you would choose to play it like that."

ALTMAN COULD have easily justified running the Grand Ole Opry interlude as a self-contained concert sequence, unfettered by plot progression. Instead, he gave it dramatic propulsion by intercutting a tense hospital-room encounter between Barbara Jean and Barnett. As the live broadcast voice of Connie White coming from the radio taunts the recuperating Barbara Jean, the bedridden star's insecurities bubble to the surface. Barbara Jean's anxiety is further fueled by her husband's intentions to bring flowers to White as a goodwill gesture. The resultant argument pushes Barbara Jean closer to the edge. She grabs at the jungle of flower arrangements around her, hurling flowers everywhere and prompting Barnett's memorable outburst: "Are you going nutsy on me, is that what you're doing? 'Cause I won't stand for that, Barbara Jean. Huh? You having one of them nervous breakdowns again? Huh? . . . Now you just settle down and shape up, you understand? The only reason I'm going over there is because I love you. I don't love to go over there and hobnob with them phonies."

Barnett cajoles his wife down from her fit, infantilizing her with a well-oiled paternalism that is as chilling to observe as it is touching. As he leaves her in the hospital room so utterly alone, we understand that this scenario has probably played itself out many times before.

BARNETT: Now where's Barnett going? Where am I goin'? Huh?
BARBARA JEAN: King of the Road.
BARNETT: And why am I goin' there?
BARBARA JEAN: To see Connie.
BARNETT: And why am I doing that?
BARBARA JEAN: Thank her for singin' for me.
BARNETT: And who am I doin' that for?
BARBARA JEAN: Doin' it for me . . .

BARNETT: That's right. . . . Now I'm walking out now.
BARBARA JEAN: Um huh.
BARNETT: Now, what do you say as I walk out? You say, "Bye-bye."
BARBARA JEAN: Bye.
BARNETT: Bye-bye.
BARBARA JEAN: Bye. [He leaves and, after a beat, she cries out.] Barnett! Barnett!

In this short scene, Allen Garfield and Ronee Blakley hauntingly convey the complex power dynamic that keeps this relationship ticking on like a precariously balanced old clock. For the politically alert Blakley, Barnett's control is deceptive. "He couldn't

Barnett (Allen Garfield) calms his wife, Barbara Jean (Ronee Blakley), strung out with anxiety and resentment at the hospital.

do a thing without her," explained Blakley. "She was the whole show. He did everything she wanted, she had him around her finger. She had a lot of power. I think of her as being strong and weak."

Blakley waived off the challenges of a downtown New York journalist who asked, "Isn't this an incorrect stereotype that the world in general has of the Southern woman singer, as weak and defenseless, when actually women like Tammy Wynette and Loretta Lynn and Dolly Parton have a lot of spunk?"

"We're talking about a business that's controlled by men," retorted Blakley, speaking from personal experience. "If you're a woman singer and have a woman manager, it's very tough. It's tough to walk into a room full of men and, first of all, be taken seriously. And second of all, not to have them trying to look up your dress. And third of all—the main thing—if you do act in any kind of solid, straight-on, person-to-person way, a lot of men will feel threatened and think that you're trying to bully them and then they'll get uptight and won't want to give you *anything*. So almost your only choice out of it is to go, 'Oh, you're such a *big strong man.*' Those are the patterns that women are trying to unlearn. But I can say that, personally, I know that there's always that temptation to pass into that little girl trip. Because when you're behaving the little girl with men, you're safe."

Blakley's intellectual grasp of Barbara Jean extended to a fastidious control of environment. Like Henry Gibson, Blakley thought long and hard about the accoutrements of her character's surroundings. For Barbara Jean's hospital room, Blakley brought in pictures to hang on the wall, as well as ceramic bird planters she felt the frail singer would have accumulated from previous infirmities. For her bedside table, there lay a couple of books handpicked for sensitive singers from the Deep South who are on the verge of going off the deep end: William Faulkner's *Light in August* and *The Letters of Vincent van Gogh*.

Blakley's sense of Barbara Jean's power over Barnett seeped into her own working relationship with the willful Garfield, who often resented his on-screen partner's attempts to commandeer the scene. "He thought that I was bossing him around," admits Blakley, "and I was told not to."

"Allen was so fucking generous with her, so generous," claims Joan Tewkesbury, giving Garfield his due. "He made her character work, in a funny way, by his generosity."

"Ronee was very self-oriented," Altman says, defending Blakley. "When Ronee was the focal point, from Ronee's standpoint, it was about her. And it's the way it should be. If we have to tolerate a little self-indulgence through that, well I do that with every actor I've ever done a film with. The only person I haven't seen too much of that sort of thing was with Julianne Moore [*Short Cuts* and *Cookie's Fortune*]; she does her job, is there for everybody, and never overstays.

"Allen Garfield really was an abrasive outsider, which was great for Barnett. He really was a terrific character. That relationship is quite clear to me. They played that [hospital scene] very well. I think Ronee had an idea of what she was doing. Where she was over the top, I was getting the same kinds of things that Barbara Jean would have given. So Ronee's bad acting was her best acting."

AT NINE P.M. on August 8, Richard Milhous Nixon resigned from office in a fifteen-minute address to the nation. Many of the *Nashville* cast and crew huddled in front of a TV set in the production office the next day and hooted wildly as President and Mrs. Nixon boarded Air Force One at Andrews Air Force Base and flew off to California. "We were cheering," recalls David Hayward. "The Antichrist was being taken away."

The euphoria that overtook the set of *Nashville* only pointed up the chasm that separated the filmmakers from their host city: But for the teamsters and extras, Republicans were in short supply on the set. "That town was in tears," said Henry Gibson. "If ever there were loyalists, they were in Nashville."

Perhaps no one reflected the anguish of a city more eloquently than Roy Acuff. The evening of Nixon's resignation happened to coincide with the filming of the Grand Ole Opry sequence, and the news crushed the small, gray-haired veteran to cinders. In tears, he approached a group of actors standing offstage and cried, "Look at what you've done to our president!" At that, he retreated to his dressing room, stage left, and slammed the door. Within moments, soulful strains of music began to emanate from behind his door. Word got around to the *Nashville* cast, who gathered outside the star's dressing room. There Roy Acuff remained for the next two hours, playing his fiddle.

CHAPTER ELEVEN

NOTHING SACRED, BUT THE SACRAMENTS

(Wherein Altman Goes to Church,
Opal Goes to the Junkyard, and
Barbara Jean Goes Over the Edge)

"Buckle up with Jesus"
—MOTTO ON NASHVILLE LICENSE PLATE

THERE WAS ONCE A GROCERY STORE near Murfreesboro, a solemn town southeast of Nashville, that was thought to be the best place to be when the Rapture came. At least one fundamentalist organization had a standing arrangement for its members to meet there at the first sign of the Apocalypse.

The Rapture was a big deal around Murfreesboro. "People looked forward to it, dreaded it, planned for it," said a former resident, who also recalls that the only TV on after eleven in the town was *The PTL Club*.

It is impossible to overestimate the extent to which religious zeal impacts upon community life in and around Nashville. The buckle city of the Bible Belt notches over eight hundred houses of worship (250 of which are Protestant, including Church of Christ and Southern Baptist). Nashville's first rabbi arrived in 1852, initiating a ripple of diversity that has deepened to embrace Baha'i, Satsung, Scientology, Course in Miracles, Hinduism, and, as late as 1994, Islam. Had it been around during the making of *Nashville*, there surely would have been a nod reserved in the film for the Nashville Cowboy Church, a honky-tonk admixture of old-time religion and vaudeville led by Dr. Harry Yates, who dresses in full cowboy regalia. (Yates's wife is Johnny Cash's sister.) This flashy, nondenominational group, which holds its performances/services at the Texas Troubadour Theater near Opryland, collects a very enthusiastic outpouring of donations in a Stetson hat.

The montage of Sunday church services that comes midway in *Nashville* is one of the film's least remarked upon sequences, yet one that contributes incalculably to the film's authenticity. Filmed over a two-day period at four houses of faith, including the Baptist church on Broadway in downtown Nashville, it locates each of the movie's characters (save for a few of the more godless celebrities, like Tom, Mary, and Bill) in their respective spiritual homes.

In a Catholic church, we find Sueleen Gay singing with the choir in the balcony, her voluptuous red hair veiled angelically beneath a halo of woven lace. Dispersed among the congregation below are Wade, Star, and Lady Pearl. Significantly, neither Star nor Lady Pearl are worshiping with their respective mates; throughout this juxtaposition of church services, Altman questions the assumption that "the family that prays together, stays together." Lady Pearl's companion, Haven Hamilton, is discovered in the next cut singing in the choir at the Protestant church (Henry Gibson has been noticeably body-miked to amplify Haven's voice from the choir—even in a performance for God, the vainglorious Haven can be counted upon to grab the spotlight). By this subtle delineation, Altman and Tewkesbury speculate that the politically antithetical Lady Pearl and Haven would also be on opposite sides of a holy war.

Among the congregants of the Protestant church are Delbert Reese and his children, who follow the service with the help of a woman who conducts the hymn in sign language. Once again, we notice a family apart in worship: Delbert's wife Linnea is off at the Baptist church (as seen in the next cut), singing with the black choir to a congregation that includes Tommy Brown and his wife.

Altman sets up a shoot for the church montage.
(*Jim Coe*)

A would-be churchgoer who never made it to the shoot was George Segal, who along with Elliott Gould was taking a detour from promotional work on *California Split*. Following the example of Gould and Julie Christie, Segal was going to enact a variation of his own circumstance: the Hollywood celebrity who blows through to check out the scene and gawk at the locals. Prior to the shoot, Segal had a falling-out with Altman, and plans for using him in the scene were dropped.

The fourth and final locale is the chapel at the hospital where Barbara Jean is recuperating. There, the wheelchair-bound star is leading the congregation in a hymn. Among the attendees are Mr. Green and PFC Kelly, who proves he'll go just about anywhere to see his beloved Barbara Jean. Intriguingly, it is the first time we actually get to hear Barbara Jean sing. The hymn she has chosen, "In the Garden," was Ronee Blakley's favorite at the First Christian Church she attended as an adolescent in Idaho. Blakley thought the lyric—"I come to the garden alone"—aptly illustrated Barbara Jean's isolation.

For a lapsed Catholic such as Altman (whose more eloquent comments on religion included the doddering bishop who stumbles through the marriage ceremony in *A Wedding* and the hymn-singing whores in *McCabe & Mrs. Miller*), the church montage is notable for its studied respect and utter lack of editorializing. It is virtually an act of penance on the director's part when compared to the scene from which he adapted it.

As originally conceived by Joan Tewkesbury, the church segment cops a smug, antirevivalist attitude with sledgehammer subtlety. In it, Kenny attends an Opryland service in which a slick preacher gives a Good Book hard-sell worthy of Elmer Gantry, presaging the yet-to-appear Nashville Cowboy Church. The shiny-suited preacher hawks Jesus and photo souvenirs of himself to the jangling underscore of drums and organ. The abrasiveness of his huckster's rant is amplified by his small congregation, in which a young couple begins to fight noisily over the wails of their crying baby. As the noisy family leaves, the preacher testifies about an Arkansas couple whose troubled marriage was saved after they attended his service and became ministers for God.

The less-than-sacrosanct regard for any one scene, actor, or character charged the multiple *Nashville* locations with a mounting air of uncertainty. "We were all in a daze most of the time," says Alan Rudolph. "It's as if you didn't worry about who was driving the bus. You knew it was a stormy, twisting road and the headlights were out, but you knew you were going to get there. The key to it was that Bob recognized that this thing was alive, that he was guiding it, and that it was going to reach its conclusion."

IF NASHVILLE was a living creature, it was like a Hydra that grew back two heads for every one that got lopped off. For every unworkable scene or lousy idea that got tossed out, a dozen inspired ones riveted the director's attention and defied his budget-conscious mandate. One afternoon, as Altman sighed over the tough editing challenges they would be facing, Alan Rudolph chimed in, "Why don't you cut it into two pictures? Not just Part I and Part II, but have them begin and end the same way, just compose them of different takes we've got. So we'd have two movies."

The suggestion sparked a flame in the director that had been smoldering "for twenty-eight thousand years, when I got into this shit." He had once had an idea for a double movie version of James Michener's *Tales of the South Pacific* with Frank Sinatra. The idea was to shoot all of the tales in two films, with Sinatra in the foreground in the first film and then receding into the background for the second. Altman could do the same for *Nashville*. In movie A, eight or nine characters would prominently figure into a scene with another eight or nine playing supporting roles; the second film would examine the same scene but in reverse focus, such that the secondary characters became the leads. They would call the two movies *Nashville Red* and *Nashville Blue*.

God knows, there would be enough great scenes slashed to fuel a *Nashville White, Plaid,* and *Paisley* to boot. In the final cut, Mr. Green is observed bidding Barbara Jean goodbye as she is released from the hospital. Ronee Blakley laments losing a scene she had written for her and Keenan Wynn establishing an empathetic rapport between the two characters in which Barbara Jean relates to Mr. Green the details of a dream she had.

Cut from the King of the Road scene, in which Connie White performs with Vassar Clements, is a piece of shtick between Allan Nicholls and David Arkin. "He was a limo driver, but he was also supposed to be a failed magician and stand-up performer," says Nicholls of Arkin's character, Norman. "He's always staring at Jeff Goldblum's character because Jeff is doing all this magic stuff. And as I am telling him I think Mary is having an affair, he's playing with these handcuffs, and we end up being handcuffed together. It was pretty funny."

(Less amusing was Nicholls's state of mind when the scene was shot. "I knew I had to get drunk in this scene. So I had a few margaritas downstairs in the hotel bar. It was midday, and there was all this waiting time while they set up the lighting. So I didn't get drunk. I ended up doing the scene with one of the worst headaches I've ever had in my life.")

Gone as well is an exchange between Geraldine Chaplin and Michael Murphy in which it becomes clear that Opal, a TV reporter who is noticeably in need of a camerman, is a fraud. Recalls Murphy, "I accused her of not being who she is. 'C'mon, I know who you are, you know who I am.' That kind of stuff. And she's hemming and hawing, 'Oh, no, really, I have . . .' I don't think Bob wanted it. She later said that people didn't understand her character because that scene was cut."

Chaplin feels that the cut may have contributed to the intensity of distaste for her strident characterization, with the heaviest brickbats tossed by the British press. "Because they didn't understand that she *wasn't* from the BBC. We shot the scene and I think someone said, 'No, it's enough of a giveaway that she says at one moment, British Broadcasting Company' [as opposed to Corporation]. But that's so subtle people wouldn't know that."

Joan Tewkesbury defends the cut. "I never thought she worked for the BBC at all. I thought she was full of shit, totally. But she never said it. Because the minute you say something like that within the reality of your movie, she becomes a cynic. And once she says, I am a cynic, I am really not this person, you go back and look at this character differently, all the way through. If she still believes her own lie, there is an element of fear in this character that drives her all the way through. And fear in that way leaves her vulnerable to experiences. If she's so cynical, she's not open to anything. So I prefer to keep Opal a little off-center."

Barbara Harris would mourn losing a song she had cowritten with her buddy Shel Silverstein for a sequence in which Albuquerque records a demo tape in a studio. With little prompting, Harris will croon for you the tinselly, character-defining country ballad with a thick Tennessee lilt:

Don't know how other girls do it,
Livin' in heaven above.
Maybe they're trying, or lying,
But I'm out here dying.
I can't figure it out at all.
Anyway I'm goin' away, anywhere I can,
Anything I will do, I'll do to get out at all . . .

I'm tied to a one-way man, doin' the best I can,
There may be stars in my horoscope,
There may be stars in my eyes,
But I got to let go, and I'm takin' so slow . . .

The scene was shot but ultimately dropped. Altman's reasoning, according to Tewkesbury, was he wanted to keep the true extent of Albuquerque's talents a mystery and thus maximize the impact of her singing triumph in the final scene. According to Harris, Altman thought the lyrics were too aware for the character. "He wanted me down and out, and the words were 'too good.' You never know when people say you're too good. Are you ever lucky you're getting cut out!"

Another Harris moment that was trimmed was the speedway scene in which she steps up to the mike to sing, only to have her vocalizing drowned out by the roar of passing cars. As filmed, Albuquerque launches into a striptease as she sings the song (Harris was actually singing "It Don't Worry Me" amid the din). Her performance is then interrupted by her husband, Star, who drags her off and throws her into the back of his truck. Presumably Altman decided that one strip per movie was enough, preferring to save the burlesque moment for Sueleen Gay.

Had *Nashville Red* and *Nashville Blue* become a reality, audiences certainly would have seen more of Lady Pearl's heartfelt tribute to the Kennedy boys, ghostwritten by Thomas Hal Phillips and performed to a bravura fare-the-well by Barbara Baxley. Lady Pearl's monologue is the first in a series of spoken arias that will be continued in subsequent scenes by divas Barbara Jean

Barbara Harris, as Albuquerque, gets drowned out at the speedway. As originally filmed, Albuquerque was launching into a striptease, but the strip was cut.

and Opal. Sliced and diced from a rambling twenty minutes to a mere minute of screen time, Lady Pearl's moist-eyed testimony to an unnerved Opal was based on Baxley's actual experiences working on the campaign trail for Robert Kennedy.

"Now the problem we got here is anti-Catholicism. These dumbheads around here, they're all Baptists and whatever. I dunno. Even to teach 'em to make change over the bar ya gotta crack their skulls. Let alone teach 'em to vote for the Catholic, just because he happens to be the better man.

"And all I remember the next few days were . . . us just lookin' at that TV set, an' seeing it all. And seeing that great fat-bellied sheriff sayin', 'Ruby, you sonofabitch.' And Oswald and her in her little pink suit.

"And then comes Bobby. Well, I worked for him . . . I worked

Lady Pearl waxes nostalgic about the Kennedys. Barbara Baxley's monologue, drawn from her own experiences on RFK's campaign trail, was tailored by Thomas Hal Phillips.

here . . . I worked all over the country. I worked out in California, out in Stockton. Well, Bobby came here and spoke and he went down to Memphis, and then he went out to Stockton, California, and spoke off the Santa Fe train at the old Santa Fe depot. Oh, he was a beautiful man. He . . . was not much like, uh, John, you know; he was more—puny-like. But all the time I was workin' for him, I was just so scared, inside, you know? Just scared."

"Baxley's script was this thick when she brought it in," says Altman, holding his thumb and pointing finger inches apart. "She came in and said, I'm going to talk about Kennedy. She had a big passion about him, which was perfect. At that particular time in history everybody had an attitude about the Kennedy assassinations, and for me to get her input was like having Dos Passos write it for me. So I told Barbara, 'You have two reels of film, that's roughly twenty minutes. I'm going to put the camera on the two of you. I'll let you know when we're out of film. But I want you to get through to what you want to get to.' Because there was no mandate. She didn't have to lead the other characters. I could get rid of it if I wanted to. And that's what we did. And Barbara's speech was impassioned. The twenty minutes are much more impressive than the snippets we had to use. As a documentary film, that is a great performance that she did."

Baxley's monologue is noteworthy for two reasons: It is the only time in the movie that actual politicians are mentioned, and it is the only conversation in the film that succeeds in stopping the normally voluble Opal in her tracks. That was not originally the case.

"Geraldine is a real radical," recalls Altman. "When we were doing *A Wedding* and Grace Kelly came to visit the set and have lunch, Geraldine wouldn't have lunch. She wouldn't be in the presence of Princess Grace. And let it be well known."

Chaplin, a chip off her father's pugnacious socialist block, had every intention of busting Baxley's balloon of reverence for JFK. "What about the Bay of Pigs?" she chimed in during a rehearsal with Baxley. Joan Tewkesbury loved that spontaneous note of dissonance, and exhorted Chaplin to say it in front of the cameras as Opal.

When the time came to shoot, Chaplin was struck mute by the sheer force of her acting partner's sincerity. "I didn't dare interrupt," says Chaplin. "I thought, She's not acting. I wish I *had* done it. I wish *Opal* had done it. But Barbara had such passionate convictions. Mine were a lot of chameleonic, you know, French intellectual shit. I didn't know what I was talking about. I felt it, but certainly not as strongly as she felt."

Geraldine Chaplin's panache for "French intellectual shit" would be put to impeccable use in Opal's two tape-recorder arias, in which she waxes poetical on the glories of a wrecked-car graveyard and school-bus parking lot. Neither of the scenes, which occur respectively on the Sunday and Monday of *Nashville*'s five-day sprint, were planned from the outset of filming. Altman had come upon the locations during his periodic rounds of the city, and they begged to be used. And Altman, enamored of Chaplin's stops-out characterization of Opal, was looking for more ways to use her.

"When I saw the bus yard, I thought, this is a great setting," says Altman. "Then the idea of busing crystallized in Geraldine's mind, so we just took that subject and had Jeff Goldblum shaving there like he slept there. Same thing with the dead cars. I thought, Let's put Kenny in there looking for a part because his car broke down. *Nashville*, as much as any film that I've made, I shot anything interesting that was happening. I would try any-

Altman came upon a school-bus yard in his location travels. It would become a subject for one of Opal's two memorable taped monologues. (*Jim Coe*)

thing. I had no linear obligations, necessarily. If something didn't work, we could always go to something else."

Accompanying Chaplin to each of the sites, he asked her to write deadpan dissertations about them as Opal might see them. The actress recalls, "Bob said, 'If you're trying to be Opal, write them as though you were really serious. Really try and write poetry.' And he did add, you know, 'Then it'll be really crappy.'"

Chaplin made it crappy, but it was crap with a purposeful edge: Opal's extemporizations satirize the tendency of foreign tourists to idealize the most kitsch elements of their host countries. The monologues bemused and bored many at the time of the film's release, but they have aged over the years like vintage purple prose.

"I'm wandering in a graveyard," begins her Sunday-morning ode to wrecked cars. "The dead here have no crosses, nor tombstones, nor wreaths to sing of their past glory. But lie, in rotting, decaying, rusty heaps. Their innards ripped out by greedy, vulturous hands. Their vast, vacant skeletons sadly sighing to the sky. The rust on their bodies is the color of dried blood. Dried blood . . . I'm reminded of . . . of an elephant's secret burial ground. Yes. *Le val de mystère. C'est l'estompe de gloire.*"

The school-bus monologue occurs the next day, a comic prelude to the hospital scene in which Mr. Green is told that his ailing wife has died. "The buses! The buses are empty and look almost menacing, threatening as so many yellow dragons watching me with their hollow, vacant eyes. I wonder how many little black children and little white children have yellow nightmares, their own special brand of fear for the yellow peril. I can't have . . . I can't start . . . Damn it. It's got to be more . . . positive. No, more negative. Start again. Yellow is the color of caution. No. Yellow is the color of cowardice. Yellow is the color of sunshine, and yet I see very little sunshine in the lives of all the little black children and the little white children. I see their lives rather as a study in grayness, a mixture of black and . . . oh, of Christ, no, that's fascist. Oh, yellow, yellow, yellow, yellow *fever.*"

Alan Rudolph, who would star Chaplin in his early directing efforts *Welcome to L.A.* and *Remember My Name,* characterizes the actress's fearlessness. "Geraldine sees the Goyaesque side of things, the perverse slant. She takes pleasure in finding a twist that makes her character look kind of foolish. There is a scene in *Remember My Name* in which she wanted a lamp and Moses Gunn wouldn't give it to her. Instead of making it sympathetic and vulnerable, she got on her knees and started mocking him like a beggar in the streets. If the front door is open, she'll climb in the window."

Encouraged by Altman, who was delighted at Chaplin's abandoned satire of old-style imperialist racism, the actress pushed the jest further when filming the recording-studio scene in which Opal coos over the black gospel singers. ". . . It's come down in the genes through ages and ages and hundreds of years, but it's there. And take off those robes and, and . . . and one's in darkest Africa. I can just see their naked, frenzied bodies dancing to the beat of . . ."

Not everyone bought the joke. Barbara Harris was appalled, and confronted the director. "It was very heavy," says Harris of the Opal remarks. "When I saw the rushes, I thought they were very strong and possibly offensive. It got very sick, over the top. Because I had friends in New York, Jimmy Baldwin, Brock Peters, who had strong feelings about these things. I said, 'We're in a time where African-Americans are really not in a happy mood. [Altman] said, 'It's irony.' I said, 'Some people would not see it as irony. You have to be careful. There are whole masses of audiences who may just not pick up on these subtle things. It's almost too English.'

"It was a mistake. I thought he meant what he said when he said he wanted everyone's opinion. I thought it was Second City. But he was very, very tender. I think he thought the scene was wonderful, and Geraldine coming from England felt she could go as far as she did. He had a fit. He was scared. He brought in his wife, and Scotty, as if I were attacking him. I thought [the scene] was tempered when it finally came out. I may be wrong."

Harris was not alone in her anxieties. Lily Tomlin expressed concern about the severity of some of the humor. "I was hypersensitive, knowing how my own family would have reacted if it were about their town. I said, 'I hope we get out of town before anybody sees any of these dailies, you know.'

RONEE BLAKLEY was disgruntled. Barbara Jean was finally getting out of the hospital, and now she was going to have to faint all over again. This would never do.

The next big scene that Tewkesbury had concocted for Barbara Jean was her first public appearance since her hospital release, singing at the Memphis Shopping Center. (Shortly before the August 24 shoot, the location would be switched to the *Opry*

Ronee Blakley chats with some acquaintances before shooting her nervous breakdown scene. Despite Blakley's cheerful demeanor, she was in ill health that morning. (*Jim Coe*)

Belle riverboat theater at Opryland, an infinitely more flamboyant setting.) In the midst of her second number, she would suddenly collapse and be spirited off in an ambulance accompanied by a consoling Barnett.

As fashioned for the actress originally cast as Barbara Jean, Susan Anspach, the second fainting made a certain amount of sense. "Susan was pretty fragile too, very eggshell," claims Joan Tewkesbury. "She had a little more fame [than Blakley]. There might have been a little more competition between her Barbara Jean and Karen Black." The latter, not incidentally, costarred with Anspach in *Five Easy Pieces* opposite Anspach's onetime lover, Jack Nicholson.

"As written, Barbara Jean used fainting. That was how she got out of life, out of a situation. She didn't want to deal with Barnett. She'd check out. It wasn't that she was a victim, it was that she was using it as a device to get out of Dodge. Ronee saw it more literally. I kept saying, no, no, no, it's your ticket on the bus, that's how you use fainting."

Whatever Tewkesbury's intentions, Blakley felt she needed to up the ante of Barbara Jean's instability. "She's already fainted once," she protested gently to Altman. "In phrasing something,

Opry Belle outdoor theater scene at Barbara Jean's breakdown.

Sound man Jim Webb prepares the 8-track sound truck for Barbara Jean's *Opry Belle* appearance. All concert scenes were recorded live.

in the phrasing of a musical piece for example, it needs to go somewhere, not just up and down, up and down. It needs to build to a new place to make sense. I wanted to keep it climbing."

Altman responded, simply, "Why don't you go catatonic?"

Ask a diva to go mute for her big scene? Preposterous. Blakley needed to find another route out of Dodge. Preferably the scenic one.

The solution she came up with would emerge as one of the most memorable high-wire acts in all of *Nashville*. Sequestering herself in her Jack Spence cell the night before the shoot, she opened up her journal and devised an aria of mental collapse as mortifying to behold as Lady Macbeth scrubbing the spots from her hands.

"... Last night I thanked my lucky stars that I could be here at all today to sing for you. And I heard on the radio the cutest little boy. He was nine years old and you know how sometimes the DJ'll play a tune and ask everybody to phone in and say how they like it, you know? And, uh, I was listening to it and, uh, they asked for callers to call in. This little nine-year-old boy called in, an' the song had voices in the background like the way they usually back up voices these days sometimes, you know? Sounded like little munchkins? He called up and the DJ said, 'And how old are you son?' And the boy said, 'I'm nine and I think it's

Ned Beatty and Michael Murphy arrive at *Opry Belle* for shooting of Barbara Jean's concert. (*Jim Coe*)

gonna be a hit.' And the DJ said, 'Why?' And he said, 'Oh, be-cause it had those little chipmunks in it.' And I thought that was so cute because—well, I can sing like a munchkin myself. I don't know about you, and I'm real fond of *The Wizard of Oz*, plus I live out y'know just a ways out here on—offa Highway Interstate 24 on the road to Chattanooga, so you can see why I kinda related to that, and I–I dunno. I think me and the boys are gonna strike up another tune for you now. Let's go, boys."

At that, the band kicks into the next tune. Barbara Jean looks up at the sky and continues chattering.

"I think there's a storm. Seems like it's a-brewing. That's what my granddaddy used to say all the time before he lost his hearin'. Once he got deaf he'd never talk much no more. Except some-times he'd say, 'Oh, gosh,' or 'Durn it,' or 'My word.'"

The band stops. Barbara Jean doesn't.

"My granny, she'd go round the house clickin' her teeth to the radio all day. She was a lot of fun and cooked always my favorite roast beef and she was a sweetheart. She raised chickens, too. She, uh, in fact, did ya ever hear a chicken sound? You know how chickens go? [She clucks like a chicken.] Here chick, chick, chick, chick, chick, chick, here chick, chick, chick. Well, anyway I guess we better strike up this tune before it's too late. Okay, boys."

The boys try again, but Barbara Jean won't quit.

"I'm thinkin', y'know, about the—first job I ever really got was when Mama—[the band gives up] my grandma, she, she's the one who clacked her false teeth to the radio all day? She taught my mama how to sing an' mama taught me. One time she took me down 'cause we was gonna get a new Frigidaire, an' she took me down to the Frigidaire store where the man was doin' the ad-vertisin', and this little record was goin' round and round an' my mama told him that I knew how to sing. He said if she really does, if she learns this tune and comes down and sings it to me, I'll give y'all a quarter. So Mama and I went home, and then what happened—let's see, I think—oh, yeah—we went home and I learned both sides of the record in half an hour and we went back there and pranced in real fancy, and told 'im that I'd learned 'em, and he said, Well, let me hear this, so I sang 'im both sides of the record instead of just one, so he gave us fifty cents and we went across the street and had us a soda. Ever since then I been workin.' I don't—I think ever since then I been workin' and doin' my . . . supportin' myself . . ."

Barbara Jean's hazy, stream-of-consciousness breakdown was stitched together from the real-life detritus of Blakley's own Idaho family album. (The sole detail that was appropriated was grandma's false teeth chattering to the radio, which she got from

Altman confers with Ronee Blakley and Richard Baskin
before the breakdown scene.

Barbara Jean sings "Dues" at *Opry Belle* riverboat
theater before a crowd of locals.

Lily Tomlin.) Blakley committed it to memory, and tried to get some sleep.

The next morning, Blakley headed down to the production office to find Altman. The director recalls, "We were getting ready to leave for the location. She was going to do the songs and

Barbara Jean is scurried offstage. Barnett
(Allen Garfield) tries to calm the protesting crowd.

we didn't have anything written for her. She came up to me and said, 'I've written something. Can I read this to you and see what you think?' I said, 'I don't have time for that. Just do it. I'm just going to put you onstage, and do what you think is right.' It was all her invention."

As written, Barbara Jean's breakdown was an uninterrupted monologue that would follow Barbara Jean's renditions of two Blakley songs, the rollicking "Tapedeck in His Tractor" and a piercing ballad called "Dues." Before shooting, Altman decided to break it up into three "beats," punctuated by the frustrated attempts to dislodge the singer from her reverie.

The credibility of Blakley's fever-dream of a monologue was no doubt enhanced by her own borderline state of health the Saturday morning of the shoot. The actress was running a temperature and taking medication to stave off the woozy effects from lack of sleep and starving herself for two months to stay thin. She was also nervously trying to remember the words to the breathless "Tapedeck in His Tractor," which she had just composed in the weeks prior. Blakley took comfort in the presence of her brother, Steven, who hovered amid the Opryland audience.

Seated among the crowd of Barbara Jean watchers at Opryland is an obstreperous convention of Shriners in an unusually subdued pose. Throughout their four-day visit to Nashville, the belligerent and often inebriated group of Shriners was a constant headache for Altman and the crew, as they noisily insinuated themselves in the filmmaker's activities on and off the set. Geraldine Chaplin remembers, "They got really wild and drunk. They went berserk. They drove into the Jack Spence Motor Hotel on motorcycles and wrecked the place."

"We were shooting downtown one time, and there were thirty of them," says Tommy Thompson. "They wouldn't let us shoot. They were walking into the scenes and hitting on the girls. Bob said, 'We got to get these guys out of here.' So I went to them and said, 'Guys, we really need you for this scene. If you'd go around the corner and let us get started, when I call, you come running around and do your thing.' And they said, 'Great! Yeah! We'll get it this time!' And around the corner they went. And we shot our scene, cut the cameras, and then called them. They came running around, whooping it up like crazy."

Along with Steven Blakley, Opal, and the Shriners, the Opryland crowd is notable in that it is the first time the reflexive characters of Kenny and PFC Glenn Kelly surface in a scene together. Significantly, there is also a sea change in our impression of the two men for the first time, as Kenny takes his seat in the crowd just feet away from Kelly. All at once, it is the sheepish Kenny who prods our suspicions, rather than the stoic Kelly. Who is really the benign presence? Who is the stalker?

CRISTINA RAINES should have known the jig was up the night she lost the Toyota Land Cruiser. It was raining, a summer storm as fierce and over-the-top as a good Southern Gothic yarn. "I was parking Keith's Land Cruiser, that heavy-duty, four-wheel drive, monster-eating car with the winch on it," recalls Raines. "Why we had that car, I had no idea. I drove it up to the top of the hill to the hotel where we were rehearsing. It was pouring rain. Lightning and all that stuff. The guy that was playing guitar behind me, lightning struck him. It came through the roof and zapped him and burned a hole in his guitar. I remember thinking, This is totally wild.

"When we were leaving, I went outside to go get the car, and the jeep wasn't anywhere in sight. I looked down the hill and it was at the bottom. I hadn't put the brakes on, and it

Suspicion trades places: Loners Kenny (David Hayward) and PFC Kelly (Scott Glenn) await Barbara Jean at the outdoor Opry.

Bill (Allan Nicholls) in a moment of dissonance with his wife, Mary (Cristina Raines).

rolled all the way down into the trash bin. And I just thought, Well, this has been quite a day."

The scene could have been a metaphor for the downhill trajectory of her relationship with Keith Carradine. A SEVEN YEAR ITCH TO STAY UNMARRIED, teased a fawning *People* magazine feature on the pair, referring to the loving if unholy bond that kept the two together since meeting on the set of the ill-fated *Grasslands*. The headline was reaffirmed by Carradine's older brother Chris, who attested that "theirs is the best marriage I've ever seen, with or without the piece of paper."

To most of the *Nashville* cast and crew, Keith Carradine and Tina Raines were the golden couple of the set, beautiful Hollywood lovebirds kissed by the grace of God. "Cristina Raines was so radiant, you smiled to see them so in love," recalls Henry Gibson. "Keith was madly in love with Tina, and later drove her to complete distraction," reaffirms Alan Rudolph, who first met the couple when he was assigned to photograph them with Allan Nicholls for a mock album cover of Tom, Bill, and Mary.

Only Keith Carradine could see another Tina. "Things are never what they appear. She was suffering from her own demons. She was terrified of singing. And the demons of our relationship. The fact that it was doomed. I think with us, as with everybody in the cast, there was a perverse blending of life and fiction there."

Raines's "demons" shadowed her character Mary, who is smitten with Carradine's character, Tom, but trapped in a souring marriage to their partner Bill (Allan Nicholls). There is a palpable sadness in the scene in which Raines lies in bed with a sleeping Carradine, whispering an unheard "I love you" into his ear. Even more transparent is the yearning gaze that escapes from Raines's face in the Exit/In scene, as Mary harmonizes with her would-be lover on "Since You've Gone."

The fragile state of affairs of the Carradine–Raines alliance would be deflected in an explosive motel-room confrontation between Raines and Nicholls, filmed over two days at the King of the Road Motel. In the scene, which Altman considers to be one of the best realized and acted in the film, Mary expresses her contempt for her husband from behind a tragic white mask of cold cream. "Fucker!" she yells at his efforts to get her out of bed, then dumps the contents of a drawer onto the floor.

Into this chaotic tableau walks John Triplette, attempting to charm the couple into performing for the Hal Phillip Walker rally. With the appearance of a stranger, the embattled couple instantly put on their best doting-couple pose. Triplette's flattery works on the easygoing Bill but strikes out with the less impressionable Mary. She waives away the request, saying she is a registered Democrat. With one last "Fuck you," she adds that "Tom's a registered Democrat and he won't do it."

Chris Hodenfield, reporting for *Rolling Stone* magazine, observed the scene being filmed.

"Pan back from the twelfth-floor view . . . She is buried asleep. He is in the next bed, idly stitching his guitar, his cigarette jammed into the tuning knobs. 'C'mon wake up, will ya?' She sleeps. 'You wanna talk about it now?' He sees the balloon hanging there, swings his guitar neck so the glowing butt pops the balloon. She wheels out of the covers, spits 'Fucker' at him, clomps over his bed, splashing his breakfast tray.

"'Terrific!' says Altman. Zooming back, there stood Altman waltzing by the Panavision, watching Raines and Nicholls. 'That balloon thing was terrific.' It was new on him. 'Are there more balloons so we can do another take on that?' No. Messengers were dispatched. 'And get some blue ones.'

"Waiting for the balloons, he prepared the twosome for their fight scene. 'Now, the situation is this. Tina, why don't you go into the bathroom and, Allan, you're banging on the door. You know: 'Get the hell outta there!' And then Tina, you come out here and take your things out of the drawer. Does that drawer come all the way out?'

"Altman yanked the drawer out of the chest. 'Yeah, good, why don't you dump all the clothes on the floor there. And here, then hand him his turtle.'

"Privately he warned her not to call Nicholls a 'fucker,' because he was looking for a PG rating here. For once.

". . . Michael Murphy paced the floor, repeating his lines on silent lips. Now he was memorizing them . . . *in case all else fails.*"

Hodenfield captures the loose dance between script and improvisation that actors negotiate in an Altman film. You do what works for you. Recalls Nicholls, "Michael and I were comfortable with improvising. Tina wasn't comfortable with that. She wanted lines to say. So we just fed off of her lines. The fight scene was ad-libbed, and then when Michael came into the room it was scripted." In fact, the bristling three-way tango between Bill, Mary, and Triplette, in which Mary claims to be a registered Democrat, hugs close to the original dialogue that Tewkesbury first envisioned for the scene.

"It was sort of like one of those seeds or pills that you stick into water and it turns into a dinosaur," explains Raines. "The deeper you would go into a character, the more you would find out and things started happening. I felt like a deer with the headlights on my face. I really didn't know which way to go. So Bob said, 'Why don't you put some cold cream on?'"

Murphy added his own little grace note to the encounter. "Right before we started shooting, I said to Bob, 'I should have the hots for her. You know, she's real cute and he's such a square guy. There's such a cultural divide there. For him to come in and be sort of knocked off his pins by some sort of hippie chick is sort of a good idea.' So we did just that."

The Pirendellian interplay of fiction and reality eventually got the better of Allan Nicholls, who had observed the on-again, off-again relationship of his buddies Carradine and Raines from as close as the corner bed of their Laurel Canyon house. Nicholls threw himself into the on-screen role of Raines's husband with such totality that he was completely unnerved when, at the dailies, he watched a scene unfold in which Carradine and

On-screen and off-screen lovers Cristina Raines and Keith Carradine.

Raines bed down together. The actor had not been apprised that his "wife" Mary was having an affair with his "friend" Tom, and went ballistic at the discovery.

"It hadn't been that long since he had been through that himself in real life," explained Nicholls's buddy, Carradine. "The scene kind of brought all of that back."

"It was the weirdest thing," said Nicholls. "I was floored at the dailies. It's not the old story of tunnel vision and not knowing what you're doing. We're so into being this trio, and I knew Tom was supposed to be this bed-hopping kind of guy. I never read that part of the script where he hops into bed with Mary. Because Bob told us not to read the script. And after the dailies I went back and grabbed my script and went, 'Shit, I never saw that!' I was thrown. I was totally upset. I went to Keith and Bob, and Bob just smirked. That all-knowing smirk."

"That's the thing about Bob, he's the Cheshire cat from *Alice in Wonderland*," adds Cristina Raines, who finally got to keep the "fucker" in the motel-room scene. If Altman was at all concerned about blowing his PG rating, he must have realized on some level he had a lot more to worry about than a single off-color word.

CHAPTER TWELVE

GETTING NAKED, GETTING ENOUGH

(Wherein Gwen Welles Takes Her Clothes Off and Lily Tomlin Keeps Her Clothes On)

"I never get enough, I never get enough
Of the love I'm hungry for.
I never get enough, I never get enough,
I always want more and more.
Even if we stay together
Our whole lifetime through,
I'll never get enough, I'll never get enough
I'll never get enough of you."

—"I NEVER GET ENOUGH," WRITTEN BY RICHARD BASKIN
AND BEN RALEIGH FOR THE CHARACTER SUELEEN

FOR LONGTIME NATIVES OF NASHVILLE, THE at-home murder of the beloved performer Stringbean and his wife had an instantaneous greenhouse effect that altered the climate of well-being forever and a day. For outsiders, it was merely a confirmation of what they had long suspected: Beneath the smile-button facade, Nashville was a rough-riding town. Violent expression was merely the yang that complemented the yin of religious fervor. To the visitor, it was only a wonder it didn't happen more often.

Where else could you find an artillery superstore called Gun City, where consumers piled weapons and ammunition into shopping carts as if they were stocking up on Duraflame logs for the winter? Where else did one find each of the teamsters on a film crew, to a man, walking tall with a gun strapped to his belt? Where else was one likely to see a bullet hole in a sound booth window, as Altman discovered at the recording studio where Barbara Harris cut Albuquerque's demo record?

Barbara Baxley was unnerved to discover that her hairdresser packed a .38 revolver in her handbag, and that just about everyone else she encountered in Nashville carried a gun.

"There was a definite undercurrent of violence," says Cristina Raines. "They have their way of doing things there, and you needed to be aware of it. There was a girl who got murdered who was an extra on the set. She didn't show up one day."

Henry Gibson learned at close range that it didn't take much to expose the town's underside of menace. One afternoon, Ned Beatty, Keith Carradine, Bert Remsen, and Gibson found themselves with an hour and a half to kill before dailies, and decided to go for a bite. Gibson recalls, "We're sitting there having our beer and pizza, then our second beer. And I excused myself to go to the men's room. I opened the door to the men's room, and like this [he claps down on his hands] a guy turned around from the urinal, pulls out a gun and says [viciously], *Nobody walks in on me when I'm taking a leak!'* The blood just drained out of me."

All things considered, Altman showed restraint in depicting some of the more bellicose aspects of Music City life in the seventies which Daryl Duke's 1973 film *Payday* confronted with a gritty and unsparing hand. But for a hotheaded Barnett and a drunken outburst by Wade, overt acts of violence are side-stepped in *Nashville* prior to the climactic assassination. Wade's outburst at the Old Time Picking Parlor was a significantly altered version of an old-style barroom fight Tewkesbury had envisioned at Lady Pearl's establishment involving Bill, Kenny, and a local rowdy who has mistaken Kenny for a despised adversary. When Bill steps in to defend Kenny, the yahoo takes Bill for a pot-smoking out-of-towner, and the tension escalates into a fist-swinging, table-turning brawl.

Notwithstanding David Arkin's assault on a journalist, the only incident that came close to that on the set of *Nashville* was an encounter between Altman and a couple of visiting producers from *California Split*. Rumor had it that Altman knocked one of them into the swimming pool after they suggested cuts they wanted to make on that film.

"I never punched anybody in my life," says Altman, denying the charges. "Ever. Mainly because I'm afraid they would hit me back. We had a screening of *California Split* at a pool party at the Jack Spence Motor Hotel before we started shooting *Nashville*. These guys came down. Leonard Goldberg came over after he saw the picture screened, made some comment I didn't like, we should change this or do this. And I threw him out of there. But he never went in the water. It would be a better story."

Despite Altman's hands-off method of showing folks the door, actors and coworkers witnessed a hair-trigger volatility from their director that could be easily set off if he was insulted, hurt, ambushed, or felt betrayed. Sue Barton, the film's unit publicist and a devoted friend of Kathryn Altman, got a taste of this mercurial behavior when she, Kelly Marshall, and Altman's secretary, Elaine Bradish, decided to throw an anniversary party for the Altmans. Barton had spearheaded a number of birthday celebrations over the summer (including Carradine's twenty-third, Keenan Wynn's fifty-eighth, and Geraldine Chaplin's thirtieth), family affairs that usually consisted of a big cake at dailies. For the Altmans' fif-

Press liaison Sue Barton (right) was fired for throwing an anniversary party for Kathryn and Bob Altman.

teenth anniversary, they felt that something a little more festive was in order.

"At the end of dailies we announced that we'd like to invite everybody next door to the conference room for cake and champagne for Bob and Kathryn. I could tell by the look on Bob's face that this was not going down very well. Why, to this day, I have no idea. We all trouped over, but Bob and Kathryn didn't go right away. When they did, Bob was in a really nasty mood. He insisted that he and Kathryn sing this song that was their song, and he was just as nasty as can be. It was very unpleasant. Finally people drifted away.

"I was going to go out to dinner with Jeff Goldblum and a few others, but I wanted to get something from the office first. My room was upstairs, but in the living room downstairs Bob would sometimes stay at night if he had to be out real early in the morning. So I started down the alleyway, and Bob and Kathryn were coming toward me from that same room. And Bob said, 'Who's idea was this?' I said, 'Well, I guess it was mine.' And he said, 'Well, you're fired.' And kept walking. I said, 'Wait a minute, you can't do that and run!'

"So he came back—this is actually very funny—and started in, 'What's so great about an anniversary? What do anniversaries celebrate? Marriage is ridiculous!' Kathryn is standing there. And he said, 'Your mother just died, right?' I said, 'Yes.' And he said, 'Why aren't we celebrating that?' And on and on he went. And he and I were actually in the bedroom, Kathryn was in the living room. And ABC had sent a huge basket of fruit for their anniversary. At one point at some particularly nasty remark Kathryn picked up the basket of fruit and threw it at him. There was stuff all over the place. With that Kathryn and I walked out. The next morning, I was ready to leave, and Kathryn kept saying, 'No, don't, wait, he'll just ignore the whole thing if you ignore it.' So I remained till the picture was finished."

Barton's alliance with the Altmans endured, although she did not work for the director again. Years later she would express her prickly affection for her former boss at a party. "I have no idea why I did it, but I poured my glass of wine over his head. It was something I wanted to do for a very long time. He took it very well. He laughed, and everybody laughed. And he told me that I reminded him of Glenn Close in *Dangerous Liaisons*."

Twenty-five anniversaries after the fifteenth-anniversary fruit toss, Kathryn Altman recalls her husband's flare-ups with a smile: "I was always having to run in and tell people, 'Don't worry, it's not about you!'"

What it was about, in many cases, was the incendiary effect of alcohol on the pressures of making an epic on a shoestring. "I think this had to be the movie that worked, or else he was out of Hollywood," speculates Barbara Harris. "Even though he had fans, he was going on a wing and a prayer."

"Stoned and drunk out of his mind," says Geraldine Chaplin of Altman's postshoot equilibrium. "We all were. It was wonderful."

Altman concedes, "I'd be drinking at night when we were finished and looking at the dailies. We'd go back, have some drinks and look at film. And there were miles and miles of film."

PRIOR TO the assassination of Barbara Jean, the most disturbing violence that plays itself out in the film is of the psychosexual variety, predatory gestures in which men—acting alone and in groups—violate the dignity of women.

Sueleen Gay's reluctant striptease before a hooting roomful of men at a fund-raising "smoker" strikes the audience with the force of a gang rape. The scene is loaded with ambivalence, given the in-your-face quality of Sueleen's willful, if clueless, musical seduction that prompts the strip. For a bunch of guys out on the town, any woman wearing a slinky, lime green gown and swiveling her hips to the provocative lyrics of "I Never Get Enough" would appear to be ready to fulfill their most salacious dreams.

For Joan Tewkesbury, the smoker is nothing less than the moral centerpiece of the film. "It's the key to the movie, the metaphor: If you want to make it, at some time you're going to have to take off all your clothes."

The moment only gains in its queasy power by the seamlessness with which Altman folds the striptease into a scene at the Exit/In, in which Tom performs his own musical seduction on a number of his recent female conquests. Altman intensifies our discomfort with a pair of postperformance interludes in which Tom cavalierly beds Linnea and Delbert hits on a spirit-shattered Sueleen. The climactic pileup of human violations reminds us, in case we had forgotten, that the screenplay was conceived by a woman traveling alone in Nashville.

LILY TOMLIN took a seat by herself in the back of the Exit/In, just as Joan Tewkesbury had done a year and a half earlier. She was wearing a tastefully alluring ensemble, white dress with a dark kerchief accent, of the sort that Linnea might pull out of the mothballs just to wear to the theater or a celebratory dinner. Her hands clutched a purse tooled together in a prison crafts shop out of Camel cigarette wrappers, a treasure that she had found at a local thrift shop.

The purse was Tomlin's subtle nod to Wade Coolidge, the luncheonette counterman who would do his best to pick up Linnea at the Exit/In ("romancin' the stone," as Robert Doqui called the impossible effort). Tomlin and Doqui had rehearsed an extended dialogue in which Wade revealed he had just been released from prison three months previously after serving twenty-eight years for premeditated murder. The conversation, wherein Wade exhausts a menu of come-on lines ranging from recreational drugs to religion, was lifted with literal fidelity from Joan Tewkesbury's Exit/In encounter with James Broadway. Like so much of Tewkesbury's character shading for *Nashville*, the Linnea–Wade dialogue would be filmed in its entirety and shaved down to the barest details. Along with the excised barroom brawl, the scene was another of Tewkesbury's (largely ignored) attempts to raise the thorny issue of Nashville's incipient drug culture.

In the film, Linnea's visit to the Exit/In to initiate a clandestine rendezvous occurs after a series of three phone calls from Tom in which he gradually chips away at her faithful-wife resistance. Another phone conversation that would have dulled the ambiguity of Linnea's true feelings (in it, Linnea is palpably disappointed that it is not Tom on the other end) was dropped. Instead, Altman went with the subtler signals sent out by a phone call from Tom in which Linnea doth protest too much, knowing that her husband is listening in on the other end. "Listen," she barks, "I don't know who you are or why you are callin' me, but I want you to stop." We are left to infer that if Delbert did not pick up the extension phone in the other room, Linnea and Tom would have had a very different conversation.

"Someone like Linnea would never make that move unless someone made that move toward her first," says Lily Tomlin, ex-

Altman sets up a scene at the Exit/In as Joan Tewkesbury listens in.
Seated (left to right) are David Arkin, Geraldine Chaplin,
and Cristina Raines. (*Jim Coe*)

plaining the progression of seductive phone calls that leads her
to the Exit/In. "She's not hip. She doesn't know how to handle
someone like this on the first go-round. It shakes her up a little
bit. And instead of her saying, 'Don't ever call,' and hanging up
on him, part of her is led in there just out of her niceness or pro-
priety. Then, because she hasn't said it, she has to cover up the
next time. It's a funny shifting thing that I like."

"Basically she is a woman who is at a crossroads in her life,"
says Tewkesbury of Linnea. "She grew up in the fifties and said,
you guys are having a lot more fun than I am. And this young

man calls her up and tells her that she is attractive? My God! She's never thought about these things before, but someone's put candy on the plate and said have a piece. She's going to have it."

As Linnea takes her seat at the Exit/In, Paul Lohmann's roving camera steers us away from her nervous presence at the rear of the club to two other tables. At one are Tom and L.A. Joan, continuing her tireless, and largely successful, campaign to snag every handsome stud in Nashville. At the other is Bill, Mary, their chauffeur Norman, and the ubiquitous Opal. The insufferably loose-lipped reporter reveals to a mortified Mary and an amused Bill that she has had an affair with Tom. "We sort of got to know each other in the Biblical sense. . . ."

For his part, Allan Nicholls actually *didn't* know what Chaplin meant. When Bill responds with a captivated smile and says, "You went to church?" it is an accurate reflection of youthful Nicholls's naïveté regarding the wild jungle of sexual euphemisms. Nicholls now admits, "At the dailies, I couldn't figure out what everybody was laughing about. I had to ask. For some reason, that part of Bible class left me at that moment."

Both of the Exit/In numbers—Bill, Mary, and Tom's rendition of "Since You've Gone" and Tom's plaintive rendering of "I'm Easy"—were rehearsed once before the audience (assembled from locals and *Nashville* crew members) to establish the camera setups and adjust the sound levels from the sixteen-track van parked out in front.

For the singing-shy Cristina Raines, it was the moment of truth. The joint was crawling with local pros, including veteran guitarist Jonnie Barnett, who is seen and heard singing at the top of the scene. "There were real Nashville people out there. These are people who listen to Loretta Lynn. I look at them and all I can hear in my head is, Who is this person getting up and singing a song? The guy playing the guitar behind me said, 'You don't have to worry about it, you're just singing for these people.' And I looked at him and said [in withering tones], 'That is a camera, the audience is a lot bigger than this room.' He just went totally ashen."

Raines's agitation registers on her face during the song, which she nevertheless sells with creditable confidence and sensitivity for a recent refugee from the Ford modeling factory. Altman, ever the stickler for documentary reality, decided to leave in a telltale nervous cough. Of the unheralded musical moments in *Nashville,* the tight Crosby, Stills and Nash–like harmonizing by two real-life lovers and their close buddy on Gary Busey's tune is a buoyant highlight.

For all of Raines's misgivings, no one was more anxious and uncertain about filming that scene than Lily Tomlin. Says Henry Gibson, her former *Laugh-In* colleague, "Lily was in great anguish. She would say, 'I just feel wrong about what I'm doing, Henry. I can't imagine I can pull this off.' And I would say, 'You are doing what you are doing with incredible simplicity and credibility.' She just let that character be. Rather than emphasizing and underlining."

Gibson articulates the restrained beauty of Tomlin's presence as Linnea sits in the rear, taking in Tom's crooning of "I'm Easy." Tomlin insists she had no idea where the camera was as it floated over the rapt stares of Mary, L.A. Joan, and Opal, each of them imagining Tom is singing to them, and landed upon Linnea as she touches her chest with palpable longing. It is a devastating moment, an iconic tableau that arguably contributed as much to Tomlin's eventual Oscar nomination as any of her speaking scenes in the film.

In her self-doubt, Tomlin just assumed she blew it. "I knew this was an important scene for me. I was working for a place for myself internally. I thought I was putting out so much. This kind of conflicted yearning. I was counting on my eyes being so expressive. And the next night, when we saw the dailies, my eyes seemed to be mostly in shadows. I left the screening early, because I was just in tears.

"Scotty called me after. 'You left the screening in the middle. The scene was great!' And I started sobbing. 'No, I was horrible!' I was overcome with grief. I thought I had really failed that scene."

NED BEATTY'S phone rang at ten o'clock the night before shooting the strip scene with Gwen Welles. It was Altman. "We talked," said Beatty. "And we talked. And talked. And talked. And talked. And *talked!* And what it was all about was: How are we going to get this to happen?"

The setup, on the face of it, was simple. Sueleen had been hired by John Triplette and Delbert Reese to entertain a stag-party

Sueleen (Gwen Welles) descends from the ceiling for her unexpected striptease at a smoker fund-raiser for Hal Phillip Walker. Ned Beatty and Michael Murphy watch (rear left).

crowd of potential donors to the Hal Phillip Walker campaign. She assumed she had been invited to sing, but once there, she would realize that she would be expected to take her clothes off.

When Altman called Beatty, he still hadn't figured out the strategy for moving an unsuspecting Sueleen into a place where she would strip before a catcalling crowd of men. As originally written by Tewkesbury, Sueleen's awareness of the true nature of her job would arrive in stages. Her first suspicions are aroused as Triplette asks to see her costume.

"She has chosen to wear something that makes her look like those pictures of a frosty glass of gin and tonic on a hot day. Triplette stares at her blatantly, and Reese can hardly keep from touching her. At this point, Sueleen starts into the routine that is done as a matter of survival. It is not pleasant for her to do, but it keeps things moving and it keeps her from her fear of getting raped. She does several turns."

After ladling on flattery with a trowel, Triplette puts his arm around the now-spellbound Sueleen, saying, "Have you ever done this before?"

"She doesn't respond too much [sic]. She is too lost in his embrace and the strength of his nearness. All she can do is look at him and shake her head No."

Triplette continues the seduction. "'Well, it's not too hard. You'll sing whatever it is that you want to sing. They'll applaud like crazy 'cause I can tell that you're really something, and then the piano and drum will give you a little fanfare and you can sing and take your clothes off or not. It doesn't make much difference, really, but since you've never done this before, singing might help.'"

"She stops walking and starts gulping back all the promises she made to St. Theresa and all the dictums about how far one will go for one's art. They are near three enormous beef legs that are waiting to be carved."

Triplette goes on. "'Now this is for charity to raise money for the people who are less fortunate than us, and the more you take off, you see, the more money we can raise.'"

"Sueleen has moved into that state of mind that allows her to be there in body but not in mind. She is totally detached now and will function like a robot through the rest of the evening."

In the remainder of Tewkesbury's setup, Sueleen is enthusiastically received after her first song and tries to weasel out of the strip by suggesting another song. Triplette is determined, however, and a glazed Sueleen goes through with the strip as Albuquerque—forever waiting in the wings for her big chance—watches from behind a stage curtain.

Despite the explicitness of Tewkesbury's script descriptions, the game plan was still uncertain by the time Beatty got off the phone with Altman.

At least the machinery was in place. For the banquet hall, Altman and his team had landed upon Chaffin's Barn Dinner Theatre on Highway 100, a kitsch-rustic affair that dished up barbecued chicken and Shakespeare in comparably heavy servings. Opened in 1967, Chaffin's boasted a stage that descended from the ceiling that would be reconfigured to convey Sueleen Gay to a ravenous mob of three hundred men. Despite the wholesome red-and-white checkered tablecloths and the high-minded aspirations, Chaffin's exuded just the right aroma of grunge. "It was very sleazy," attests production coordinator Kelly Marshall Fine, "like getting your own personal tour of a striptease joint."

Finding the three hundred guys was another story. "We couldn't get extras to come," recalls Tewkesbury. "No one wanted to be seen on screen watching a striptease."

Thomas Hal Phillips came to the rescue, once more, luring three hundred of Nashville's finest with the promise of a Disneyland trip and TV set giveaway. "I think the winner took the money instead of the trip to Disneyland," says Phillips.

When the cast, crew, and expectant extras assembled at Chaffin's the next morning, Tewkesbury was unnerved to hear the upshot of Beatty and Altman's phone conversation.

Tewkesbury recalls, "Ned came in and said, 'You know, Bob, I don't think this guy would ever do this. She'd come to this club knowing that she was going to do a striptease.' I said to Bob, 'If you do that, it lets Ned off the hook, it lets everybody off the hook. The point is that everybody is in collusion here. Sueleen is more complicated than that. Sueleen heard it, but she never paid attention to it. As far as she's concerned, she's got a singing gig. Otherwise, it totally turns Sueleen's character into a cliché. It turns Ned's character into a cliché if there isn't that other complexity, that complicity with ambition.'

"Thankfully, Thomas Hal Phillips walked by. Bob said to him, 'Does this stuff go on like it does in the script?' And Thomas Hal said, 'Are you kidding? It goes on all the time.'"

So, it remained that Sueleen would come in like a lamb to slaughter. Still, it was apparent that neither Beatty nor Michael Murphy was willing to play the blackguard with the intensity demanded by the script. Consequently, Triplette's Svengali-like seduction was omitted and Delbert's leering was toned down. Instead, Sueleen would be prodded into doing the strip by the crowd, who would interpret her song ("I Never Get Enough") and her ooh-la-la outfit as an invitation. When Sueleen protests, Triplette and Reese would play dumb.

The mortification on Sueleen's face as she resigns herself to the strip was amplified by the apprehensions of Gwen Welles, who dreaded the strip nearly as much as would her character. "She was very nervous about how she was going to look naked," explains Tewkesbury. It was not a first for Welles, who had gone the nude route in her affecting turn as a woman of easy virtue in *California Split* and in a *Playboy* spread during her days as Roger Vadim's muse. But she had put on a few pounds since joining A.A., replacing her heroin habit with chocolates.

"This was the most vulnerable period in her life," says her companion at the time, record producer Richard Perry, who observed her obsessive-compulsive tendencies at close hand. "She could eat a box of doughnuts at the drop of a hat. Gwen was a very paradoxical person. Her holistic nature ran very strong, but had gotten blurred over by that drugged-out, alcoholic haze that had permcatcd her life for years."

Welles disseminated her health obsessions with an almost evangelistic ardor. She proselytized to Ronee Blakley on the miraculous power of Laszlo cosmetics. She cajoled Richard Perry into doing yoga with her on their first date. "She knew more about nutrition than anyone I'd ever met," claims Geraldine Chaplin. "She'd say to me, 'Look at my skin, look at my skin.' And she had the most incredible skin you'd ever seen. Absolutely alabaster. She'd say, 'It's because I'm a vegetarian.' She got me seriously thinking about being a vegetarian."

Welles's anxiety over going through with the scene was felt by Ned Beatty, who said, "I remember her chanting, 'I don't believe I'm going to do this, I don't believe I'm going to do this.'"

Coupled with Welles's apprehensions was a technical conundrum: how to keep an actor who is about to strip wired for sound. Recalls Jim Webb: "On the second verse of the song she was going to take off her clothes. I said, 'Bob, I can't figure out how I'm going to mike her.' He said, 'You'll figure it out.' 'I don't think so.' It keeps getting closer to the day we're going to do it. I said, 'I can't even hide the mike on that elevated stage, there's no place to do anything.' And he didn't want to loop in her singing afterwards. He often told me, 'I'd rather sacrifice a movie than loop it.' Which is why she doesn't sing the second verse when she strips."

When the time came to shoot, Altman revved up the extras with a few mock bump and grinds, undulating his pot belly like the sailor performing in drag in the song "Honey Bun" from *South Pacific*. Nashville graphic artist William Myers, who was corralled into being an extra on the scene, recalls, "Our assignment was to yell and scream like a bunch of good old boys. Altman announced to everybody that Gwen didn't want to do this, but that she was going to go through with it anyway. So there was a certain amount of empathy; we felt like we were egging her on. This older fellow next to me, he was a banker or a Sunday-school teacher. He really enjoyed behaving like he never got to before. We really got into it. We were all jumping and getting out of our chairs and screaming and being obnoxious."

"It was kind of difficult," recalls Murphy. "Everybody got into it. I thought it was awful, but I knew that it was what it was about. I wanted to show there that I felt a little ambivalent about it. It had kinda gotten almost out of hand. You set these things up and then, Oh, what am I doin'? I told Bob I oughta feel like I took it a little too far. It seems to me he cut to me a few times, with those looks of being uncomfortable."

Murphy's discomfort only reflects our own. What makes the scene so particularly disturbing to watch is the way in which Altman and Tewkesbury render the audience complicitous, nudging us to chortle along with John Triplette and Delbert Reese at the wretchedness of Sueleen's vocalizing and the sultry absurdity of her Catwoman-goes-to-the-Emerald-City outfit. Even the honey-sweet Bud Hamilton gets sucked into the mob fever, drunkenly hurling balled-up napkins at the would-be singer. Well before Sueleen is compelled to strip, the laughter sticks in our craw.

Tewkesbury credits Gwen Welles and the crowd of local recruits for the scene's ambiguous potency. She flashes back to a conversation with the actress earlier in the filming. "Gwenny had had these gym socks in her drawer and said, 'Can I use these?' And I said, 'Can you ever!' Because we all did. And she rolls up the gym socks and sticks 'em in her bra and pushes 'em up, and I said, 'This is going to work great for the striptease later.'

"So Gwen came out and started. None of these guys wanted to be shown doing catcalls. They were very polite and gentlemanly. They had come up to me during the lunch break, after Gwen had been singing all morning, and said, 'You know, that girl can't sing a lick.' And I said, 'I know.' And they said, 'Well, are you going to have somebody do a voiceover like they do in the movies?' And I said, 'Nope, the whole point is she can't sing a lick.'

"Finally she does the thing, after she takes off the top part of her dress, where she pulls out a gym sock. That flipped some of them out. Then she pulls out the other one. (I said to Ned and Bob, 'If she knew she was going to do a striptease she would have gone out and bought pasties and a G-string.') And when she took

Delbert Reese (Ned Beatty) encourages Sueleen Gay
to go through with the strip as the crowd cheers her on.

off her underpants and walked offstage, every single man stood
up and gave her a standing ovation. Then we did it again and
they did it again. And the same guys came up to me and said,
'I've never seen a braver girl in my life.'

"And that was the consensus of opinion. Because Gwen did it
without attitude, without ambivalence. She played it dead, the
way you do when you separate your head from your body.
Dancers do it all the time. That was the complexity for me in
writing the scene. Because there is a kind of beauty when you see
somebody just kind of rise to the occasion and do something that
is so shocking. 'Cause you *expect* pasties and a G-string. This girl
stood up, looked you in the eye, and tossed you her underpants.
There is lot of ambivalence in the various behaviors of the men.
And that is for me what this movie is all about: ambivalence

toward fame, toward ambition. What does it take to do it? How do you get there? It's all right there in that strip."

When the smoker scene was wrapped, the apprehensions expressed during Altman's marathon phone conversation the night before had vanished. "What were we worried about?" says Ned Beatty. "One of my favorite stage directions was, 'You can't play that *you're* the king, the other guy has to play that you're the king.' When Gwen stripped, we weren't the king. The 'audience' was the king. And they were brilliant. There was no question that that's what they came there to do. Wherever that is in the male psyche, they just went there. It was simple."

ON ITS own intimate terms, the filming of the motel bedroom scene between Lily Tomlin and Keith Carradine proved to be as fraught with dissension and discomfort as the mob-filled smoker scene with Gwen Welles.

"They took the whole day and the next day and the next day," recalls Geraldine Chaplin, who had to wait to do her scheduled scene as a result. "Because Lily did not agree on what Robert and Keith wanted her to do. And she brought them around to her way of thinking. She really stood up to him. And the scene as a result is so lovely and tender."

"I remember how much tension was in the air that day," says production coordinator Kelly Marshall Fine. "The biggest trauma was Lily and her concept of that love scene. She was so miserable. Jane [Wagner, Tomlin's partner] was with her. Scotty and Keith were trying to help. It was the only time I remember being afraid. Bob's temper was so short that day, if anybody crossed his path he just bellowed at them."

The scene as eventually filmed runs a rapid course from tender exchanges to rude awakening. We find Tom in bed with Linnea, the last and most surprising in a succession of women the musician has bedded throughout the film. Semicovered by a sheet, she is wearing a slip while he appears to be in his usual bedside nude repose. Unlike the other women with whom we have seen him in bed, Linnea seems to have captivated Tom. There is an unfamiliar warmth in the way he responds to Linnea as she teaches him how to say "I love you" in sign language. Correspondingly, there is a new familiarity in the ease with which Linnea chides him on his smoking, then playfully asks to take a drag of his cigarette.

The tableau of postcoital bliss is all too short. The moment Linnea hops out of bed to return to her family, we can feel the air chill. As Linnea dresses in the bathroom, she listens as Tom attempts to summon another girlfriend over the phone to replace her for the night. Linnea waves goodbye with a shy smile and shuts the door behind her. Tom lies to the unseen voice over the phone, explaining away the door noise. "Room service . . . uh, there's fifty cents on the desk there, just pick it up," he yells into

Linnea Reese (Lily Tomlin) teaches Tom (Keith Carradine) how to sign "I love you."
The gambit was the idea of Tomlin, who made significant changes in the scene.

the empty room for the benefit of his would-be date on the phone.

Altman had intended something even harsher. Tewkesbury's original script called for Linnea to discover a large black cockroach in the bathroom (a metaphoric correspondent to the slabs of meat Sueleen discovers at the smoker). Tom laughs at her repulsion, then momentarily interrupts his phone call to get out of bed and kiss her goodbye. He returns to the phone as she searches the room for her panties. As she gives up and heads to the door, Tom throws the underwear at her.

"Lily made a significant shift in that scene," says Tewkesbury. "I had been trying to get to a way to have this woman leave with dignity."

Tomlin demanded that the panty toss be deep-sixed, claiming that Linnea would not allow him to get away with that. Wearing a modest slip was also her call. "As a teenager, I had an affinity for 'bad-women' movies," she explains. "They were the only interesting women in the movies during that time, the only ones who had any independence or autonomy. In the fifties, they always wore a full slip. My reference was Lana Turner in *The Flame and the Flesh*."

For all the B-movie bad-girl posturing, Tomlin saw Linnea's relation to Tom as maternal. Signing "I love you" evolved out of that decision. "I had actually planned a lot of different stuff. Because she had children, I wanted to do this little rhyme that had an ironic twist to it. Something like, 'Little Miss Molly, with brow furrowed down/Ironing her dolly's best gown . . .' The idea is that this little girl is ironing her dolly's best gown and someone comes in and says, 'Why, don't you know that it's a sin to work on the Lord's day?' or something like that. And her rejoinder, it's all in rhyme, goes, 'Don't you know that this little iron ain't hot?' And somehow I thought it was almost a subconscious way for Linnea to say, you know, that she's really not being used."

Tewkesbury adds, "Lily said I would like to try and teach him something, to give her a little more control of this situation. Which was fine, because you didn't need another vulnerable girl in this mix. Teaching him to sign 'I love you' gives her some power, so that when she goes to the bathroom and can't find her underpants, she has the balls to go in and pull them out, wave goodbye, and get out of Dodge. It took long. We were in that room all day long with all the different people. We would always save Lily to the last because she would always ask the most questions. You would have to process with Lily very differently than any of the other actors. She would need to talk about it, try it on, try it out."

"Lily was not always the most trusting person," said Altman. "She'd not done a film before. She's hands-on everything. And she's very private, she and Jane. The way they work together, you never saw the wheels, but man, there was work going on!"

If Tomlin had had her way completely, the scene would never have been attempted. She recalls, "I said, 'I don't think Linnea can go to bed with this guy. He has no character.' And Bob said, 'Well, when the time comes, if she can't do it, she just can't do it.'"

It was in the nature of Altman's working methods that actors would often fudge the line between their characters' motivations and their own. Altman seemed to understand that, when Tomlin insisted Linnea would not bed this guy, what she really was saying was that *she* wouldn't. "A lot of that is Lily speaking. That happens quite often. When an actor has that much input, you're going to get it back. I have to say, 'No, this is the way I see this character.'

"Lily was partially in the closet then about her own sexuality. She wasn't really out. But she played it so emotionally honestly, I totally believed that situation. I think that is the kind of guy she would have gone for. I don't think she would have had an affair with Michael Murphy or any of the other characters. She did some of her sexiest responses in the picture. She said, 'You don't have to be one to act one.'"

According to Ned Beatty, who got to know Tomlin when they acted out a volatile sister-brother relationship in an experimental play at Washington's Arena Stage, Tomlin's struggles with the character touched a nerve of her own demons. "She told me something about what her feelings about men were shaped by.

And it was very revealing. She'd had a terrible experience in New York one time, a kind of Mafia-type guy beat her up in a bar with about six other men watching. Nobody helped her.

"One of my proudest moments is when she told me that she liked me as well as any man she'd ever known. Which really got my heart. And that night, when the brother and sister get into a fight, she proceeded to kill me onstage."

TOMLIN WAS not the only actor in the room who was tense about her assignment. "I don't think she was anywhere as skittish as I was," says Keith Carradine. "Of all the three actors [I did bed scenes with], I was most in awe of her. I considered her a force to be reckoned with. And I've never been comfortable in those [bedroom scene] situations. I'm so walking on eggshells in those circumstances. I'm terrified of offending someone or making them unintentionally uncomfortable. It's a terrible position for a human being to be put in. And in many ways more degrading for women. Women's bodies tend to be exploited on film more than men's. And I think as soon as we got into that room, I think Lily understood that it was up to her to make me okay."

If anything, Carradine was even more disconcerted by the requirements of his character than Tomlin was of hers. "My own ego got very much in the way of playing that guy, because I thought he was an ass. It was hard for me to play someone who I perceived as being a creep. And I was later stunned to discover that many women were disappointed that I wasn't more like the guy I played in the movie."

Barbara Harris would commiserate with Carradine over his discontent. "We would weep every night with our parts," she says. "'I hate being a masher,' he'd go. 'I hate being psychotic,' I'd go. 'I hate being the womanizer,' he'd say. And I'd say, 'You have no idea what it feels like walking around in outfits like mine.'"

Cristina Raines speculates her former companion's distaste for his character may have emerged from a certain identification with him. "I think he may have been dealing with his own dislike of certain things within himself. I think that happened in a lot of people on the set who always had to deal with parts of ourselves we didn't want to have to deal with."

Altman, who seemed to covet his own reputation as a ladies' man in a post-Woodstock culture of free love, could not share Carradine's disdain for the womanizing Tom. "I don't think he's so awful. I know a lot of people like that. Especially in those days, there were general pervasive attitudes that took place because of the times. And the age of that person. At that time I was fifty, late forties, my attitudes were different than they are now and than they were when I was thirty-five.

"I read the press on *Cookie's Fortune,* and they start talking about all those awful characters that I've delivered through the years. *Short Cuts.* I don't think they're terrible people. They're my children, they're me, my father, my cousin, my best friend. They're all of those things. I'm really kind of shocked that it is embossed on the general critical press today that we have some obligation to be nice about things."

Altman responded to Carradine's gripes with his signature Cheshire-cat sanguinity. "He didn't do anything," says Carradine. "That's how smart he is. I was so hating being this guy, I went to him two or three weeks into the shooting and said, 'Bob, I really don't feel comfortable with what I'm doing.' And he just smiled and said, 'Oh, no, you're doing fine,' and walked away.

"The genius [of his response] was that, since I didn't like being him, what you see in the movie is a guy who doesn't like himself. And that's great. I wish I could say I had anything to do with that. That was Bob knowing to put a particular person in a particular role, knowing that the juxtapostion of that actor's own makeup with who that character was would have that effect."

Like Carradine, Beatty would have some issues surrounding the harshness with which his character was conceived. "I think Ned suffered a bit too, feeling, Everybody thinks my character is a shit," speculates Tewkesbury, who decided that a drunken Delbert should forcefully attempt to have his way with Sueleen after she has barely recovered from her traumatic striptease. In the original scheme, the double assault would drive Sueleen to suicide. As filmed, the promise of appearing at the Parthenon rally saves Sueleen. Delbert still comes on to her, but Beatty's soft-pedaling of the attempted seduction, abetted by Paul Lohmann's meek long shot, softens the danger. (In Tewkesbury's first draft of the screenplay, interestingly enough, the Tricycle Man is the white knight who sends Delbert running; Wade Coolidge does the honors in the finished film).

"It was easy to find villainy in that character," says Beatty. "I didn't see any reason to play it into that. It was enough that he did what he did. And I think his intimacy in his marriage was so very lacking. I'm very much drawn to the touchy-feely aspect of intimacy, the warm puppy aspect that you can share with someone. That's where I was coming from.

"I have one memory of the scene that is hard to get past. I didn't know Gwen particularly well. I found her fairly obscure. She was standing there a step or two above me, and I started doing this scene propositioning her. The camera was behind me, looking over my shoulder. As we were doing the first take, I realized something was going on. Take two, maybe take three, it suddenly dawned on me that she was doing something into the lens that I'd never seen anybody do before. The apropos phrase people use is not very nice. It's basically 'doing it to the camera.' And I knew I might as well not have been there."

CHAPTER THIRTEEN

THE ASSASSINATION

(Wherein the Gunman Gets Poison Ivy and His Victim Gets an Earful)

"The thing at the Parthenon—I never
got to be in too many movies with
chariots and horses and legions, but
by God this was close!"

—NED BEATTY

THE SCULPTURE ON THE EAST PEDIMENT of Nashville's Parthenon depicts the birth of Athena, goddess of wisdom, from the head of Zeus, ruler of the gods. According to this myth, Zeus came down with a headache, and his son Hephaestus devised a novel cure. Acting upon pre-Oedipal impulses, the blacksmith Hephaestus split Zeus's skull open with an ax. Out jumped Athena, fully grown, fully armored, ready to rock and roll.

If Altman made one of his ten-minute home movies out of this scenario, he could have easily cast himself as Zeus, who was also god of the sky. (Altman did have his Air Force moment, after all.) Joan Tewkesbury could be Athena, dispensing jewels of character interpretation to the Olympian acting ensemble. And there are at least two or three of Altman's former producers who would have been very willing to wield the ax.

In reality, it was *Nashville,* as offered up by the messenge/scribe Tewkesbury, that sprung in all its glory from Altman's skull. Altman's headaches, however, were recurring. Altman's first headache had been how to find the money to get *Thieves Like Us* off and running; seeking relief, he offered up *Nashville* as a kind of promissory note to the gods of United Artists. And getting through the final day of filming *Nashville* would prove to be Altman's final headache.

Lacking access to the recently shuttered Ryman Auditorium, the Parthenon was as monumental an alternative for Altman's grand climax as one could hope to find in Nashville. Erected in 1897 to celebrate the city's centenary, it was a full-scale, fully de-tailed replica of the Parthenon that Pericles erected in 447 B.C. as part of his ambitious Acropolis. The bronze doors of the Nashville version, as www.parthenon.org boasts, weigh 7.5 tons each, rise to a height of twenty-four feet and are the largest set of matching bronze doors in the world. Originally constructed from an exterior-grade plaster, the building's inevitable rapid deterioration demanded that it be completely rebuilt in 1920—this time from concrete. Now featuring a lavish, new-millenium facelift, the Parthenon one visits in Nashville is consequently a restoration of a reconstruction of a facsimile of the realization of a Grecian fantasy. It is a dream four times removed: the perfect Hollywood movie set.

Alas, August 31, 1974, was a less than perfect day for filming an epic movie climax. Clouds hovered stubbornly, dropping rain in temperamental bursts that appeared to be discouraging the sort of crowd that Altman so desperately needed for his Hal Phillip Walker rally. Even under the cheeriest of skies, the logis-tics of staging the final scene at the Parthenon would require the fortitude of a Zeus, at the very least. For the first time since the freeway crash, every actor, saving Karen Black, would have to be present, accounted for, miked for sound, and assigned an appro-priate bit of business. A rally platform had been erected in front of one end of the Parthenon. Poised on the stage, ready to sing their hearts out for the Walker cause, were Linnea and her Fisk

Jubilee Singers, Albuquerque, Tom and Mary (with an anxious Norman hovering preposterously at their side, looking at his watch as he wonders where Bill is), Sueleen Gay and Tommy Brown, escorted by his wife. Mingled among the crowd would be Kenny and PFC Kelly, Opal, Wade, L.A. Joan, who has skipped out on her aunt's funeral to attend the concert rally with her final conquest—surprise—the recalcitrant Bill. Milling about the rally stage would be Barnett, Triplette, and Delbert Reese, with Haven and Barbara Jean huddled behind the Parthenon columns, waiting to do their star turns. Three cameras would be dispensed in and around the rally, tracking the movements of everyone.

Altman had used the day prior to set up the shots and rehearse the actors, taking them through their songs and dialogue. For all the preparation, if only one gear were to slip out of place, the scene's complex machinery would break down. A snaking cortege of Walker limousines had to be choreographed, a dirigible flashing Walker campaign messages had to float overhead on cue, a miniconcert had to be tightly performed before a crowd of locals (who would be lured by an advertisement promising ten-cent hot dogs and free entertainment), and an assassination had to come off with precision timing and an absence of injury to the actors, who were not using stunt doubles.

"It was the first time I'd ever seen Bob nervous," says Allan Nicholls. "He does get nervous with big crowds. The airport scene was more controlled because he had engaged most of those people. Here it was so dependent on a real-life audience. And when it rained, everyone was nervous we might have to put it off to another day.

"You had to be in character all the time. I remember walking around forever and not knowing if a camera was on me or not. As challenging as it was for the actors, it was probably more challenging for Bob, because he didn't have video assist in those days. He couldn't rely on looking at a video tracking to see what each camera was getting."

"We had all these people in position," remembers Altman, "and I'd be running around like a chicken with my head off,

Altman sets up the camera for the Parthenon scene as
Tommy Thompson (center) looks on.

yelling, okay, no, you're going to do this, now walk, Ned run up
and grab Lily away. Those people were all really on their own."

The tension fed upon itself. Some of the actors, feeling out on
a limb, chose the moment to stage little dramas of their own.
Allen Garfield, true to form, had a bone to pick with Altman con-
cerning a moment in which Barnett discovers his wife will be performing in front of full-on political regalia he had been assured
would not be there. With both director and actor on tenterhooks,
the difference of opinion quickly escalated into a loud dispute.
According to published accounts, Altman decided to make hay
out of a potential negative development by incorporating their
fight into the film. The blustering banter between the tense Alt-

man and the pugnacious Garfield would be transformed on screen into a confrontation between John Triplette and Barnett, with Michael Murphy appropriating Altman's half of the dispute.

Joan Tewkesbury's remembrances vary slightly from the media version of that confrontation: "That [fight] was really about the script. The whole point is that this man whom you haven't liked so much throughout the movie comes in, he was told this was not going to be a political event, his wife is always in jeopardy, and now she's going to have to compete with the American flag. So he gets pissed off at Triplette for going against the very thing he said he would not do. Allen all of a sudden was vulnerable. For the first time. Every character had to have a moment of being an utter shit, but also you had to realize they were whole people, that they did stand up when they needed to for the right stuff."

Michael Murphy recalls, "Bob said, 'You and Allen go out there and fight.' Then he said to Allen, 'Fight with him, but let him win the fight.' I think I won the fight."

BARNETT: I laid down some ground rules . . . And you gave me some truth, man. You're full of it, just like your man, your man.
TRIPLETTE: I have abided by every ground rule that you laid down!
BARNETT: Except what? What is that up there? What is that up there? She ain't gonna appear with that sign up there!
TRIPLETTE: I have busted my ass for you for this last week, Barnett.
BARNETT: Well, I'm gonna bust your ass, too.
TRIPLETTE: And I'm through with it. Now you can take your wife and you can take a walk . . .
BARNETT: You'd put a knife in my wife's back like that, man?
TRIPLETTE: You're putting the knife in her back, buster!

Murphy stumbled on the word "buster." "It got a little real there. I yelled at him—my voice went up about four octaves, screamin' at him—and all the color drained out of his face. It's where you get this visceral response, and it sort of threw me. Allen's pretty combative, he's pretty crazy. I thought, Jesus Christ, this guy is gonna have a heart attack."

An actor-instigated brouhaha of a very different stripe remained off camera. Lily Tomlin grins ear to ear as she relates her version of the Barbara Harris rebellion. "All twenty-four of us are in the hair and makeup room getting finished up, the last time we're ever gonna be there. And Barbara—who I absolutely adored, and also the last person you would ever expect this of— comes in waving the SAG [Screen Actors Guild] rule book. And she informs us that every day that we did not work on the set, we were supposed to be paid five dollars for lunch. So that was like, forty-five out of sixty days, three hundred dollars a person times twenty-four! So we suddenly had a little protest. We all lined up demanding our money. I'm sure Bob was real put out. The accountant was standing there peeling out the cash before we went out to shoot at the Parthenon."

"Everybody was so happy," recalls Harris with a renewed sense of gratification. "It just wasn't fair. I remember Barbara Baxley bursting into tears because she had drunk her money away, saying, 'Now I can go home with money for my husband.'"

While Harris was storming the barricades with a copy of the SAG rules, Richard Baskin was chasing all over Nashville, making an eleventh-hour dash to round up robes for Tomlin and the Fisk choir. Thomas Hal Phillips was stationed in a limousine, ready to make his first and only appearance as Hal Phillip Walker. The closeup shot of Phillips in the limousine would be cut, maintaining the mystique of the third-party phantom throughout. Instead, we hear a brief voice-over of Phillips after Triplette leans into the car to warn him that it may be an hour's wait before his appearance: "That's all right, John. It'll give me time to work on my speech."

Two days after the film was wrapped, Phillips would get a call from Altman, asking him to come up with one more speech. News announcer Howard K. Smith had agreed to do a televised commentary about Hal Phillip Walker that would be layered into the opening of the rally sequence, and Altman needed it pronto. While we never see Phillips in the final scene, we hear him once more through the voice of Smith, who ended up delivering the fatuous oranges-at-Christmas speech in toto.

> *Little more than a year ago, a man named Hal Phillip Walker excited a group of college students with some questions. Have you stood on a high and windy hill and heard the acorns drop and roll? Have you walked in the valley beside the brook, walked alone and remembered? Does Christmas smell like oranges to you? Within a commencement speech such questions were fitting perhaps, but hardly the material with which to launch a presidential campaign. . . . Hal Phillip Walker is in a way a mystery man. Out of nowhere, with a handful of students and scarcely any pros, he's managed to win three presidential primaries and is given a fighting chance to take a fourth: Tennessee. A win in that state would take on added significance, for only once in the last fifty years has Tennessee failed to vote for the winning presidential candidate. No doubt many Americans, especially party-liners, wish that Hal Phillip Walker would go away, disappear like the natural frost and come again at some more convenient season. But wherever he may be going, it seems sure that Hal Phillip Walker is not going away. For there is genuine appeal, and it must be related to the raw courage of this man—running for president, willing to battle vast oil companies, eliminate subsidies to farmers, tax churches, abolish the electoral college, change the national anthem, and remove lawyers from government, especially from Congress. Well, at this point it would be wise to say most of us don't know the answer to Hal Phillip Walker. But to answer one of his questions: As a matter of fact, Christmas has always smelled like oranges to me.*

Throughout the two-month shoot, Nashville residents were often stymied by the thin line that separated the faked political noise spewing out of *Nashville* from the real. An actual primary election for state governor was raging concurrent with the filming, and many of the locals assumed that Hal Phillip Walker was a genuine candidate in that race. A few even volunteered their services at the Jack Spence war room where Thomas Hal Phillips and Ron Hecht plotted Walker's campaign. On the primary election day, many of the local crew members had to excuse themselves to go to the polling place next door to the motel. If you look closely, you can spot real campaign posters for Democratic candidate Ray Blanton and Republican candidate Lamar Alexander.

NED BEATTY puttered around the Parthenon steps, chanting, "I can't stand the pace, I can't stand the pace." Like the other actors, Beatty was doing his best to remain focused on his character in the longueurs before shooting. He had a whole biographical scenario worked out for Delbert. In addition to an uncle from Louisville whom he used as a reference point, Beatty decided that Delbert came from the town of Smyrna, a farm community and Nissan outpost southeast of Nashville, and that his father was a heavy-equipment salesman.

"So I'm standing there talking to this extra. He's short, nice guy, at least as rotund as me. And we're talking away, and I asked him what he did. He said, 'I sell heavy equipment.' I said, 'What?' Then I asked him, 'Where are you from?' And he said, 'Oh, I live over near Smyrna.' Then I came out with this line, 'I can't stand the pace.' And this guy from Smyrna said, '—of the whole human race.' I eventually wrote a song out of it."

David Hayward was writhing in discomfort from the fallout of a canoe trip he had taken a few days before. "I saw a cliff that I could dive into the river from. So I beached the canoe and climbed up this little side path. And when I got to the top of the cliff I realized there was no way I could get to the river from there. I would hit the ground. So I had to come back down. I couldn't walk back down the cliff, because it was sandstone, so I jumped onto a nearby tree and slid down. Well, the tree was covered in poison ivy and I had a pair of cutoff shorts on. So, for the final scene, I was covered in calamine lotion."

Hayward's poison-ivy agony was exacerbated by one of the teamsters, his perennial bête noire, who gave the actor a hard time when he asked him to make a run to the store for some calamine. Like any resourceful actor, he decided to use his frustrations for Kenny's pent-up rage.

"I had this argument with him. And I was so physically uncomfortable, at some point in the morning I thought, You lucky sonofabitch, you're in so much pain right now, you won't have to do anything, just let it go. And I escalated the argument with the guy, I escalated my confrontation with the teamsters. And so I had nobody likin' me. I was gettin' really kind of pushed out. Olivier supposedly said to Dustin Hoffman during *Marathon Man*, after Hoffman said he'd stayed up all night to get worked up for a scene, 'Try acting, dear boy.' Perhaps that would have been a better choice on my part."

Altman was getting kind of pushed out, too. The shoot was set for twelve-thirty. By late morning, the rain looked as if it was never going to let up. What was worse, there were virtually no extras to be seen. Had they miscalculated, expecting they could draw a mob with ten-cent hot dogs and an unknown singer named Ronee Blakley? With Tommy Thompson at his side, he stood on a scissor lift surveying the empty field from above, a disgruntled, headachy Zeus.

In just thirty minutes flat, the landscape in front of the Parthenon would change radically. Tommy Thompson remembers: "At twelve-thirty, they came from everywhere, like ants. We almost fell off the scissor lift. Hundred and hundreds of people. Families and groups just filled the place up."

"So the crowd is building," recalls Henry Gibson. "The tension was palpable. It was an ominous day, because of the weather. And the crowd is getting their hot dogs, we're in our dressing rooms. Bob is going crazy. I had to talk to the special-effects man to put in the squibs that would be the blood when Barbara Jean and I were shot. And that preyed on my mind. What did that feel like? We did a rehearsal without a rehearsal because we couldn't ruin this incredible costume. So the timing had to be right.

"Then we learned that there was an escaped prisoner in the crowd. And once that rumor started going around, people got terrified that perhaps the mock killing might trigger something. We didn't know who the guy was. He turned out to be some poor old harmless black man in old clothing who had chains on his bare feet. He was drawn to the crowd. They caught him and removed him, but it only added to the tension of what was going on.

"Then the clouds started to open up. They rushed and got tarps and covered the instruments on the stage because they were worried they were going to screw up the music, screw up the last day. They were fighting budget time. People were all going to get on planes the next day and disappear. How could we hold this? How could we recreate this? And the rain got a teeny bit heavier. Then Altman stood there and yelled, '*Stop!*'

"And the fucking rain stopped. Sheer chance. He screamed it, the clouds parted, things changed."

Altman knew they would have to work fast or risk losing the crowd. He turned to Thompson and said, "This is it. Let's go with it. All right, everybody, tell them action."

"We had like forty-five minutes to shoot the thing," recalls Richard Baskin. "Bob was on the crane in the back, I was behind one of the columns of the Parthenon with Ronee. And Bob said to me through a walkie-talkie, 'Send Ronee out.' I said, 'Ronee, you got to go out now.' And she said, 'Well, I didn't get to rehearse yet.' It's very Ronee."

Thompson continues. "From over the radio we hear, 'Ronee's not ready. She hasn't vocalized. And she doesn't know whether she wants to do this number or another number.' Bob said, 'Get this scissor head down.' The scissor lift comes down and he takes off backstage to where Ronee is. I'm back at the scissor lift, holding the radio. It was one of the few times I've seen him really let go at somebody. He goes in and told her in no uncertain terms, when he said action, she was to get up there and sing that goddamn song as it was written bing bang boom or your ass is out of here. And he's big. He just cut over her and left her cringing. Whipped around and went back onto the scissor lift and he said, 'All right, give 'em action!'"

Baskin adds, "I thought he was going to jump off the crane

Barbara Jean (Ronee Blakley) and Haven Hamilton
(Henry Gibson) belt "One, I Love You," moments prior
to Barbara Jean's assassination. (*Jim Coe*)

and onto the stage, that's how pissed he was. I took her and I threw her out there. If you look at the film, you can actually see she's pushed out."

Baskin is presumably referring to a rough cut of the film. His Blakley shove undoubtedly made for an ungainly entrance for country princess Barbara Jean. It never made it to the final version. What we see is an abrupt cut to Blakley and Gibson, a pair of glistening milk bottles in their virginal white, harmonizing on "One, I Love You."

The final scene would be filmed in segments, allowing time for Altman to block the movements of his actors as the action progressed. Gibson ceded the stage to Blakley for Barbara Jean's final, fateful solo, "My Idaho Home," cuing a heavily calamined David Hayward to snake his way through the crowd, clutching Kenny's violin case. As Blakley sang, Hayward would remove the key from his neck, open the case, and remove a gun. It was a moment he had been contemplating for weeks. "I had worn the key to the violin case around my neck the whole shoot and had not told anyone about it. I wanted to be sure that, wherever the camera was, that that was in there. So that you could see that he had it the whole time. That it wasn't a new thing. But that you'd never seen him open the case.

"So I had all that going on, plus trying to justify what I was doing. And my thought was that I was there to shoot Walker. Without question. And then there was Ronee, this perfect woman, singing 'Idaho Home.' And it just put me over. It was every rejection. It was the oppression of my mother. And he went off too soon. Some reviewer said, 'Is this an assassin's version of premature ejaculation?' I thought, He got it. Exactly what I was going for.

"I remember when it started I was gonna plow through the extras to get closer. And I knew they weren't professional extras, so that was going to be interesting. So I was bumpin' people hard comin' through. And a couple of guys threw elbows at me, which was great."

The crowd of concertgoers was only half-prepared for what was going to happen next. According to Joan Tewkesbury, "Somebody told them from the outset that there was going to be a gunshot. But more and more people started arriving, and a lot of the people were not expecting it. It was terrific. They were terrified. You can see it."

Ronee Blakley had done some research of her own, phoning her father in Idaho to find out how she should fall when she was shot. "I asked him if I got shot by such-and-such caliber, and at what distance, how far would I go. Bob was afraid I was going to get hurt. I wanted to do it anyway. I thought it was important. Bob later told me he regretted not using a closeup camera on me. And all the boys landed on me and my arm was twisted around. It kind of ripped my shoulder out. But I'm sure that accident helped the scene."

As Kenny's shots fell Barbara Jean and hit Haven in the arm, Haven drops, his toupee flying. He quickly recovers himself and takes charge of the panicked mob with a heroic selflessness we have not seen before. He rallies his son, Tom, Barnett, Tommy Brown, and a few others to carry Barbara Jean away, then grabs the microphone to tell the crowd, "This isn't Dallas, this is Nashville. You show 'em what we're made of. They can't do this to us in Nashville."

Joan Tewkesbury describes the moment: "In a funny way this sinister edge all falls apart when he grabs a microphone and says, 'This is Nashville.' You watch his whole world shatter. And when that toupee comes flying off, everything he has ever stood for disintegrates in that moment. There was some footage that was shot by a third camera, some of it is in the movie, some isn't. But from this particular angle the guy shooting it just focused on Henry and he's fucking brokenhearted. He caught all of the desperateness and the fragility of that man."

The scene was shot twice, the first time training the cameras on the audience to capture their reactions while they were still fresh and surprised, the second time to record the responses of characters on the stage. Says Altman, "I had this camera operator from Chicago who I later used as the second cameraman on *A Wedding*. I turned him loose and told him to get shots around the crowd. I didn't have an idea what he was shooting, and he came back with some wonderful stuff. I don't know what I would have done without it."

Tewkesbury adds, "People did the damnedest things. Like they held up their babies. It was just weird shit. People are weird."

In an unabashed burst of show-must-go-on valor, Haven looks around for someone to pacify the crowd while he nurses his wounds. Albuquerque gingerly offers herself up, and Haven relinquishes the mike to her. It is her time. The odds would seem to have it that someone who is as ubiquitous and ever-ready as

Kenny Fraiser (David Hayward, center, striped shirt and jacket) takes aim.
The crowd was lured with the promise of live music and free hot dogs. PFC Kelly
(Scott Glenn) is three heads to the left.

Albuquerque would eventually be in the right place at the right time. She inches nervously into the first few bars of "It Don't Worry Me." Within moments she lets go full throttle, confidently leading the crowd in a purging sing-along. It is a tour-de-force triumph for the trailer waif, who is seemingly poised to be the next big star. It is an old-fashioned movie gesture worthy of Busby Berkeley.

When Barbara Harris took her place onstage, Altman frowned. "I was in danger of losing the crowd," he recalls. "We had to shoot this fast. She had another song by Shel Silverstein that she wanted us to go through. And she came out with this big silver bracelet that Silverstein had given her—I can still see it—that that tramp could not have had. I was on the lift and I wanted to kill her."

"Bob and Barbara Harris did not get on at all at that point," claims Geraldine Chaplin, who illustrates what she calls "the cruel side of Bob."

"At that point it was a total hate relationship. He never told her that he'd cut and that they'd stopped filming. She kept on singing, and he'd say, 'Keep on, keep on, keep on.' Until she was in total exhaustion. She sang for, I don't know, three-quarters of an hour and there was no film in the camera. And he was laughing. What a revenge. Everyone was horrified."

Joan Tewkesbury disputes that account. "Bob didn't do that out of vindictiveness. He had her sing on so we could get reaction shots of the people. So we could get the day's work done. And everyone was enjoying the day's singing. And she loved it."

Harris's soulful rendition of "It Don't Worry Me" certainly conveys the frisson of an actress devouring the moment. As the Fisk choir joins in, followed by a captivated audience, a conflicting chill of inspiration and disquiet overcomes the viewer. Altman encapsulated the ambiguity of the moment in an interview with *Film Quarterly* magazine:

"That song is double edged. In one way you can say, Jesus, those people are sittin' there singing right after this terrible thing happened; that shows their insensitivity. And on the other hand, no matter how bad things get, there's always a positive hope for the future. And we went on to mostly

A star is born: Albuquerque (Barbara Harris) captures an agitated crowd, singing "It Don't Worry Me."

children; you can't expect them to understand the undercompounds [sic] of an assassination like that when the adults don't understand it. . . . You ever watch an automobile accident? People'll sit there and gawk, then get back in their car, turn the radio on and finish their Pepsi Cola. A friend of mine was shot in a parking lot in California a couple of days ago and killed. There's no one single reason in the world why that person was killed, because whatever the people who killed her wanted, she would have given them, had it been money, or . . . she was raped about three months back in Philadelphia . . . So what you really have to wonder about is the reason for it or the lack of reason for it. We sit and demand such great answers in our drama, but in our lives we'll accept anything."

The ambiguity is underscored by the camera, which pans away from the ominous sight of patrolling policemen and the inspirational echo of singing throngs, scanning upward to a sky full of clouds fit to burst with rain.

And burst they did. Says Jim Webb, "Bob must have paid his dues to the man upstairs, because it rained in the A.M., stopped for two hours, we shot like bandits, and the minute we finished the last shot, it closed in on us again. It was amazing. We got out of there five minutes ahead of the posse."

CHAPTER FOURTEEN:

NASHVILLE Opens

(Wherein Loretta Lynn Boycotts, Minnie Pearl Demurs, and Barbra Streisand Shoots Herself in the Foot)

"I have often hoped that the arts could be wonderfully useful in times of trouble. I have seen few examples of that. *Nashville,* however, fulfills my dream."
—KURT VONNEGUT, JR.

"I think Altman just had a nightmare, and he filmed *that* instead of our town."
—WEBB PIERCE

AS *NASHVILLE* PULLED UP STAKES AND got out of Dodge on September 1, 200,000 feet of celluloid went trailing after it. At 11,800 feet per two-hour picture, that meant that Robert Altman and his editors had sixteen hours-plus of movie on their hands.

Since Altman takes charge of editing the first day of filming and maintains command throughout dailies, a good deal of the dross had been weeded out by the time the final shoot was completed. Even before editor Sidney Levin and his assistant Dennis Hill hunched over their Moviola to cut and paste, much of their job had been preempted by their director's instincts. Perhaps only a neophyte editor as eager to learn and defer to the boss as Dennis Hill could put up with Altman's hands-on approach. According to Hill, "Altman had, and always has, an uncanny sense of what's right on a take, what works, and not just from seeing it in dailies, but seeing it on the set."

For veteran editors, Altman's unorthodox working style could be exasperating. "Editors hate him," said Keith Carradine. "He drives them crazy. He broke all the rules. That terrible rule where you're not supposed to overlap lines of dialogue. As we all do all the time every day, all day long."

"To be an editor with Bob is not really about cutting," says Hill. "It's more about storytelling and letting the film take its breath. Because he's not going to do it the normal way. If it was the normal way, he'd say, 'You know, that really works, but let's do it some way different.'"

Perhaps the toughest adjustment for editors to make came from the informal screenings Altman would hold for a select group of friends, canvassing for their feedback. Only bits of the film would be shown, but anyone with a mouth and a brave heart could toss their two cents into the ring. Says Hill, "Altman would call, 'Hey, I noticed you walking down the street! You got nothing to do, would you like to come in here and watch twenty minutes of my film?' What the fuck is this? You know the *maid* came in and gave an opinion to Bob."

In the case of independent-minded editors such as Sidney Levin, who saw editing as a sacrosanct meeting of minds between the editor and director, Altman's communal edits could drive a body to distraction. "The screenings were a way of learning the film," says Levin, "but to my way of thinking, the people who Bob screened it for were either afraid of him or sycophants, who answered him in the way he wanted to be answered."

Levin expressed his resentment by absenting himself with greater frequency from the screenings. Friction grew between himself and his director. Altman, disgruntled by what he called Levin's arrogance, fired him. It would be the only dismissal of any sort from the film, at least the only one that stuck. Actors, even those as confrontational as Allen Garfield or as nettlesome as Barbara Harris, were ultimately immune from such threats. "I've never thought that way and I've never done it," says Altman, who knew from his revolving-door days in television what it was like to be given the hook by producers with tunnel vision.

In one sense, Levin never stood a chance. He was following directly in the footsteps of Altman's trusted editor, Louis Lombardo, a partner in crime since the director's formative Kansas City years, when they would toss hundreds of feet of industrial footage out the window for want of trim bins. Like Altman, Lombardo was a spirited, no-bullshit cowboy of a filmmaker who came alive on the job. It was not unusual to find him hunched over his Moviola late into the night with a scotch by his side, growling, "I'll ride this sonofabitch till it drops."

Over the sixties and early seventies, Lombardo had been amassing some formidable editing credits apart from Altman (including Sam Peckinpah's *The Wild Bunch*). By the time *Nashville* was ready to roll, Lombardo was making plans to direct his first film. Keeping the "family" intact, Altman hired on Lombardo's son Tony to be one of two assistant editors, along with Tony's chum, Dennis Hill. When Levin was fired, Hill was promoted to editor.

By the time Hill's chance came, the young editor was ready. After spending 1968 in Vietnam, Hill quicky acquired a technical job for Paramount, then apprenticed with Louis Lombardo for the next six years. He possessed all the requisites for the Altman family: energy, quick humor, openness, malleability, and, perhaps most critically, an absence of ego. Like so many of the bright twenty-something pups whom Altman glommed onto for *Nashville,* he could be molded. "In no way was it me sitting there saying, 'I'm the editor,'" says Hill, "because we'd still be working on the fucker right now.

"Coming out of Vietnam and going to Bob Altman was like going from one kind of controlled madness to another kind of controlled madness. And genius."

As Altman and his editing team whittled the picture down, he decided it was time to try out Alan Rudolph's two-*Nashville* notion on the moneymen. Martin Starger recalls, "He came to me one day and said, 'The movie is so good, there is no way it can be one movie. I have a great idea. We'll do two movies. The first one will be called *Nashville Red* and the second one will be called *Nashville Blue*. The stories will interconnect, but there'll be one set of characters that you'll follow in *Red* and another in *Blue*. They'll each be two hours long, and we'll run *Red*, say, on Monday night, then *Blue* on Tuesday night.

"I was beginning to worry because I saw there was a lot of material, and I didn't want my first movie to be sixteen hours long. I wanted to make a small, intelligent movie, and now I've got four hours of *Red* and *Blue*. I said, 'Bob, it's not going to work. It's too complicated. People will line up on one day to see half a movie, and then they have to come back and see the other half. You've got to get it down.' There was no way for him to, unless I locked him up in a room somewhere. The compromise, and the right one, was to do one movie and do it as short as you can do one movie. It's not the easiest one, because you could lose some of the stories. But every time I see the picture I feel like you can take a dart and throw it at the screen and say, 'Cut here.'"

Red and *Blue* were dead in the water. With the picture down to three hours, Altman decided it was time to unveil a full cut before a select group of friends and A-list strangers. Among the chosen twenty who crowded into the Lion's Gate screening room on Westwood were Martin Scorsese, Harvey Keitel, Barbra Streisand, and her beau of the moment (and soon-to-be *A Star Is Born* producer), Jon Peters.

Alan Rudolph recalls, "The screening was at eight o'clock. He said to me, 'Go out in back and mix the movie so we can show it.' You couldn't just show it, you had to mix it down. It had twenty-four tracks, and he'd go through all this effort to break down the tracks—he called it unmixing—so that everyone had their own individual things going, talking all over the place. He'd separate enough so that they were all clearly competing with each other.

"So he'd come out every so often and say, 'How're we doin'?' It was supposed to be finished at six, but now it's seven o'clock. The projector broke halfway through. It wasn't like you could look in the yellow pages to have it fixed because it was a special system, all jerry-rigged by Jac Cashin. And I'd say, 'Jesus, I got two more reels to go!' And he'd say, 'Well, hurry up.'"

The screening started an hour late. By the time the lights went down, many of the guests, whom Altman had been plying with drinks, were well along the road to blotto. The partying continued after the movie. Barbra Streisand, busily taking mental notes for her upcoming remake of *A Star Is Born,* cozied up to Richard Baskin and grilled him with questions about sound techniques for live concert sequences. Altman was not pleased.

"She came up to me in my office afterward," says Altman, summoning the encounter with palpable relish, "and didn't say diddly-squat about the film. She came to talk about getting her boyfriend pointers about directing her picture. She said, 'Now listen, I want you to talk to Jon!' I just said, 'This is not about you, or Jon, or anybody. This is my picture, and we're here to sit here and wallow in it. Just take your unappreciative ass and walk out the door!' And I threw her out. And then Peters had the audacity to come back in and say, 'Can we meet tomorrow?'"

Accolades started trickling back to Altman's office after the Westwood screenings. *Casablanca* writer Howard Koch called it "the *Citizen Kane* of this generation of moviemakers.' Dominick Dunne hailed it "a masterpiece." Sidney Lumet quipped, "Now I can take things when they are good—but *brilliant?* Then I get sick. If I were you now, they'd have to lock me up somewhere." Dinah Shore confided, "I'm *from* and *of* Nashville, and it hit me hard. I don't mind telling you that it scared the hell out of me . . ."

Reading the tea leaves blowing over from Westwood Avenue, executives at ABC and Paramount chose to be cautiously enthusiastic. A rough-cut screening was held at the Fifth Avenue home of Charles Bludhorn, head of Paramount's umbrella organization, Gulf and Western. Attending along with Altman, Bludhorn, and his wife, was former ABC exec Barry Diller, whom Bludhorn had newly installed at the top of Paramount's hierarchy. Dennis

Hill recalls, "Charlie and Bob were out in front running the film, and I was back in the kitchen with the projectionist having a beer. Diller came back with a notepad and said, 'Excuse me, you're the editor?' 'I'm the editor.' He said, 'Um, mind if I ask you a few questions? Because everybody loves this picture and, between you and me, I can't fuckin' figure it out.'"

Paramount's bemusement was not lost on Altman, who noted that Diller seemed to be on the telephone through much of the screening. The director communicated his impatience with the top brass in subversive ways. When the time came to splice in the company logo and credit sequence, Altman took the negative of the Paramount logo, threw it on the ground, and mashed it into the floor with his feet. He then picked it up, handed it to an editor, and said, "Cut this one on."

"It was kind of Bob's way of saying, Hey, fuck you," says Hill. "It ended up making this sound like static on an old radio. Sure enough, a week later, some guy calls and says, 'Dennis, you won't believe this, but somehow the worst goddamned negative of the Paramount logo got cut on. We're gonna change it. Just calling to tell you we're on top of it!' 'No! No! Leave it on!' 'You're sure?' 'Per written note from Altman, had to do it that way to get it on.'. . . I'm sure they changed it. They don't get the joke anymore."

Altman contends that he was merely trying to give the opening the antique feel of "an old silent film that had been scratched." What ended up in the film was an eerie series of producer credits in fragile white letters that echo themselves in ghostlike fashion over a mournful black screen. Then, with a jolting punch, a splashy record album cover spins out of the dark. Over the sound track, we hear the strident clash of *Nashville* tunes and a barking salesman's pitch in the manner of oldies song-collection ads on TV that begins, "Now, after years in the making, Robert Altman brings you the long-awaited *Nashville,* with twenty-four, count 'em, twenty-four of your very favorite stars . . . !"

The kaleidoscopic credit sequence, created by an authentic radio adman, thrusts the viewer into the hard-sell world that is

Nashville while providing a clue into the cascading visual and aural narrative style to follow.

The album cover art, a bouncy collage of all twenty-four characters, was the serendipitous eleventh-hour contribution of Nashville graphic artist William Myers. Unbeknownst to Altman, Myers had been trailing the cast for the last two months, photographing them in costume and fashioning caricatures with a kind of whimsical realism. He was ostensibly on a freelance assignment for the *Los Angeles Times*, but hoped to parlay his work into the poster art for the finished film. At the end of the final day of shooting, Myers collared Bert Remsen and showed him his handiwork. Remsen, Myers, and Myers's family chased after Altman's mobile office as it was pulling out of Centennial Park. Altman scoured the artwork and said, "When in hell did you do this? You've captured my movie." Myers's contribution made the opening credits, as well as the sound-track album cover, but was deep-sixed by ABC and Paramount for the poster campaign in favor of a dancing microphone with an Uncle Sam hat.

Aside from Diller, another note of dissonance arrived in the form of a handwritten letter from Allen Garfield to Altman that pushed the art of backhanded compliments to unparalleled heights. ". . . I think you've made an unforgettably great movie with *Nashville*—I say that despite the fact I feel the entire guts and beauty of my performance and of my relationship with Barnett and Barbara Jean has been deleted virtually from the film— still and all, I feel *Nashville* will be a long-remembered American film, to your beautiful and creative credit, despite how I personally feel about the vital stuff of mine that (1) is left out, and (2) the weakest and least powerful takes of mine being left *in*—especially in the Parthenon argument between Michael Murphy and myself, not to mention the hospital scenes with Ronee and me."

WHEN *NEW YORKER* critic Pauline Kael stepped into New York's Magno screening room one January evening in 1975, it was not her first encounter with the world of

Nashville. She had visited the set one afternoon during a brief so-journ to the city to tape a one-hour discussion for European television about Altman's movies with the director. She was one of a small cadre of journalists (including the *Los Angeles Times* free-lancer and faux pas whiz Harry Haun, *Playboy*'s Bruce Williamson, and Chris Hodenfield, who would whip up a marvelously at-mospheric making-of story for *Rolling Stone*) who had been permitted entrée to Altman's *Nashville* carnival during its two-month shoot.

Kael remembers little of the visit. She was in and out only long enough to get a sense of the unique participatory axis between director, actor, and screenwriter. But a European television sta-tion could not hope to find a more ardent supporter of Altman from the critics' ranks than Kael, who enthusiastically embraced U.A.'s black sheep *The Long Goodbye* and *Thieves Like Us,* and whose rave for *McCabe & Mrs. Miller* prompted a resistant critical community to give it a second look.

Kael was not alone among the Altman well-wishers at Magno, a popular midtown screening venue memorable for its hideously futuristic decor of gold-painted acoustical disks. Among the handful along for the ride were novelist Kurt Vonnegut, Jr., with whom Altman had hoped to film an adaptation of *Breakfast of Champions,* and actor Paul Newman, who hunkered down for the three-hour experience with a six-pack of beer. (Altman had re-cently visited Newman's Connecticut home to discuss plans for their upcoming movie, *Buffalo Bill and the Indians.* While there, he suggested to the actor that they form a production company that would take its title from one half of each their surnames: The Altman Company.)

After previewing a cut of the film, which was eleven minutes longer than the final release version, Kael phoned Altman's of-fice the next day to find out if it was kosher to review the film. "After I saw it, it occurred to me that he might want it reviewed to keep the studio from hacking away at it," says Kael, who had a growing reputation for exploiting her media muscle in and out of the studios. She had been invited to the screening by Altman's

production office rather than through the standard media pro-
tocol of invitation via the distributor's publicity office. Paramount
had not set a release date for the film, and Kael was convinced
that they were not supportive of it. Altman's assistant returned to
the phone, saying simply, "That's what the screening was for."

The review of *Nashville* that ran in the March 3 issue of *The
New Yorker* was one of those advance cannon shots that film buffs
and buzzmakers live for. Brazenly acknowledging its own scoop
status with the title "Coming: *Nashville*," Kael's eight-column
lovefest had the reader salivating from the first sentence: "Is
there such a thing as an orgy for movie-lovers—but an orgy without excess?" She answered her own question with feverish glee
long before the last sentence, a quintessentially Kaelesque flourish of hyperbole: "*Nashville* is the funniest epic vision of America
ever to reach the screen."

Kael's little-kid thrill at seeing *Nashville* for the first time was
only outpaced by her big-kid perceptions. Picking up on the spiritual link between the realms of *Nashville*'s political and show-
business celebrity, Kael wrote, "Country stars are symbolic
ordinary figures. In this, they're more like political demagogues
than artists. The singer bears the burden of what he has become,
and he keeps saying, 'I may be driving an expensive car, but that
doesn't mean I'm happier than you are.' Neither he nor the
politician dares to come right out and confess to the audience
that what he's got is what he set out for from the beginning. Instead, he says, 'It's only an accident that puts me here and you
there—don't we talk the same language?'" . . . *Nashville* is about
the insanity of a fundamentalist culture in which practically the
whole population has been turned into groupies."

The movie would not be released for three and a half months,
but already the media frenzy had begun. Kael's column-long
valentine to Ronee Blakley (". . . she puts most movie hysteria to
shame; she achieves her effects so simply that I wasn't surprised
when someone near me started to cry during one of her songs")
prompted a full-page Richard Avedon photo and Leo Lerman
tribute to the budding star in *Vogue*. The "People Are Talking

Henry Gibson, Ronee Blakley, and Keith Carradine sing numbers from
Nashville in a publicity concert at the Central Park bandshell
in New York City. (© *Waring Abbott*)

About" spread was buttressed with an essay by Kurt Vonnegut
fulminating with importance ("Robert Altman has used the camera to produce a ribbon of acetate which, when illuminated from
behind, projects onto a flat surface in a darkened room anywhere a shadow play of what we have truly become and where
we might look for greater wisdom"). *Newsweek* was inspired to reserve a cover spread for the movie, disinterring Walt Whitman's
much-abused "I hear America singing" passage from *Leaves of
Grass* one more time to kick off a spacious tribute to the film. A visual pun was conjured for the cover, with Altman standing behind a camera lens "shooting" Ronee Blakley. Accompanying
Charles Michener's combination review and news story was another photo of Altman, glowering wildly from behind a camera
like a deranged scientist who had just emptied a lethal virus into
the nation's drinking supply.

The critics, predictably enough, seethed with jealousy at Kael's
scoop. Those who were not tantalized by the promise of a masterpiece around the corner were resentful of Kael's unladylike

breaching of the gentleman's agreement between the media and movie publicists, wherein critics agree to hold their piece till a film's release date. Perhaps no critic was crankier in his protestations than Vincent Canby of *The New York Times*. Instead of whining, Canby adopted a wry pundit's pose in a satirical essay that dubbed Kael's early-bird maneuver "The New Criticism" and speculated, with tongue planted firmly in cheek, about the can of worms she had opened with her review.

"If one can review a film on the basis of an approximately three-hour rough-cut, why not review it on the basis of a five-hour rough-cut? A ten-hour one? On the basis of the screenplay? The original material if first printed as a book? On the basis of press releases? Gossip items? I've been high all week inventorying the possibilities. . . .

"*The Last Tycoon* with a Harold Pinter screenplay, based on the uncompleted F. Scott Fitzgerald novel, hasn't yet gone into production, but so what? I can safely say that it was a mistake for Elia Kazan to direct the movie. Why should Kazan, a bad novelist who has written too many novels (three), be entrusted with the work of a great novelist who wrote too few (five), without expressing his resentment?

"*Three Days of the Condor,* directed by Sydney Pollack, was shooting on location down the block from The Times ten days ago, where it was easy to see that any movie that changes its title from *Six Days of the Condor* to *Three Days of the Condor* is going to be stingy entertainment . . . *The Other Side of the Wind,* an autobiographical comedy directed by Orson Welles with John Huston as the Welles surrogate, is a mess, but it's a beautiful mess . . . His movie is a ham that needs twenty-four hours of boiling . . ."

Canby's hissy fit had its intended cathartic effect, at least for himself. When *Nashville* opened, he shrugged off his initial irritation with Kael and joined the chorus of praise.

Kael defends her preemptive review, saying, "There is nothing unusual about what I did. It is standard practice for many magazines to see films in an early unfinished state. *Time* and *Newsweek* go early to see if it's something for the cover." In point of fact, magazines do send representatives early to scout out features, but the privilege is usually limited to editors who will not be writing on the film.

What perhaps rankled many critics more than the ego-deflating idea of being scooped was the insider's undercurrent of Kael's densely insightful review, spiked as it is with an awareness of the film's creative process that only someone who had been sidling up to the director would be privy to. There is a dig reserved for Altman's loathed former employer ("U.A.'s decision [to withdraw backing] will probably rack up as a classic boner, because this picture is going to take off into the stratosphere") that flirts with industry-speak and seems almost calculated to warm the cockles of the director's heart. With an uneasy balance of journalistic integrity and smug triumph, Kael makes it clear that she was attending the film "informally . . . before even the Paramount executives had seen the picture," reasserting her burgeoning role as a critic with a hot-line connection to major film artists and the power to impact on the fate of a film's release, if not its content. The breach of journalistic boundaries evidenced in "Coming: *Nashville*" would reach its ultimate evolution two decades later with the chummy, interview-laced *New Yorker* theater reviews of John Lahr, jumping not just the gun but the Atlantic Ocean to fast-track an event.

By the time *Nashville* opened in New York City on June 8 in an unprecedented double booking at two prestigious East Side houses, the adjacent Baronet and Cinema II, the critics tumbled over themselves in the effort to outdistance one another for placement in the quote ads. "After I saw it, I felt more alive," crowed Roger Ebert. "I felt I understood more about people. I felt somehow wiser." CBS's David Sheehan insisted that "it should be enshrined in the Smithsonian." Frank Rich, the only critic to appreciate the film's aesthetic relationship to *A Chorus Line*, wrote for *New Times*, "The tragedy implicit in *Nashville* . . . has to do with the price we must pay for our freedom, for, to maintain the democratic illusion, we must believe the myths we create about ourselves, the nonsense that is enshrined in the music." He concluded, "I don't see how anyone who cares about the state of the nation, not to mention the state of film, can possibly fail to see *Nashville*."

Married critics Andrew Sarris and Molly Haskell, their thumbs enthusiastically up for *Nashville,* indulged in a chatty, pre–*Siskel and Ebert* tête-à-tête for the *Village Voice,* in which Haskell anointed it "a Chaucerian musical pilgrimage whose Canterbury is Nashville," with Sarris picking up on Altman's "novelistic" canvas. Sarris noted a religious pattern in the "ritualized slaughter" of Altman denouements, while Haskell located a religious layer to the film's fatalism: "As Blakley sings a song of lost innocence . . . we feel not so much that America was a paradise, now corrupted, but that each of us must experience his own personal loss of innocence, as we 'outgrow' the roots, the family, the 'folk heritage' that spawned us."

Folk, shmolk, said Rex Reed, who led a small but incendiary counterattack against the film. Reed stepped gingerly into the fray in his June 13 column for the *Daily News* with an equivocating, "For now, let me say that it is better than most Altman films (faint praise) and not nearly as good as most of the hysterical hype would lead you to believe."

Three days later, he removed the white gloves on *The Merv Griffin Show* and came out punching. Disposing of the *New Yorker* review peremptorily ("Pauline Kael is always foaming at the mouth about something"), he then went on to brand *Nashville* as a "snob picture" and tackle Altman with the sort of bare-fisted populism cum Addison De Witt bitchery that made Reed a favored bad boy of Tinseltown journalism in the 1960s.

". . . [The critics] built this great big monolith out of a dunghill. I mean, this man is really not very talented, when you come down to it. He makes movies that are very pretentious, they're self-indulgent, they're too long, they need to be edited, they have no point of view. It's all just private moviemaking time; and the public really lets him know it, I guess, 'cause his pictures are always total flops.

"I thought it was just awful. I thought *Nashville* was the most

underrated [sic] picture of the last five or six years. It's totally underrated [sic] . . . In this picture a crazy fan just murders a girl
onstage in a hillbilly thing and it makes no sense whatsoever, and
the whole picture just falls apart, and that's why I don't see—I
think it's easy to say that the country is in danger, the country is
mindless, the people are brainless, that everything stinks, and
everything is negative. It's easy to say that and show a group of
people in Nashville trying to get into the Grand Ole Opry and
say that this is a metaphor of what's wrong with America. It's not
what's wrong with America. To find out what's wrong with America, you don't have to go to Nashville. I mean, it's like, Let's get
the grassroots people, let's make fun of the lower classes, let's
make fun of the country-and-western music."

When Reed's written assessment came out in a June 22 column of the *Daily News,* it was clear that beneath the superhero
mask of a champion and defender of the country-world lumpen
proletariat was a supercilious city slicker. "*Nashville* is a vicious,
malicious, occasionally witty look at grassroots America as it floats
like navel lint into the vulgar Vegas of country-and-western music, that plunking, planking citadel of bad taste called Nashville,
Tenn., where trash is the one locally produced commodity that
never wears out."

Easily trumping Altman in the condescension game, Reed was
nevertheless drawing a line in the sand between America's skep-
tics and her love-it-or-leave-its, her effete snobs and her just-
folks. Depending on which side of the line you identified yourself
to be, the perceived negativity of *Nashville* was either a virtue or
a menace.

Exemplifying this Nixon-influenced schism were *The New York
Times*'s Tom Wicker and *The Washington Post*'s George F. Will.
Wicker, struggling to process a myriad of *Nashville* images in an
odd blending of Altman interview and essay, said, "Far more is
there than merely the American mobility culture, with its autos
obsolete and crunchable the day they're sold, its fast-food par-
lors, plastic motel rooms, take-out orders, transient sex, and junk
music. This is a culture in which old people are thrown aside as

carelessly as Colonel Sanders' chicken bones, patriotism and sentimentality salve the hideous wounds of progress, and madmen peer mildly from benign eyes just before they strike. The greatest reward in this world is prime time, the greatest achievement is visibility, the most profound corruption is not that of the con men but that of the conned who march willingly into their delusions and falsities.

". . . The dark perceptions of *Nashville* are not, moreover, apocalyptic. The vitality of the culture is double edged; dreariness and vulgarity and falsity affirm life if only by opposing death. In the end there is even an aspiring singer who gets an unexpected chance to go on and makes it big, while the country-music crowd, seen earlier as callous and threatening, joins in a rousing sing-along—'You may say that I ain't free/But it don't worry me.'

"These final scenes, confirming both the vitality and the heedlessness of American life, form what Altman calls 'a total negative and a total positive.'"

Lacking Rex Reed's flair for purple prose, Will proffered a more buttoned-down rejection of the "everything stinks" interpretation of *Nashville*. Will quoted liberally from Wicker's column, turning Wicker's cultural critique on its head so that both the *Times* writer and the movie he was defending were befouled by the taint of cynicism.

"An unglued female star clips her toenails and approaches a nervous breakdown in a motel room while her porcine husband-manager munches fried chicken and calculates how to keep her earning powers healthy. A sausage-necked father of two deaf children won't bother to learn their sign language. Get the point? Callousness, exploitation, failure to communicate.

"Other characters shriek at each other in parking lots, wander in auto junkyards, have multicar freeway crackups. Where would today's artistic imagination be without the automobile as symbol of our heedless vitality, crunchable culture, etc.?

"Really, Altman's *Nashville* is to America what country music is to music—not a close approximation. But Altman was approxi-

mately correct when he said what he would achieve with
Nashville, his depiction of American hysteria, hypocrisy, vulgarity,
deceit, cruelty, cynicism, greed, materialism, etc.

"He said: 'I'm gonna make all the money in the world.'"

Will found an unlikely ally in liberal essayist Griel Marcus, who
located in the warm reception accorded *Nashville* and the recent
publication of E. L. Doctorow's *Ragtime* a glaring abscess in the
state of criticism. His *Village Voice* piece, "*Ragtime* and *Nashville:*
Failure of America Fad," was illustrated with a doctored shot of
Barbara Harris singing atop the base of the Statue of Liberty,
captioned, "The Statue of Gliberty: Empty characters propped
up by grand ideas."

Marcus argued: "As *Ragtime* and *Nashville* are proving, a stylish
work that 'proclaims the failure of our civilization'—of America,
to be precise—has become the artistic equivalent of the sucker
punch . . . All of this—the book, the movie, and their reception—
seems particularly suited to the spirit of passivity and fatigue that
animates, if one can use that word, the times."

Marcus goes on to characterize in both works a "coldness, manipulation of characters both alive and stillborn, with distortion
and occasional fraud, with cheap shots and setups. . . . This is accompanied, in both cases, by the artist's distance from his subject.
Neither Altman nor Doctorow are even, for a moment, impli-
cated in the stories they tell, the lessons they draw, or the actions
of their characters. . . . Both men maintain this distance—a
deadening distance that ultimately kills their works—because instead of discovering the fate of their characters as they emerge,
the artists have imposed that fate.

". . . It is probably spoiling the fun to point out that before a
work can be convincing as a 'metaphor' for something as big and
complex as 'America' . . . before it can work as anything so grand
as an epic of 'our fall from grace,' a book or movie must be convincing on the much more basic, if seemingly tiresome, level of
plot, character, motivation, detail, and so on. One feels out of
place noting that the most chilling scene in *Nashville*—the vicious, heartless reaction of the crowd to Barbara Jean's onstage

breakdown—cannot possibly be a metaphor for anything save the director's cynicism and disinterest in his ostensible subject, since no country audience anywhere in America would respond to the crisis of a singer as well-loved as Barbara Jean is supposed to be with anything less than sympathy, compassion, and fear."

UNCERTAINTY, IF not fear, accompanied the belated opening of *Nashville* in Nashville on August 8, two months after its initial premiere. The largely ecstatic critical response from points north was tempered by a barrage of suspicious articles by Bill Hance, the city editor of Nashville's conservative (and now-defunct) news organ, the *Banner,* provoking anxieties that Altman and company were whipping up a put-down of the city and its country-music industry.

In a defense that coincided with the movie's New York opening, Altman attempted to nip those concerns in the bud in an interview with the more sympathetic Eugene Wyatt of the *Banner's* rival paper, the *Tennessean.* "If I put down anything, it was me and my impression of what I consider America is today and doesn't need to be. I can't understand how they can take a picture like *W.W. and the Dixie Dancekings* and have a big premiere and have everybody think it's great. All they're talking about is some two-bit hustler. But then everybody says it's Burt Reynolds and so everything is just fine. They'll do a *Walking Tall,* which treats Southerners like a bunch of damned cretins. Then this picture comes along and somebody thinks somebody might be offended. I just can't believe it. People are smarter than that.

". . . I had an interview with Frances Taylor of the *Long Island Press,* and she said that in all my films she had detected an affection for people but she didn't think I showed it for the musicians in *Nashville.* That astounded me because I think that, of all my friends, the largest category would have to be musicians. And there were many, many such friends in *Nashville.* She also said the musicians in the picture didn't seem to care about their music. That astounded me even more. I can't imagine anybody more dedicated than Barbara Jean in the film. She loved her music, and I loved it too."

Despite Altman's affection for musicians, he opted to skip the Nashville premiere, choosing instead to hover in Canada where he was well into production on *Buffalo Bill and the Indians*. The writing on the Nashville wall was not promising. After an early press screening at the Belcourt Cinema that preceded the premiere by a week, local TV morning-show host Stanley Siegal sneered, "It stinks," but "Karen Black could be a country singer." More representative of the tentative local media response was radio celeb Roger Schutt, who liked the film but didn't understand it. "And if someone explained it to me, I probably wouldn't like it."

For a time it seemed that Paramount was going to ignore Music City as well, eschewing a splashy hometown premiere in favor of an unobtrusive opening. Nashville, not a town of small effects, would have none of that. Two months after the New York and Los Angeles openings, Nashville's publicity machine pulled out the stops on Friday, August 8, with a baton-twirling, cornet-blaring, and star-studded event that, for sheer spectacle, echoed if not eclipsed the airport sequence that kicks *Nashville* into high gear.

The choice of venue, the Martin 100 Oaks, was fitting. The boxy, state-of-the-art twin theater (RELAX IN OUR LUXURIOUS ROCKING CHAIRS, beckoned the flat marquis) exemplified the city's, if not the nation's, shift away from decaying downtown splendor to contemporary shopping-mall minimalism. The barren parking-lot sprawl of the Martin's exterior was tarted up with a red carpet and animated with a procession of entertainment that included a country group called the Silver Spurs, followed by the Rutherford Country Square Dancers and an antique car parade. The crowd of four thousand spectators began gathering at one o'clock for the seven o'clock premiere. Among those waiting in line that afternoon to buy one of the seats that had not been set aside for Nashville's dignitaries were newlyweds Billy Jo Spears and Mike Edilin, who had heard so much about the movie they decided to set aside a chunk of their honeymoon for the opening.

The Tennessee Twirlers were recruited once more to flank the arrival of Ronee Blakley with a flag-bearing honor guard, as they do in the film. As Blakley emerged from her limousine, she was presented with a bouquet of roses by Cindy Green, the "little beauty" with a tiara from Dalton, Georgia, who does the same honors for Barbara Jean in the movie. Blakley was accompanied by four other emissaries from the film, Henry Gibson, Dave Peel, Merle Kilgore (who plays Trout, the bartender at Deemen's Den), and Keith Carradine, the last of whom was made an honorary deputy by Metro Sheriff Fate Thomas and presented with a gold-plated key to the city jail. Posted by the entrance to chat with each star as they whisked through was Channel 2's Bill Jenkins, the anchorman who broadcasts Barbara Jean's arrival at the top of the film.

The greatest oohs and aahs, however, were reserved for the local stars: Brenda Lee, Minnie Pearl, Ronnie Milsap, Webb Pierce, Jeannie Pruett, Dottie West, Del Wood, songwriter Larry Gatlin, Mayor-elect Richard Fulton. Roy Acuff, who was holding the fort at the Grand Ole Opry, arrived in a bright plaid jacket to pay his respects and then return to his duties before the picture started. Noticeably missing was Loretta Lynn, who had no intentions of ever seeing the film. "I'd rather see *Bambi*," she huffed at a reporter.

Opening-night ticket holders had been asked to gather at one end of the parking lot, where a phalanx of limousines was stationed to transport them the short distance around the corner of the building to the carpeted entrance. Recalls Bill Myers: "It was getting late, and they didn't have enough limousines to keep the traffic moving. So the people were really backing up. Finally they got to the point where they were only going to take the stars. Minnie Pearl and her husband, Henry, had offered us a ride in their limo. They were told they could get in but their six or seven friends would have to walk. And Henry would not get in the limousine unless everyone could ride. So we all walked around the corner and walked in the door."

The lights finally dimmed at 7:40. Loud cheers greeted the word "Nashville" as it flashed across the credits, and two hours and forty minutes later, the closing credits were met by polite applause. There were a handful of walkouts. As the remaining crowd headed out the door for a reception at the Exit/In, Brenda Lee was heard grumbling that the film was little more than "a dialectic collage of unreality."

That was about as high-minded as the industry reaction would get. Songwriter-producer Billy Sherrill set the tone for the primal screams of protest that would spill from country-music circles when he grunted, "I'll tell you what I liked best about the film—when they shot that miserable excuse for a country-music singer."

The offal-slinging competition had officially begun, with an extra pile of manure reserved for the music. The most tempered of reactions came from Minnie Pearl. Diplomatically noncommittal at the premiere, she later owned up to her disdain. "I'm afraid a lot of people who love our music will be offended by the film. The music was terrible. I *know* they did a bad job with the Opry. There was a plastic look about the fans that turned me off. They took a group of regular Opry fans who were scared about bein' in a movie, and they had them do the scene over and over. It showed in their faces. Also, they left out the most important part of Nashville: the fellowship and love that exists between country singers and their fans."

Jeannie Pruett called it "a rip-off . . . a bunch of dressed-up, eccentric people parading around in a circus atmosphere . . . Those songs never would've made it out of Nashville. I'd be hard pressed to name the one I hated the most."

Lynn Anderson, who had been likened to Connie White, cried exploitation. "I was *personally* affronted by the music. They didn't make it clear that it was tongue-in-cheek. They didn't *say* it with a smile. Parts of the movie were painfully true—realistic to the point of hurting people. Other parts were blatantly overdone. There are some performers who are egomaniacs and some performers who are pious to the point of being ridiculous. But you find that in any business. . . . The producer, writer, and director obviously had a preconceived notion that Nashville and all it stood for was trash. They left a lot of hurt feelings because everybody opened doors for them, accepted them, helped them—and didn't expect a kick in the chops. . . . The part I hate the most is that the uninitiated will think all of us must be bad or that all of us create that horrible music they had. I hope to God *my* music doesn't sound like that!"

Webb Pierce invoked a vengeful God when he said, "I don't think [Altman]'ll ever be able to come back here again—he'll get hanged!"

Haven Hamilton role model Hank Snow avoided the film along with Loretta Lynn, insisting, "I'm not a moviegoer. . . . I have better things to do than to go see a movie where somebody's supposed to be playing me. . . . And I'm not pompous at all. I'm just a quiet, bashful country boy."

Any suspicions that the country-music world was pressing sour grapes over the film's music were waived away by *New Leader*'s music critic Bruce Cook, who attacked the film's "counterfeit" music. "It's simply not true that *anybody* can write songs," complained Cook, who went on to label Timothy Brown and "the hapless" Karen Black as "embarrassing" after damning the contributions of Keith Carradine and Ronee Blakley with faint praise. Cook quotes session musician Lloyd Green, who worked on a couple of the background tracks for the film. " 'I thought the music was atrocious . . . unlistenable. The background music and the studio work came off fine, but we had nothing to work with. If Altman thinks that this is our kind of music, he has another thing coming.' " Cook saved his sharpest arrows for the sound-track album: ". . . At least half of the tracks are so poorly sung that you might think you were listening to a put-on if you didn't know better."

The great *Nashville* music debate, if one could dignify it with that term, was intensified by a counterreview of the album in *The New York Times*. "However it may irk country buffs," wrote pop music critic Shaun Considine, "as a sound-track memento, *Nashville* is one of the finest scores ever transferred from film to vinyl." After claiming hit-single potential for Blakley's "Dues" and "My Idaho Home," Karen Black's "Memphis," and Barbara Harris's rendition of "It Don't Worry Me," Considine closed with a suggestion that assuredly had *Nashville*-phobes quivering in their cowboy boots. "Depending upon the success of this soundtrack LP, and the possibility that the five hours cut from *Nashville* will show up on TV this fall, a second and third album of music may be released."

There were a handful of warm responses from Nashville circles, notably from redheaded singer Dottie West, who regretted that the only redhead in the picture had to strip. Carl Smith was unalloyed in his enthusiasm. "Great! Fabulous! I haven't enjoyed a movie like that in ages. I've been here twenty-five years and I've seen it all. Maybe it hit too close to some people. There's no doubt the major characters were Loretta Lynn and Hank Snow. The film is exaggerated a little in terms of what they would do, but the main characters are based on them. It's *definitely* about Nashville."

Perhaps the pluckiest, if not last, word, came from Barbara Jean's ostensible role model. Loretta Lynn, maintaining her resolve to steer clear of the picture as long as she could, reviewed the hearsay with humor and humility. "I don't care if they have me kinda crazy, because I am. I don't care if they have me goin' in and out of hospitals, because I do. But when I hear they're cartin' my dead body off and havin' an unknown take my place— *that I don't like!*"

CHAPTER FIFTEEN

THE SEQUEL: LINNEA VS. GODZILLA

*(Wherein Louise Fletcher Wins the Ultimate
Consolation Prize and Lily Tomlin
Runs for Office)*

A LIMOUSINE SHUTTLED TWO ELDERLY LADIES through the narrow side streets of London's Soho district. Anna Freud, at age eighty the younger of the pair, took in the rows of sex shops and Chinese restaurants with a childlike wonder. It was all so glamorous. Her eighty-five-year-old companion, Dorothy Berlingham, got into the spirit as well. Like many of the actors in *Nashville*, they were the second generation of celebrity who had achieved fame in their own right (Anna Freud was the daughter of the father of psychoanalysis, Berlingham was the daughter of Louis Tiffany). Moreover, they were not shy about public displays of overt sexuality.

The two friends were en route to the London offices of Paramount Pictures, where a screening of *Nashville* had been specially arranged for them. They would never have thought to see the film if Joan Tewkesbury were not preparing a documentary on the life of Anna Freud, who, in fact, had not been to a movie in three years. (The last film she had seen was *Fiddler on the Roof.*) When she asked Tewkesbury if she could arrange for her to see *Nashville,* the screenwriter warned her, "This is not *Fiddler on the Roof,* babe."

Two days after the screening, Tewkesbury arrived in London and headed over to Freud's house to meet her for the first day's shoot on the documentary. Freud was out in front, walking her dog. Tewkesbury recalled, "Her eyes were just twinkling. She said, 'Yes, I want you to come in and sit down. I want to talk about what you've done.'

"When we got inside, she said, 'It would have pleased my father very much to see this movie.' And I said, 'Really?' She said, 'Yes,' and then, 'Does everybody look like that in Nashville? Do the women dress like that? Do they all sound that way? They sound so strange. Is all of Hollywood like that?' And I said, 'This is very particular to this part of the country.' She was absolutely fascinated. Then she went on to ask questions about each of the characters, the women in particular, and her linkage was absolutely correct. She was operating on the same internal psychological level that I had been operating. She got the stories within the stories and the back behavior that I had brought that no one else got. Particularly the characters of Linnea and Sueleen Gay. She got it all. And she said, 'What I liked was the fact that you showed all sides of the characters.'

Tewkesbury called Altman shortly afterward and crowed, "We've gotten the best review we could ever have had."

At least one more memorable review would also be generated from London, in the form of a telegram to another daughter of a twentieth-century superstar (and granddaughter to still another one). Geraldine Chaplin was in Calgary filming *Buffalo Bill and the Indians* with Altman when she received a telegram from her mother, Oona O'Neill Chaplin.

"NASHVILLE BEAUTIFUL FILM DADDY SO MOVED AT PARTS OF IT HE
WAS WILTED AT THE END SAID HE WOULDNT HAVE HAD THE
COURAGE HIMSELF STOP YOU WERE PERFECT VERY FUNNY CONGRATU-
LATIONS LOVE KISSES
MOMMY

"My father especially loved the film," Geraldine Chaplin af-
firms. "He was getting on then. He didn't go much to the movies.
I think that that's the only one he saw. He adored it because,
well—what do you call it?—all his bitterness about the United
States. And this, I mean, this *parody,* this absolute—everything he
ever thought about the States, this was it. Right there on film.
That's probably what he meant when he talked about the
courage to do it."

In concert with the aging Tramp, the reviews for *Nashville*
were unequivocally adoring in England, where the excesses of
American Southern culture are venerated from a safe distance.
Where would the once-unsung plays of Tennessee Williams be
without the West End theater discovering and validating them
every five years? According to England's reigning playwright,
Tom Stoppard (who attended the London premiere of *Nashville*
with director John Boorman), audiences were ready to be captivated by the film even before the curtain went up. When Altman
came out to say a few words of introduction, he eschewed any insider insights or nuggets of wisdom: "Listen, this is quite a lot of
film. If you need to go to the john in the middle, just go, don't
worry about it. I perfectly understand. I won't be watching."

Not surprisingly, British critics seemed to care even less than
the American critics about the authenticity of the film's music
and milieu. The British critics demonstrated that they could be
as wrongheaded in their enthusiasm as American critics were in
their condemnation. Russell Davies likened the film, incorrectly,
to a "superanimated Norman Rockwell painting." Dilys Powell of
the *Sunday Times* made the claim that "the American cinema has
a genius for telling other people about America" and that "the

British have never had the same gift with their own scene," a remarkable statement given the sharp contrast between the potent social realism of British cinema in the sixties and the Hollywood fantasies of America that Altman was rejecting. Powell also insisted that *Nashville* "looks much truer than *Woodstock,* much more real," explaining that "fiction has this advantage over fact, that it can eliminate the boring and emphasize the believable." Truth is apparently in the eye of the passport. The rococo slang and period mannerisms that fix *Woodstock* so immovably, and credibly, in its time are the very sort of thing that Altman minimized, if not eliminated, in his film. As a result, *Nashville* gains a certain timelessness that *Woodstock* lacks.

Pushing the limits of credibility—not to say bearability—was the character of roving BBC reporter Opal, who clearly had struck a nerve with bona fide British journalists. "Stupid, charmless, and lacking even basic tact," groaned Hugh Herbert in the *Guardian,* "she would never get to read the stock-market report, much less make documentaries about Kenya, Israel, and the other place names she carefully drops. I hope." Precisely.

The most insightful British-spun observations, ironically, would come from a writer who, like Opal, had recently enjoyed a stranger-in-a-strange-land experience of America. Writing for the *Evening Standard,* Alexander Walker aptly caught the film's undercurrent in a mostly laudatory review titled "Altman's Grand Motel" by saying, "The thing that strikes any traveller in America—where I was last week—is how politicised it and everyone is, how aware and shaken the people are by Vietnam, by Watergate, by the energy crisis, by the recession. How apprehensive they are. How plagued by the suspicion that for the first time in history they can see an end to the American future."

Even with its finger on the pulse of the American zeitgeist, however, Walker found that *Nashville* fell off in its political concerns.

"The whole political theme, anyhow, looks stuck in for a significance that it could never have in a place so traumatised by its self-importance that minutes after gunshots have left a bloodied body onstage the townsfolk are nodding and clapping again in time to their staple industry."

Despite the predominant chorus of praise from both sides of the Atlantic and one side of the Pacific, at the box office, *Nashville* did not "take off into the stratosphere" according to Pauline Kael's earliest predictions. On opening day, the forecast from *Variety* was as optimistic as Kael, claiming that "Robert Altman appears on the verge of shaking off his unpredictable and artistically self-indulgent reputation that's dogged his career—and frightened big production coin sources—since he made *MASH* seven years [sic] ago. . . . Few films in recent memory has [sic] evoked pre-opening critical paens [sic] of the same intensity."

And for a time, *Variety*'s crystal ball seemed to be in sound condition. The summer of '75 spelled S.R.O. houses for *Nashville* in its biggest-city venues. Once it wandered off to the middle-American territory it professed to be capturing, *Nashville* failed to catch fire. Kael (who owned up to her missed prediction in her last collection of reviews, *For Keeps*) blamed in part the platform release strategy, which prevented most of the country from jumping onto the bandwagon at the height of the film's big media blitz. "The lumpen proletariat never got near it," she said. "I never met a Southerner who didn't hate the movie, and it's hard to explain. The Italians, after all, hated *Shoeshine* [Vittorio De Sica's dour neorealist classic]. There is a kind of reaction, as if the movie is meant to be critical of them."

As *Nashville* readied to move into three hundred theaters cross-country after a seven-month first run, *Variety* reported that the film's domestic box office totaled $7 million from 1,532 venues by mid-December. This was considerably short of Paramount's projected $30 million. By way of comparison, *Variety* reported that Paramount's blaxpoitation epic *Mandingo* had pulled in $8,684,000 in one week at 4,625 theaters, while *Once Is Not Enough,* based on the Jacqueline Susann novel, took in $7,865,000 on 4,978 screens, "and the end is not in sight for either." If any picture would hit the stratosphere in 1975, it would be the summer megahit *Jaws,* which mustered a jaw-dropping

$406 million in worldwide ticket sales. By 1994, the total gross receipts for *Nashville* would total $11,241,296: respectable, if very much within the atmosphere.

BUT AWARDS began to fall from the sky. Both the New York Film Critics Circle and the National Society of Film Critics honored *Nashville* with awards for Best Picture, Best Director, and Best Supporting Actress (Lily Tomlin). The National Society of Film Critics went one further by naming Henry Gibson as Best Supporting Actor, offering a particularly moving career cap for two alums of *Rowan and Martin's Laugh-In*. There were also some arresting footnotes to be found in the voting tallies of the New York Film Critics. *Nashville*'s Best Picture and Best Director awards were decided on the second vote, with *Nashville* taking forty-five weighted votes to thirty for *Barry Lyndon,* and Altman beating fellow maverick Stanley Kubrick for directorial honors, forty-four to twenty-eight. In perhaps the most provocative run off, Lily Tomlin also won by a forty-nine-to-twenty-eight vote over *Nashville*'s would-be Linnea, *One Flew Over the Cuckoo's Nest*'s Louise Fletcher. (Tomlin, who had not been aware of Fletcher's participation in *Nashville*'s seedling period until late in the filming, wrote to the actress soon after to commiserate and sympathize.)

If you walked into the New York Film Critics Circle awards ceremony held at Sardi's on January 25, 1976, you might think you had walked into a luncheon for the PEN club. In line to present the awards for Best Director and Best Picture were E. L. Doctorow and Kurt Vonnegut, Jr., each of whom was about to conspire with Altman on film adaptations of their books, *Ragtime* and *Breakfast of Champions,* respectively. Also loitering around the red banquettes was dramatist Marc Connelly, who had been tapped to present the screenwriting award to Suzanne Schiffman for *The Story of Adele H.*

Doctorow presented the director prize, stating with book-jacket hyperbole, "It is the first time I have ever seen a film that is at the same time an act of prophecy." Andrew Sarris, reporting for the *Village Voice*, yawned over the novelist's performance. "Doctorow never let us forget that he was an accredited emissary from the royal realm of literature, and that our two rival kingdoms had had an uneasy relationship over the years." Ever the critic, Sarris gave four stars to Vonnegut, who "[tore] into both *Nashville* and *Ragtime* as anti–White Protestant manifestations. He then paid mock tribute to the power of the critics in determining that *Nashville* and *Ragtime* were each the best in their medium. He then repeated the old suggestion that critiques should be written first, and then works of art created to conform with the critiques. It was a rollicking performance (even from a prepared text) that brought the house down. We had come to laugh at Lily Tomlin and stayed to guffaw at Kurt Vonnegut."

Stepping up to accept the Best Picture prize, Altman instantly upstaged Vonnegut with a shoulder-shrugging, "I didn't understand what he said, but I'm sure it'll sell to the kids."

When the Academy of Motion Picture Arts and Sciences announced its own nominations a month later, it was one more reminder that Oscar was not about to be browbeaten by anyone so inconsequential to the box office as a film critic. Leading the pack with nine nominations was an also-ran among the critics' prizes, Best Picture nominee *One Flew Over the Cuckoo's Nest*, released by the studio (U.A.) that had kissed off *Nashville*. Included among the nine nominations was one for Louise Fletcher, whom Oscar had promoted from a supporting player to the Best Actress category. Second in line with a total of seven nominations, including one for Best Picture, was the epic *Barry Lyndon*.

Nashville took third place with a modest five nominations: Best Picture, Best Director, two Best Supporting Actress nominations (Tomlin and Ronee Blakley), and a Best Song nod for Keith Carradine's "I'm Easy." So much had been made of the actors' contributions to the film that there was no hope of a screenplay nomination for Joan Tewkesbury. Likewise, Altman's thumbprints were on so much of the film that the technical divisions could not justify acknowledging any individuals for the film's innovations in sound and editing. Given the extent to which Jim Webb and Dennis McLaughlin's meticulous sound mixing and the serpentine cutting of Sidney Levin, Dennis Hill, and Altman contributed to the flow and personality of the film, one can only infer that either Oscar did not get it or found the final result too messy for award consideration.

The one snub that pushed Altman to the mat, however, was the musical-score category. The complicated nature of *Nashville*'s song score, with its multiple composers (many of whom were rank amateurs) and original songs, two of which had been previously recorded on Blakley's debut album, blew a fuse in the Academy's tightly plugged system of eligibility. Certainly the loud chorus of boos blowing in from the country-western community couldn't have helped matters either. When Altman learned that *Nashville*'s score had been disqualified for consideration, he fired off a Mailgram to Academy president Walter Mirisch. ". . . The reason given by the executive committee of the music branch was that at least five songs were not written by the same team of composer and lyricist. We believe that the score meets this requirement because its composer, Richard Baskin, wrote the music and lyrics for more than five songs, although he collaborated with other artists on the lyrics. Moreover he arranged and adapted all the music in the film for dramatic purposes.

"More importantly, this is the latest decision by an executive committee which has consistently interpreted and reinterpreted its rules with the obvious intention of excluding the score of *Nashville* and its composer, Richard Baskin, from Academy consideration. As the producer and director of the film, I know that the song score was centrally contributive to whatever the movie is and to its artistic worth. I feel I must publicly state my firm personal and professional objection to the exclusion from Academy consideration of the score and its composer, Richard Baskin. Whatever recognition may or may not ultimately be accorded the film, me, and the other artists, will not rectify the destructive effect of the discriminatory and arbitrary action of the executive committee of the music branch regarding Baskin's score."

In this instance, Altman couldn't beat city hall. "I was very pissed," says Baskin. "Because I probably would have won an Academy Award." The Academy tried to make amends by appointing Baskin to its executive branch ("largely because I was so screwed"), where the composer remained for a few years before quitting. "It was just silly."

On the night of the awards, it became clear that *Nashville* did not stand a chance against the *Cuckoo's Nest* juggernaut. The popular Milos Forman film took the top prize, along with awards for its director and its lead actor and actress. When Louise Fletcher ascended to the podium to accept her Oscar, she thanked her parents in sign language. Among those who applauded her from the audience were Altman and Tomlin. In a historically typical move, Tomlin and Blakley would appear to have split the *Nashville* vote, sending the Best Supporting Actress prize to Lee Grant for *Shampoo*.

The only gold statue to go to *Nashville* would be won by Keith Carradine for the song he had written years ago to romance the mother of his daughter. But first, Carradine had to perform "I'm Easy" before the star-studded crowd, accompanying himself solo on the guitar as he had in the film. He was so terrified that he vamped an extra quarter bar at the end of a stanza to give himself time to recall the next lyric. Carradine's win was watched from the audience by his two dates, a beaming Cristina Raines ("She was wearing a lacy cotton thing that Altman said looked like an unmade bed," recalls the winner) and his father, John Carradine.

The *Cuckoo's Nest* rout would not be the first, or last, rebuff that Altman would get from the Academy. (He would be nominated again, and lose again, in 1992 for *The Player.*) When he and *MASH* lost to *Patton* and Franklin Schaffner in 1970, Altman quipped to his wife, "They gave it to the wrong war." In the case of *Nashville*'s defeat to the rabble-rousing but distinctly lesser *Cuckoo's Nest,* one can only conclude that they gave it to the wrong inmates.

BETWEEN THE Oscar defeat and a sub-blockbuster showing at the box office, ABC's initial flurry of interest in assembling a ten-hour miniseries of *Nashville* from edited material rapidly waned. The proposed bicentennial project never happened. To this day, no one, including the director, knows exactly where the edited footage is sleeping.

While it was not the director's habit to leech off his former successes for new projects, even Altman could not help but feel wistful about the glory days of *Nashville* during some of the less-than-glorious years that followed. During the mid-eighties, when Altman was generating a series of screen adaptations of stage plays whose budgets were as low as their attendance, the oft-kicked-around notion of a sequel to *Nashville* seemed more and more attractive. In May of 1986, a contract for the sequel was drawn up by Altman's venerable agent, Sam Cohn, signing Robert Harders (Altman's associate director on *Secret Honor*) as chief writer and listing Joan Tewkesbury and Jane Wagner.

It was a surprise choice, on the face of it. Harders had no history with *Nashville*. A transplanted New York actor (and by his own accounts a bad one, relegated to "playing younger brothers and boyfriends on TV shows"), Harders parlayed his MFA from Sarah Lawrence into directing gigs in the L.A. Actors Theater. Altman was enamored of one of them, a one-man play by Donald Freed and Arnold M. Stone called *The Last Tape and Testament of Richard M. Nixon*, with a tour-de-force performance by Philip Baker Hall. Under the new title *Secret Honor*, Freed and Stone's play went on a small tour around the country. When it arrived at the University of Michigan in Ann Arbor, Altman put it in front of the cameras, with Harders as his associate director.

Over the coming three years, Harders embarked upon writing a series of projects for Altman that would ultimately fizzle, including an adaptation of Hemingway's *Across the River and Into the Woods*. Over dinner at his Malibu home, Altman stunned Harders by asking him to write *Nashville 12* (a working title referring to the number of years that had elapsed since the events of the original), which proved to be the most formidable nonstarter of them all. "The prospect of living up to *Nashville* was terrifying," recalls Harders, who was afraid to ask Altman why he wasn't using Joan Tewkesbury again lest the director change his mind. In actuality, Altman and Tewkesbury went their separate ways, maintaining a respectful friendship over the years after their planned participation in a film version of E. L. Doctorow's *Ragtime* broke down.

Altman took his new writer with him to Paris, where Harders remained for the next three months working on *Nashville 12*. Unlike Tewkesbury, Harders had not even had an experience of Nashville. Not surprisingly, the series of drafts that evolved were less dependent on the city itself than on the characters' preexisting relationships with one another, however tangential they may have been. Working from two- or three-sentence notes that Altman sketched out to give his sense of what might have become of each of the characters twelve years later, Harders worked up an occasionally screwball series of scenarios that were simultaneously more cruel and more compassionate than the ones Tewkesbury had originally cooked up.

Harders's theme, cribbed from Christopher Lasch's *Culture of Narcissism,* would be the tendency of Americans to repeat their mistakes because of an inability to learn from their history. In Harders's scheme, the rich get richer and the poor keep drinking. Haven Hamilton had become the host of a popular Christian TV show modeled loosely on *The 700 Club*. Wearing his new televangelist's hat, Hamilton exploits the grief and vulnerability of his viewers, raking in thousands of dollars by doing special TV spots on their recently deceased loved ones in exchange for donations. Still traumatized by the shooting at the Parthenon, Hamilton has also become security-conscious to the point of obsession, and has turned his home into a fortress buttressed by guards and elaborate alarm systems. Despite his costly and elaborate efforts, he is shot at from out of nowhere.

Lady Pearl has left Hamilton, throwing her energy and support behind Tennessee gubernatorial candidate Linnea Reese (!). Linnea's left-leaning politics lead to a nasty incident in which she is smeared with paint by a conservative troublemaker while on the campaign trail; rather than wash it off, she decides to wear the paint like a badge of honor. Linnea's campaign is supervised by none other than former Hal Phillip Walker manager John Triplette. She has divorced Delbert, who has remarried Sueleen Gay (a truly perverse turn of events given his exploitive role before, during, and after the fund-raising smoker).

Albuquerque, having enjoyed a brief splash of fame and success in the wake of her impromptu Parthenon debut, has returned to obscurity and is back at square one, trying to make it in the business. Her husband, Star, drowns his bitterness over the failure of their marriage and her aspirations in alcohol. At a bar, he encounters Wade, who has apparently not honored his own threats to flee to Detroit. As they chat, Star becomes progressively drunk and Wade offers to drive him home. In his stupor, Star misdirects Wade through a wealthy neighborhood and then suddenly grabs the wheel. The car hits a young boy, who turns out to be the son of country star Tommy Brown, whom Wade had verbally assaulted at the Picking Parlor twelve years earlier. The boy is badly hurt, and eventually dies (Altman fans will note this provocative precursor to a similar incident in his adaptation of Raymond Carver stories, *Short Cuts*.) In the follow-up investigations, it is initially assumed that Wade is the culprit because of his skin color. Harders deliberately complicated the issue of racism by making the arresting cop and the assistant D.A. black. Wade is eventually cleared, but not before his name is muddied in the community. That is the happy version. In the first draft, Harders had Wade being beaten to death in a modern-day lynching.

In a more comic vein, Tommy Brown is again compelled to confront racism when Haven presents Tommy with a song he wants him to sing on his show called "Black Sheep," about a guy who is the outcast of his family. (The song was cowritten by Altman and his songwriter friend Danny Darst, who appears as the mumbling cop in *Cookie's Fortune*.) Tommy initially refuses to sing the song, based merely on the title, but is eventually strongarmed into doing so by the persuasive Haven.

Connie White has become a lush and a floozy, picking up a total stranger for a one-night stand at her home (an over-the-top
nightmare of Barbie-pink accoutrements). The stranger turns
out to be John Triplette. White gets stupefyingly drunk to the
point of passing out. When she comes to and asks Triplette to
make love to her, he lies and says they already did, then slips off
into the night. Connie White is now managed by Barnett, the
widower of her former rival, Barbara Jean.

Professional heel Tom Frank has married L.A. Joan, now
Martha again, having fully embraced the life of a Tennessee
mother and housewife. For a moment we are led to believe that
he hasn't changed his stripes—he is overheard arranging another motel assignation—until it is discovered that the clandestine partner is none other than Martha. Celebrity and marriage
have had redemptive power on the least likely candidate.
Martha's uncle, the widower Mr. Green, was written out with a
funeral scene of his own when Keenan Wynn passed away in the
midst of one of the drafts.

The recording world has been less than kind to Tom's former
singing partners. Mary has left the business altogether to become
a schoolteacher. Bill's singing career has also run aground, and
he now works for his former chauffeur, Norman, who has taken
over the whole limousine service. (In one of Harders's unkinder
cuts, Bill is sent to the airport to pick up a client, who turns out
to be Tom.) Norman supplements his wealth by installing security systems, and has made a small fortune off the fears of Haven
Hamilton.

Harders has reserved his most bizarre pairing for Opal and
the Tricycle Man, who revile each another as rivals working at a
local TV station. It is later revealed that they are living together.

The woebegone assassin Kenny is now rational and coherent,
appearing briefly in a television interview to accept responsibility
for what he did and acknowledge that people hate him so much
that he will never get out of jail.

The only characters unaccounted for in Harders's several versions are Buddy and PFC Kelly. Dave Peel, who was moving away

from show business and deeper into religion, was not available to reprise his role as Haven's browbeaten son. Harders avoided dealing with the taciturn PFC Kelly altogether. "I blanked him out because I never knew what was going on with him," he admits frankly.

The sequel was structured to begin with the last eight minutes of the original film at the Parthenon, then launch into a memorial service for Barbara Jean at the Nashville Cemetery twelve years later. (Amusingly, if improbably, the Hal Phillip Walker van was going to snake its way into the procession, its unrelenting p.a. system finally conking out midway.) Throughout the different drafts, Harders struggled with ways to bring Ronee Blakley back into the sequel. His solution, which arrived at the eleventh hour, was his most harebrained and inspired conceit: She would reappear as a Barbara Jean impersonator. In keeping with Harders's theme of history doomed to repeat itself, Barnett would fall in love with her.

But how to end the sequel? How do you follow a climactic act as stunning as the one Altman devised for *Nashville?* "I know how I would do it now," says Harders. "I'd have Barbara Jean assassinated again."

The climax would become a bone of contention. Jerry Weintraub, it seemed, was insisting upon an upbeat ending. Perhaps even more alienating to the director was what Harders called the "schoolmarmish" efforts of one of Weintraub's executives to get Altman to adhere to a script. "If it wasn't on the page, it wouldn't go on the stage," says Harders, evoking the same rigid cost-control mind-set that Altman had encountered from the studios throughout his career. "Weintraub was going to teach Altman how to make a film. It was going to be his way or none at all."

Beyond the executive rumblings, Lily Tomlin purportedly had reservations about the script, which appeared to be moving further away from an ensemble effort and more toward a star vehicle with her character at the center. Harders speculated that the impetus for the focus on Tomlin's character was generated by

Weintraub's office, hoping to capitalize on Tomlin's star appeal in the eighties.

According to Martin Starger, the new emphasis on Tomlin's character drew protests from her agents, who weren't ready to settle for the same favored-nations agreement. But for these hitches, few of Altman's ill-fated projects have come this close to fruition. The actors were lined up and ready to go, locations had been chosen, a script, however unfinished, was percolating.

On May 1, 1987, the New York *Daily News* ran a story announcing, "The *Nashville* sequel won't shoot this summer as planned," then quoted Jerry Weintraub as saying it was pushed back to the following spring in fear of a directors' strike and because of "scheduling problems" with Lily Tomlin, who was set to film *Big Business* with Bette Midler.

That was the last that was heard of *Nashville 12*, whose genesis was becoming so drawn out that it was being called *Nashville 13*. One person who regrets its demise is Martin Starger. "Again, I'm not sure it would have been a blockbuster. But I remember when I tried to get the rights to ABC. I said you should retain something of it. Run the original *Nashville* on Sunday night and this on Monday night. You have a miniseries. It's the story of America in political terms."

Tomlin would also come to express regrets about her reluctance to do the sequel. "I think I was stupid, because I think it was worth doing. I wish we had done it now. You know, to have all those actors back together was extraordinary, and I was too ignorant to forget my own subjective thoughts. I have much more appreciation for that kind of continuity and history than I did then."

Years later, when asked about the fate of the *Nashville* sequel at a Television Critics Association press tour, Altman said, "The commercial dragon roared. They wanted to be sure there would be a happy ending. And I just don't know how to make a happy ending."

Epilogue

In 1987 I had the privilege of interviewing the original cast of *A Chorus Line* as the show was winding down from its record-breaking Broadway run at New York's Shubert Theatre. Perhaps only more enthralling than watching that magnificent team from a mezzanine perch in 1975 was the opportunity to hear the cast members contemplate their subsequent careers from across a coffee-shop table twelve years later. It was a bittersweet journey, for both the actors and their one-man audience; more than once did I bite down on my lip, pondering the temporary fit of sanity that pushed me out of the path of a runaway life in show business and into a career in writing. Why audition when you can get your work rejected, cleanly and impersonally, by mail?

Remarkably, all of the cast members had survived, no mean feat when one considers that the arc of the show's run had coincided with the insurgency of a virus that would wipe out some of the theater's brightest lights (including the show's director and choreographer, Michael Bennett). They talked of marriages, divorces, children; one baby who had been conceived in tandem with the show's opening was now a precocious twelve-year-old. A few had managed to eke out respectable careers in the theater as actors and choreographers; the majority had been compelled to reinvent themselves after learning the hard way of Hollywood's antipathy toward Broadway gypsies. There was some bitterness, but most had made peace with their fates; many radiated joy at the thought of their families, their new careers, and the unseen gold lurking just over the next hill. To a person, the landmark musical they shared in common had been the ne plus ultra of their performing careers.

Correspondingly, the cast of *Nashville* represents the full spectrum of scenarios that can play out for people compelled to inhabit other people's lives for their daily bread. Many lost their footing on the road to celebrity. Some who signed on to the Altman film as unknowns became players for a time, then, after the

The *Nashville* players assemble for a group photo op. (© *J. William Myers*)

fashion of the Albuquerque character as projected in the unrealized sequel to *Nashville*, they returned to obscurity. One or two crested on the A list of Hollywood's fickle casting agents, then settled into the relative comfort, if unpredictability, of the B lists. There were marriages, divorces, lots of children, and some surprising new career choices. Five have died, two of them with a cruel and unsettling prematurity.

There are those who are haunted by the demise of their link with the director who offered them one of their most exhilarating, if not most enduring, moments before a camera. To be welcomed into the Altman family is a heady experience; to be cast aside by the head of the household scars some for life.

David Hayward, an affable soul with a vigorous survivor's spirit, lives near Malibu. After a modest flurry of TV and film roles, he has kept his acting muscles in shape through local stage appearances. He is wistful in speaking of Altman, for whom he would not act again. "I don't know why Bob and I didn't click better. I remember him coming to me one night before we were going to work. Which he did; he'd go to everybody the night before if they hadn't worked for a few days, to get them back in sync. And he said, 'I just want to be sure our relationship tomorrow is'—I forget what he said, but then he said, 'but not arch.' Which I really didn't understand at the time. And then I realized that he was saying we shouldn't be at loggerheads. And I had no idea why we should be. I certainly would have liked it to be better." When we spoke, the actor who played Barbara Jean's assassin was readying for a revival of Mark Medoff's *When You Comin' Back, Red Ryder?* as a psychopath who terrorizes patrons at a diner.

Twenty-five years after Altman cold-shouldered Timothy Brown at a *Nashville* screening, the former actor and football pro is pained by the memory. "For some odd reason which I've never understood, Robert fell out with me," he reflects. "I always felt like a son. He had a kid who was half-black who reminded me of me, and he and his wife were always very nice. I don't want to sound bitter. Another thing that might have hurt me: I beat him in chess." Brown's acting career dissolved by the end of the eighties, when he took a job with the Los Angeles probation department taking ballplayers around to the probation centers. He now works for the probation courts. He lives in Van Nuys, and is very proud of his thirteen-year-old son.

A quintessential family member with seven Altman pictures to her credit, Shelley Duvall was dropped from the fold after *Popeye*. For Altman, the sticking point was her leaving *A Wedding* at the last minute to pursue a relationship with singer Paul Simon. (She was replaced by Pam Dawber. Duvall's *3 Women* cohort, Sissy Spacek, also fled the *Nashville*-esque wedding chronicle and was replaced by Mia Farrow.) There was some life after Altman, most notably as Jack Nicholson's terrified wife in Kubrick's *The Shining* and as the producer of *Shelley Duvall's Bedtime Stories* for Showtime. When we last spoke, she was in the process of moving back to the city where the Altman camp first discovered her, Houston, to build a computer business.

The first of the *Nashville* family to expire was also the oldest Altman acquaintance of the group. Keenan Wynn died of cancer at the age of seventy in October of 1986, having notched some two hundred fifty television shows, one hundred stage productions, and two hundred twenty movies.

Barbara Baxley, who had known Altman since working with him on TV's *Bus Stop* in 1961, would try without success to woo Altman for other roles. There is some evidence that she alienated her boss during and beyond the *Nashville* shoot. "Barbara used to be a letter writer," says Bert Remsen. "She used to drive Bob nuts. Instead of calling him up on the phone she would write him a letter about her feelings and give it to him." After playing Sally Field's mother in *Norma Rae*, her career nose-dived. Baxley died of a heart attack in 1990 shortly after completing work on *The Exorcist 3*. She was sixty-three.

Politics would trail the career of the man who played Hal Phillip Walker's handler, Michael Murphy. A prolific Altman family member, Murphy would enjoy one of his greatest acting triumphs as the eponymous Democratic presidential candidate in Altman and Garry Trudeau's extraordinary HBO series, *Tanner '88*. He lives in Northern California with his wife and two very athletic daughters. When we met to discuss *Nashville,* he had recently completed *The Island* opposite Sally Kirkland in which they played JFK and Marilyn Monroe thirty years later. A screening of the film, which he had attended the night before, was projected by Altman's son, Michael.

Geraldine Chaplin would become a familiar face in the Altman entourage immediately following *Nashville,* playing Annie Oakley in *Buffalo Bill and the Indians* and the bossy wedding coordinator in *A Wedding*, as well as lead roles in Alan Rudolph's *Welcome to L.A.*, *Remember My Name,* and *The Moderns*. While the seventies proved to be her busiest decade, Chaplin continued to divide her time over the next two decades between a multiplicity of European and American films, including *White Mischief* and *The Age of Innocence.* She played the title role in *Mother Teresa: In the Name of God's Poor* and her grandmother Hannah Chaplin in *Chaplin.* She lives in Spain, Switzerland, and Miami Beach. Her son, Shane, with whom she was pregnant during the making of *Nashville,* is now twenty-five. When we met, he was completing university and had very long hair.

While Lily Tomlin's Hollywood star rose on the strength of her subtle dramatic turn as Linnea, it was primary-color fluff on the order of *All of Me, Nine to Five, Big Business,* and *The Incredible Shrinking Woman* that kept her there for a time. Arguably, the Altman shoe fit best. She would be shown to her best advantage opposite Tom Waits in Altman's *Short Cuts,* in which they played a hardscrabble L.A. couple; a brief but witty cameo in *The Player;* and in the Altman-produced *The Late Show.* (Altman had talked writer-director Robert Benton, who had written the role for a sex kitten, into casting Tomlin instead.) The pet project that led Tomlin to Altman's door, *Maiden,* went as far as a rewrite by Joan Tewkesbury but never came to fruition.

Nashville alum Scott Glenn would also resurface in Altmanland with a cameo in *The Player.* After creeping stoically through *Nashville,* Glenn enjoyed a breakout success via director James Bridges as John Travolta's antagonist in *Urban Cowboy.* Since then, he has danced between the commercial zone of such films as *Courage Under Fire* and *The Silence of the Lambs* and the indie territory of Ken Loach's *Carla's Song* and Norman Rene's *Reckless.* He lives in New York City with his wife, Carol Schwartz, and their daughters, Rio and Dacota.

The future also proved bright for *Nashville*'s other phantom figure. In fact, Tricycle Man Jeff Goldblum soon became too expensive for the director who discovered him. Who could have predicted that the strange tall guy on the long bike with the funny glasses would endure as *Nashville*'s most recognizable veteran (not to mention the only one with anything that resembled an enduring music career)? But the funny glasses and mute posturing of the Tricyle Man concealed an actor with a slouching sexiness and oddball insouciance that came to the fore time and again in *The Big Chill, The Fly, Silverado, Jurassic Park,* and *Independence Day.*

As is often the case in Hollywood, the *Nashville* actors with some of the more durable careers were among its least glamorous: the character actors who could always be counted on to fill their niche with élan. Ned Beatty has amassed a catalogue of 115 screen appearances, extraordinary for their variety and consistent high standard. Notable among the list are roles in *Network, All the President's Men,* the first two *Superman* films, *Hear My Song,* and *Life.* He made his second Altman appearance as a sociable Mississippi cop in *Cookie's Fortune.* When he is not shuttling back and forth for another gig, he dwells in a redneck renaissance cabin deep in the hills of Tulare County, California.

Allen Garfield would continue to rack up credits (albeit not for Altman) playing gangsters, newsmen, rabbis, and magnates with such names as Bernie, Abe, Abbadabba Berman, and Vinnie Vidivici. At press time, he was in prime form as an old-style movie mogul on AMC's series *The Lot.* Similarly, Robert Doqui stayed in demand throughout the next two and a half decades, running the gamut of the cop and military-officer field. A Los Angeles family man with a rich and gracious heart, Doqui was gearing up to fly out to Australia for another movie the day after our chat.

Days before I spoke to him, Bert Remsen had just returned from North Carolina, where he had been filming a scene for the Sandra Bullock–Ben Affleck comedy *Forces of Nature.* Despite his most dogged efforts to stay out of acting, the phone kept ringing with requests for his ingratiatingly crusty screen presence, right up until his death from heart failure on April 22, 1999. He was seventy-four. Remsen was a charming, effortlessly good-humored man, a jewel in the crown of Altman actors.

For better or worse, the singing stars of *Nashville* were never able to parlay their musical debuts into recording careers. Henry Gibson rolled his eyes as he recalled Jerry Weintraub's attempts to trade on his *Nashville* success. "Weintraub wanted to manage me—his notion of managing me was to make the rounds of fairs and do country songs. I thought, Jesus, suppose I played a bloody killer, where would he send me?" Gibson went on to do roles in two of Altman's most maligned films, *A Perfect Couple* and *H.E.A.L.T.H.*, signaling a spotty string of film and TV roles that never quite fulfilled the breadth and promise of Haven Hamilton. In 1999, he made a poignant impression as a gay gentleman barfly in Paul Thomas Anderson's very Altmanesque *Magnolia*.

If Haven Hamilton's future as Nashville's Pat Robertson was nipped in the bud with the shelving of *Nashville 12*, his aspirations have been borne out more modestly by his son Buddy. When last heard from, Dave Peel had abandoned his path as a country singer and actor to take his vows; word had it that Peel was ministering somewhere in California. He was the only cast member born and bred in Nashville. I regret that he could not be located in the process of researching this book.

The fates of the actors who played Tom, Mary, and Bill loosely reflected those that Robert Harders had envisioned for their characters. Of the three, Keith Carradine kept a solid acting career spinning after the initial Oscar hoopla over "I'm Easy" faded away. As the song climbed to number nineteen on the *Billboard* chart, Carradine was offered a record deal by David Geffen. The two albums that resulted generated marginal interest, and Carradine focused on his film work. Although he never acted for Altman again, he maintained strong ties with the Altman circle, starring in Joan Tewkesbury's film-directing debut (*Old Boyfriends*) and a succession of Altman-produced films by Alan Rudolph, including *Choose Me, The Moderns,* and *Mrs. Parker and the Vicious Circle.*

The acting careers of Cristina Raines and Allan Nicholls fell by the wayside as the two reinvented themselves in and out of show business. As Nicholls handled small roles in five of Altman's subsequent films, he segued into assistant-directing with *Streamers* and producing (Altman's *Quintet* and the non-Altman films *Bob Roberts* and *Dead Man Walking*). His first credit as executive producer was *Cradle Will Rock* in 1999. Wearing his new mogul hat,

Nicholls traipses frequently between New York City and Montpelier, Vermont, where he and his wife have raised two sons.

In *Nashville*'s original draft, Joan Tewkesbury ventured that Mary should have been a nurse. Cristina Raines, well on the road to fulfilling her character's unrealized potential, was studying to be a nurse when we last met. She soon parted romantically with Keith Carradine after *Nashville,* and made a specialty of bad TV movies for a good part of the eighties. She shares a home in Pasadena with her graceful thirteen-year-old daughter and disarming second husband, a computer animator.

While the actors playing Tom, Bill, and Mary arrived at points of emotional stasis and career gratification independently of one another, the same could not be said of the man who played Norman, their hapless chauffeur. After *Nashville,* David Arkin's film career fizzled. Following brief appearances in *All the President's Men* and a British production called *Cannonball,* Arkin would make his last screen appearance courtesy of his former boss, appearing in the ensemble of Robert Altman's *Popeye.* Two decades later, Arkin's name would surface in the papers one more time, after he committed suicide on January 14, 1990.

Barbara Harris, like her glorious and resilient character, would keep on keepin' on. Harris's film career crested in the late seventies with such films as Hitchcock's *Family Plot* and *The Seduction of Joe Tynan,* but only Hitchcock (who found her to be a consummate professional) would tap into the actress's off-center genius. The jobs diminished in the eighties, when she made supporting appearances in *Dirty Rotten Scoundrels* and *Peggy Sue Got Married.* Her last role was in *Grosse Pointe Blank* in 1997. She lives in the city of her earliest triumphs, Chicago, where she teaches and directs.

Harris would be reunited with *Nashville* foil Karen Black in Alfred Hitchcock's *Family Plot,* in which Black was cast as a jewel thief. In turn, Black would team up again with her *Nashville* director for both the stage and film versions of *Come to the 5 & Dime, Jimmy Dean, Jimmy Dean,* in which she glowed as a glamorous transsexual who returns to the small town of her youth. The otherworldly aspect of these projects would set the tone for the rest of Black's career, which has been characterized by innumerable parts in horror and science-fiction films. After Tobe Hooper's *Invaders from Mars,* the indefatigable Black would pursue dozens of independent and low-budget jobs with titles such as *Evil Spirits* (with Virginia Mayo and *Nashville* costar Bert Remsen), *Haunting Fear, Plan 10 From Outer Space, Oliver Twisted,* and *Auntie Lee's Meat Pies.*

Sueleen, who is left standing against a Parthenon column while Albuquerque grabs her chance at fame, would never get to sing her song. All of Gwen Welles's most diligent efforts at living a holistic, vegetarian life failed her during a protracted fight against anal cancer that claimed her life in 1993 at age forty-two. She was married to actor Harris Yulin at the time. Filmmaker Donna Deitch, who featured Welles in her movie *Desert Hearts,* chronicled the actress's last months in the wrenching documentary *Angel on My Shoulder.* Welles thought it would be her greatest role, and in many ways it was. The spectacle of this stunning and gentle-spirited actress succumbing to the ravages of a humbling, contorting cancer conceals ironies of almost mythological proportions.

Perhaps no *Nashville* actor personifies the vagaries of fate as powerfully as Ronee Blakley. The poster girl for *Nashville* with a *Newsweek* cover, an Oscar nomination, and multiple profiles touting her improvisational gifts, Blakley was unable to maintain her stride after the initial star burst of Barbara Jean. The problem: getting people to believe she wasn't Barbara Jean. Talk show hosts required her to appear in full-on Barbara Jean wig and regalia. Studio executives assumed Blakley was a fragile, Southern-twangy belle who had exhausted her full range with *Nashville.* Recalls Altman, "When Michael Ovitz and Ron Meyer started C.A.A., they came to my office in Westwood and I showed them all about Ronee, who had come to see some footage of her. They weren't very interested. They said, 'Yeah, she's a country singer.' I said, 'No, she's not.' She was a very supercontemporary girl when I met her, and the furthest from country. I said, 'No, that's acting.' They just didn't buy it."

No one seemed to. The offers to follow were unmemorable but

for a stint as a heavy in Walter Hill's *The Driver* and one of Freddy's victims in Wes Craven's *A Nightmare on Elm Street*. After touring with Bob Dylan in his Rolling Thunder Revue, Blakley played Mrs. Dylan in the misbegotten fictionalized account of the tour, *Renaldo and Clara*. Despite Altman's boosting of the actress to C.A.A., he would not employ Blakley again.

Blakley attributes the falling out with Altman to a misunderstanding over her second album, released in the wake of her *Nashville* success. "He didn't approve of the ad that came out. The ad said, 'Hello Ronee, goodbye Barbara Jean.' That made Bob furious. I think he thought, I took her and gave her everything that she has, and now she says goodbye to it? Alan Rudolph had cast me in *Welcome to L.A.* And I was replaced, with Geraldine [Chaplin]. That was heartbreaking for me. I screamed and cried."

Neither Altman nor Rudolph recall her would-be involvement with *Welcome to L.A.*, which Altman produced. "I assisted him with the casting but I never got in his way," says Altman. "She was never up for it. That's just her perception of what was taken from her. And she was suddenly taking these songs, like 'Tapedeck in His Tractor' and 'Dues,' trying to strip the country side out of them. I said, 'You can't do this, you can't make an album, you don't own the rights to your songs.' It wasn't just me. Legally she was not allowed to. And she said, 'We've already done them and it's really important to me.' That's what that was about."

The other shoe began to drop for Blakley. Her first marriage, to German film director Wim Wenders, began to crumble long before it ended after seven years. (Their charged relationship would be chronicled in *I Played It for You*, a fascinating documentary-style drama directed by Blakley, featuring herself and Wenders in the full heat of their marriage). Her beloved brother Steven, who cheered her on during the filming of *Nashville*, died of AIDS. Blakley herself began to fall ill, developing a spinal fluid leak that put her on her back for two years and led to problems with weight and arthritis. As I was completing research, Blakley was studying for a degree in film at a community college in the San Fernando Valley and living with her delightful twelve-year-old daughter (from a failed second marriage to a screenwriter, which she prefers not to discuss). She continues to write songs, many that convey a beauty and emotional ache that outdistances anything she wrote for *Nashville*.

It is as if Ronee Blakley and Barbara Jean merged. That is the explanation offered by at least one of Blakley's best *Nashville* buddies. Says Geraldine Chaplin, "She seemed extremely vulnerable [during *Nashville*]. I met her later and she had put on weight and was strong, a completely different personality. I think she went into this personality so deeply that she really became this singer, this very feeble, sick woman. She wasn't well. She *became* her."

Blakley reflects upon that time. "A year later, when Geraldine Chaplin and I went to the Oscars together, I think she felt betrayed, that I had lived my part to the extent that perhaps she didn't know that I was another person. I'd just been on tour with Bob Dylan, and as I talked to her in the car, as Ronee, she looked at me [with surprise]." Blakley mimes a look of astonishment, then adds with empathy, "I loved Barbara Jean. It was hard to let her go, but I had to be Ronee Blakley. I *was* Ronee Blakley."

FOLLOWING NASHVILLE, Joan Tewkesbury was awarded the prestigious task of writing the screenplay for Altman's upcoming version of Doctorow's *Ragtime*. Dino de Laurentiis had bought the rights for Altman, and de Laurentiis would soon take them away. There would be many bones of contention between Altman and his producer, not the least of which was de Laurentiis's determination to cast Robert Redford as Mother's younger brother. Altman would soon be dropped, but not before the director let go of his *Nashville* screenwriter, who was locked in her own war of wills with Altman aide-de-camp Scott Bushnell. "My sense was that Bob knew the handwriting was on the wall and there was no sense of it going any further," explains Tewkesbury of her preemptive firing. "And I was desperate to keep my friendship, because I had no idea what the ins and outs of what was playing out with Dino."

Tewkesbury, one of the more articulate and perceptive writer-directors I have had the pleasure of meeting, would have a creditable, if not earth-shattering, career as a writer and director of TV films in the coming twenty-four years, including an evocative adaptation of Olive Ann Burns's fin de siècle novel, *Cold Sassy Tree*, with Faye Dunaway and Richard Widmark. She also carries the mantle of her early dancing career and continues to choreograph dances and ballets. When we last met, she was directing segments of the well-received TV series about teenage angst, *Felicity*.

It is hard to discuss the career of Robert Altman without acknowledging the invaluable partnership and camaraderie of Tommy Thompson, who died suddenly of a heart attack on March 3, 2000. Like Tewkesbury, he would also flee the Altman scene for a time as a result of dissonances with Bushnell. Jumping ship with the double-punch failures of *A Perfect Couple* and *H.E.A.L.T.H.*, he would assistant-direct on only five non-Altman movies (including *Twice in a Lifetime* and *Black Widow*) before patching things up with his old friend. Thompson returned to the fold with *Cookie's Fortune*, and capped off his alliance as first assistant-director on *Dr. T and the Women*. His passing is an incalculable loss to Altman. He was one of the good guys.

Scott Bushnell and Robert Eggenweiler would carry on and flourish in their roles as Altman's associate producers. Bushnell was dropped from the Altman team after she suffered an aneurysm during the making of *Kansas City*. I regret that neither of them were able to participate in the research for this book: Eggenweiler was suffering from respiratory problems that had him in and out of the hospital with troubling regularity, and Bushnell politely declined, explaining that she had been burned by journalists one too many times. Their absence leaves holes in the *Nashville* story that could fill another volume, I am confident. Editor Sidney Levin would weather his dismissal from *Nashville* with aplomb. Beginning with *The Front, Casey's Shadow,* and

Norma Rae, and moving on to *Cross Creek* and *Clara's Heart,* he evolved a flair for small, nicely acted and conventionally directed human-interest dramas.

Arguably the biggest star to emerge from behind the camera was Altman's longhaired second assistant director, Alan Rudolph. In many ways, Rudolph's directing career would prove to be as bumpy as his mentor's, albeit minus the iconographic peaks to compare with *MASH, Nashville, Short Cuts,* and *McCabe & Mrs. Miller.* Rudolph has generated an arresting, quirky body of films mining the prickly territory of relationships between men and women, most notably *Choose Me* and *Afterglow.* Like his mentor, he has favored a rotating ensemble of actors that have included such *Nashville* veterans as Geraldine Chaplin and Keith Carradine. He eventually took on a project Altman had long abandoned, a film version of Kurt Vonnegut's *Breakfast of Champions* (with a screen-play much revised for the one he had done for Altman over twenty years back). It opened in September 1999 to skeptical re-views. At press time, he was embarking upon a long-delayed noirish comedy called *Trixie,* with Emily Watson in the title role.

Wayne Simpson nearly lost his job as director of the Franklin High School Band when *Nashville* was released and the mother of one of his young charges was outraged to see that her daugh-ter was in an R-rated picture. A *Playboy* photo spread featuring all of *Nashville's* younger actresses (plus Keith Carradine) in var-ious stages of undress did not help his case. In a school fracas that prefigured *South Park: Bigger, Longer and Uncut,* the mother threatened to sue Simpson, who argued in his defense that he had been promised it would be a PG movie. He kept his job. Twenty-five years later, he is still the director of the Franklin High School Band. As a result of the publicity and prestige gar-nered through its appearance in the film, the band's ranks have swelled from sixty to three hundred, and it has emerged as a prize-winning, nationally acknowledged musical organization.

And John Denver, that self-styled "country boy" whose Carnegie Hall concert debut was a turning point in the realization of *Nashville,* would be awarded the Entertainer of the Year award by the Country Music Association. That was in 1975, the year of *Nashville*'s release. For many country music diehards, the simultaneous attention showered upon someone they felt was the ultimate crossover pop artist and a movie that seemed like the ultimate put-down was too much to take. The end of the Nashville world, as they knew it, was near.

A TALL, black skyscraper with funny black wings has gone up in Nashville in the twenty-five years since Robert Altman came to town. Called "the bat building" by the locals, it is one of many bank and hotel concerns that now rival the Equity and Life Building for dominance of Nashville's bursting skyline. Despite the tangible corporate sprawl that has grown to accommodate the phenomenal new international market for country music, it would be an oversimplification to say that Nashville has changed in leaps and bounds since 1975. Tootsie's Orchid Lounge still beckons the visitor on a noticeably decaying lower Broadway. You can continue to buy vintage Roy Acuff at Ernie Tubbs Record Store, where the records have mostly been replaced by compact discs and it is not uncommon to hear English-accented tourists asking the salespeople for recommendations. You can still be overcharged for a box of Goo Goo Clusters at one of the Broadway souvenir shops, but now you can munch them while you ride the whimsical and gleaming new Red Grooms carousel at the waterfront.

With the happy exception of the Exit/In, all of the clubs that served as locations for *Nashville* have been either razed or turned into other clubs or stores. The former Picking Parlor, on the spankingly renovated Second Street, is now a boutique for tony country-western clothing. Along with many of the surrounding businesses, it has been struggling to stay afloat since Opryland Park shuttered and the dazzling, Las Vegas–style Opryland Hotel complex began to lure tourists away from downtown. The shop's proprietor, a svelte, forty-something native Israeli who worked as a cabdriver in New York City before moving south, is typical of the new global wave of emigration to Nashville. When asked if she saw *Nashville,* she smiles sullenly and says with the spiky directness of a Manhattan cabbie, "Yeah, it was too long and didn't go anywhere."

Despite the shopkeeper's polyglot background, chances are you can find a number of people in town who'd say the same thing about the film. For that matter, you'd probably hear similar opinions from a number of people in and out of the American Film Institute, which shunned *Nashville* when compiling its list of all-time top one hundred American films in 1999. For all of the acclaim accorded *Nashville* over the years, Altman has maintained a wary regard for both the film and his audience ever since he attended the first screening in Boston. Altman recalls, "Some woman walked up the aisle, very butch, masculine-looking, short hair, striped overalls, and she had a baby. She stood in the back of the theater, turned around, and yelled out, 'I could take a *shit* and it would be better than this!'"

Her words hung like a curse over Altman's output over the next fifteen years. Critics and audiences alike began to turn away from Altman with a resentment that approached anger, as if he had betrayed them somehow by not sustaining the brio of *Nashville.* Even Pauline Kael, arguably his most passionate press enthusiast, would only go to bat for *Vincent & Theo* in 1990. After the disappointing *Buffalo Bill and the Indians,* Altman attempted to outdo his promiscuous narrative technique honed in *Nashville* with *A Wedding,* in which he doubled the character count to forty-eight. The film holds up beautifully today (it's currently being turned into an opera), but after accolades in Europe it was greeted tepidly in America. His anxiety-dream inspiration, *3 Women,* may be the most effective film from the years immediately following *Nashville.* A string of flops—*A Perfect Couple, Quintet, H.E.A.L.T.H.,* and the big-budget *Popeye*—undermined his credibility with the Hollywood studios. If *Short Cuts* reenergized Altman's multinarrative technique, it wasn't until the cocky and confident insider satire of *The Player* that Altman would be welcomed back into the fold. The irony of the film's success, in which Altman flipped the bird at all of the business's most artificial conventions, was sweet. *The Player* earned Oscar nominations for Best Adapted Screenplay, Best Editing, and Best Director, and for at least a day or two it seemed as if Altman was a player again. Just a few short years later, he would be back on the mat again, wrestling studio executives for the final edit of his film *The Gingerbread Man*.

It is hard to weigh the influence of *Nashville* on the film scene in the years following its release. The American independent film spirit that Altman fostered has exploded in the years since. Young upstarts such as Todd Haynes, Kevin Smith, and Spike Jonze seem intent on pushing the envelope on both the means and ends of the indie industry, which has its own festival in Park City, Utah, in which to flex its considerable muscle (and where *Cookie's Fortune* was the premier attraction in 1999). While directors and cineastes rate *Nashville* high on their list of most life-changing films, only one young director stands out as a true son of *Nashville*. Paul Thomas Anderson attempted to refine Altman's kaleidoscopic daring, bumping a multiplicity of characters against one another in *Boogie Nights* and especially *Magnolia,* with ensemble casting that was Altmanlike in both size and incongruousness. As spiritual scions go, Anderson is more literary than his mentor: Thematic connections that Altman tended to make in the editing room are already preplanned and polished to a tee by Anderson in the writing. For an auteur so fascinated by chance occurrence, Anderson leaves far less to chance once the shoot has commenced. But *Magnolia*'s long tracking shots are an indisputable homage to Altman, as is a cast that includes *Nashville*-ians Henry Gibson and Michael Murphy, as well as Altman veterans Julianne Moore and Phillip Baker Hall.

For all the fights, for all the pans, for all the angry women screaming "shit" from the back of the movie house, Altman continues at the age of seventy-five to be baffled when his films fail to connect. Contrary to the suspicions of some detractors, Altman never endeavors, like Zero Mostel and Gene Wilder's wily entrepreneurs in *The Producers,* to ferret out scripts calculated to send audiences scurrying for the exit en masse (he should only have had their luck). On the contrary, he charges into each new project confident in his soul that moviegoers will naturally want to join him for the ride. All too often, his faith has gotten him *bupkis*. At the time of our last interview, *Cookie's Fortune* was in its third week of release, and he was contemplating the possibility that his most lauded film in years might gross less than one of his most maligned, *Prêt-à-Porter.*

"I'm always shocked," he admitted with palpable wistfulness. "I'm just now starting to understand what this mass-audience distribution thing is, the full extent of the great unwashed. When I did *Images,* I thought, Well, this is the best picture that's ever been made. I could never see beyond my own little village."

If Altman is not able to see over the next church steeple, any lack of commercial sense is more than compensated for by a preponderance of sixth sense. There is a prescience to Altman's best films that give this self-styled heathen the aura of a prophet. Five years after the release of *Nashville,* a young man stalked John Lennon outside his New York apartment building and shot him to death. Days after, Altman received a phone call from a reporter at *The Washington Post.* She mentioned the Lennon killing and asked him, "Don't you feel responsible?" Altman was stunned. "Why?" he wanted to know. "I don't know how you can say that." She responded, "Well, you were the first person who got into that."

After pondering that logic for the briefest of moments, Altman said the only thing he possibly could: "Well, somebody should have paid notice then."

Notes

AI indicates "Author's interview."

Introduction

p. 14   "I try to get in," Sally Quinn, *The Washington Post,* June 18, 1975.

p. 17   "I wouldn't have," Robert Altman, AI, January 14, 1999.

p. 22   "Metacontemporary," Alan Rudolph, AI, October 16, 1998.

p. 22   "Has fiction become fact," Kevin Phillips, *TV Guide,* February 21–27, 1976, p. A-3.

p. 22   "no 'ideas,'" Robert Mazzacco, *The New York Review of Books,* July 12, 1975, p. 19.

Prologue

p. 25   "more than anything," Ned Beatty, AI, March 12, 1999.

Chapter One
"Robert Altman Goes to a John Denver Concert"

p. 29   "Robert Altman is like," Kathryn Altman, AI, April 20, 1999.

p. 30   "We'll call it Lion's Gate," Robert Altman, AI, April 16, 1999.

p. 30   "It couldn't have helped," Patrick McGilligan, *Robert Altman: Jumping Off the Cliff,* (New York: St. Martin's Press, 1991), p. 216.

p. 30   "Altman forged an alliance," Robert Altman, AI, April 16, 1999.

p. 30   "The project soon collapsed," McGilligan, p. 262.

p. 32   "It was like a men's club," Tommy Thompson, AI, May 14, 1999.

p. 32   "It was just sort of," Scott Glenn, AI, October 28, 1998.

p. 32   "Not knowing," Rudolph, AI, October 16, 1998.

p. 34   "He was up in his apartment," Keith Carradine, AI, April 19, 1999.

p. 36   "I just wanted," Carradine, AI, April 19, 1999.

p. 38   "They had hoped for," Jack Viertel and David Colker, "The Long Road to Nashville," *New Times,* p. 55.

p. 38   "Peter Bogdonavich, who," Elliott Gould, AI, January 29, 1999.

p. 38   "He was not enamored," Gould, AI, January 29, 1999.

p. 38   "Sterling Hayden had serious," Gould, AI, January 29, 1999.

p. 38   "I didn't realize," Gould, AI, January 29, 1999.

p. 39   "A downer," Viertel, Colker, "The Long Road to Nashville," p. 56.

p. 40   "This is not a movie," Joan Tewkesbury, AI, April 16, 1998.

p. 40   "There were probably," David Picker, AI, May 22, 1999.

p. 41   "It did not leave," Picker, AI, May 22, 1999.

p. 42   "Weintraub had dreams," Jerry Weintraub, *The Charlie Rose Show,* November 10, 1998.

p. 43   "He had made," Starger, AI, March 10, 1999.

Chapter Two:
Joan Goes to Music City

p. 48   "You should come with me," Joan Tewkesbury, AI September 15, 1999.

p. 48   "It invigorates him," Sam Cohn, AI, May 19, 1999.

p. 49   "She said 'I want,'" Altman, AI, April 5, 1998.

p. 50   "Would you like," Tewkesbury, AI, September 15, 1998.

p. 50   "Nashville the city," Helene Keyssar, *Robert Altman's America,* (Oxford: Oxford University Press, 1991), p. 159.

p. 51   "Mary was being pursued," Tewkesbury, AI, April 6, 1999.

p. 53   "This girl looked like," Tewkesbury, AI, September 15, 1998.

p. 53   "You did four," Tewkesbury, "A Conversation About Screenwriting with Joan Tewkesbury," *Columbia College Film Department Journal,* November 1975, p. 4.

p. 54   "I had a sense of," Tewkesbury, "A Conversation about Screenwriting with Joan Tewkesbury," p. 4.

p. 54   "It was at the point," Michael Murphy, AI, March 15, 1999.

p. 55	"It was bullshit," Tewkesbury, AI, April 16, 1998.
p. 56	"It was one of the most," Tewkesbury, "A Conversation About Screenwriting with Joan Tewkesbury," p. 7.

Chapter Three:
Will the Circle Be Unbroken?

p. 59	"Your movie is in here," Tewkesbury, AI, April 6, 1999.
p. 60	"I suppose someone's," Tewkesbury, AI, April 6, 1999.
p. 60	"Jerry Jeff was," Tewkesbury, AI, September 15, 1998.
p. 60	"He was so in with," Tewkesbury, AI, September 15, 1998.
p. 62	"The whole music industry," Tewkesbury, AI, April 6, 1999.
p. 62	"Personification of," Tewkesbury, AI, September 15, 1998.
p. 63	"If you look at Albuquerque," Tewkesbury, AI, September 15, 1998.
p. 63	"She was one of those," Tewkesbury, AI, September 15, 1998.
p. 65	"The original idea," Geraldine Chaplin, AI, January 7, 1999.
p. 65	"He was short," Tewkesbury, AI, September 15, 1998.
p. 65	"I said, 'This has to be something,'" Altman, AI, April 5, 1998.
p. 66	"She thought Bob had wrecked," Tewkesbury, September 15, 1998.
p. 66	"She's a very ballsy," Altman, AI, April 19, 1999.
p. 66	"Sometimes these things," Tewkesbury, AI, September 15, 1998.
p. 67	"He wanted to go where," Ned Beatty, AI, March 12, 1999.
p. 67	"Okay, then the nicest guy," Tewkesbury, AI, April 16, 1998.
p. 67	"Keith was the nice guy," Tewkesbury, AI, September 15, 1998.

Chapter Four:
How to Invent a Political Party

p. 70   "The main reason," Altman, AI, April 5, 1998.

p. 71   "He didn't give many instructions," Thomas Hal Phillips, AI, March 22, 1999.

p. 71   "I attacked the whole business," Phillips, AI, March 22, 1999.

p. 72   "Altman got more fun," Phillips, AI, March 22, 1999.

p. 72   "I didn't change anything," Altman, AI, April 19, 1999.

p. 72   "He was an obnoxious, pushy asshole,'" Altman, AI, April 19, 1999.

p. 73   "Bob said, 'Well, we have to have,'" Tewkesbury, AI, September 15, 1998.

p. 74   "I knew a guy in college," Michael Murphy, AI, March 15, 1999.

p. 75   "Michael's character came out of," Tewkesbury, AI, September 15, 1998.

p. 75   "What Michael brings to it," Rudolph, AI, October 16, 1998.

p. 76   "rumor has it that," Tewkesbury, *Nashville* screenplay, first draft.

p. 77   "All of the other characters never," Tewkesbury, AI, September 15, 1998.

p. 79   "It became too expensive," Altman, AI, April 5, 1998.

p. 79   "We had to get songs," Altman, AI, April 19, 1999.

p. 79   "That's a brilliant piece of work," Altman, AI, April 19, 1999.

p. 80   "By that time, I decided," Richard Baskin, AI, March 8, 1999.

Chapter Five:
Doing the Replacement Party Shuffle

p. 83   "Being firstborn," Ronee Blakley, autobiographical resume, 1972.

p. 85   "She was the first person," Altman, AI, April 5, 1998.

p. 86   "Singing was not her thing," Baskin, AI, March 8, 1999.

p. 86   "He said, 'Look foxy,'" Blakley, AI, March 7, 1999.

p. 87   "We were talking about the scene," Blakley, AI, March 7, 1999.

p. 87   "Bob was talking to me one night," Murphy, AI, March 15, 1999.

p. 88   "He really is the puppeteer," Sue Barton, AI, April 20, 1999.

p. 89   "He had cut his hair," Altman, AI, April 16, 1999.

p. 90   "We lost an actor," David Hayward, AI, March 8, 1999.

p. 90   "I always thought that Kenny's insecurities," Hayward, AI, March 8, 1999.

p. 91   "They do such a cursory judgment," Altman, AI, April 19, 1999.

p. 92   "He wouldn't let her go," Altman, AI, April 5, 1999.

p. 93   "It was very hard to cross over," Lily Tomlin, AI, September 14, 1998.

p. 93   "The next thing I knew," Tomlin, AI, September 14, 1998.

p. 95   "I told you, Bob, I quit," Bert Remsen, AI, September 15, 1998.

p. 96   "Shelley Duvall may not be an actress," Pauline Kael, *The New Yorker*, February 4, 1974.

p. 97   "Shelley opened the door," Tommy Thompson, AI, March 11, 1999.

p. 98   "He was the one," Henry Gibson, AI, September 14, 1999.

p. 99   "I have a role for you," Tewkesbury, April 6, 1999.

p. 99   "They sent a young man," Gibson, AI, September 14, 1999.

p. 101   "He mentioned that he was going to," Karen Black, AI, September 20, 1998.

p. 102   "I was out of work," Barbara Harris, phone interview, April 3, 1999.

p. 102   "We were painting and building," Mike Nichols, *Life Magazine*.

p. 106   "If you tell me what to do," Tom Wicker, "In the Beginning: Miller's Creation," *The New York Times*, December 5, 1972.

p. 106   "Although her reactions are spontaneous," *Newsweek,* November 1, 1965, p. 84.

p. 107   "He looked like the person," Allan Nicholls, AI, January 13, 1999.

p. 107   "I was vacationing in Miami," AI, January 13, 1999.

p. 107   "It didn't work out," Altman, AI, April 19, 1999.

p. 108   "She said, 'I just finished writing,'" Scott Glenn, phone interview, October 28, 1998.

Chapter Six:
Basic Training

p. 109   "It's the one job," Glenn, phone interview, October 28, 1998.

p. 109   "He's not rehearsing any of this," Murphy, March 15, 1999.

p. 110   "Hey killer, what're you doing," Glenn, phone interview, October 28, 1998.

p. 112   "When we were young," Eugenia Shepherd, "Inside Fashion," *New York Post,* September 6, 1974, p. 42.

p. 112   "So she could sing badly," Hayward, AI, March 8, 1999.

p. 112   "Oh, God, don't," Tewkesbury, AI, September 15, 1998.

p. 112   "You earned them, Sueleen," Viertel and Colker, "The Long Road to Nashville," *New Times,* June 14, 1975.

p. 112   "Ironically, I didn't want to work," Timothy Brown, phone interview, May 26, 1999.

p. 113   "We treated ourselves as a trio," Nicholls, AI, January 13, 1999.

p. 113   "Staying there was a test," Nicholls, AI, January 13, 1999.

p. 113   "I was extremely shy," Christina Raines, AI, March 9, 1999.

p. 113   "She had this incredible voice," Nicholls, AI, March 9, 1999.

p. 113   "I took daily lessons," Jeff Goldblum, AI, April 20, 1999.

p. 115   "I got put up against a wall," Hayward, AI, March 8, 1999.

p. 117   "to just try and be the least bit proficient," Tomlin, AI, September 14, 1998.

p. 117   "Because Linnea, being a Baptist," Tomlin, AI, September 14, 1998.

p. 118   "I started drinking rum," Robert Doqui, AI, September 17, 1998.

p. 120   "He said, 'Come join us for dinner,'" Blakley, AI, September 17, 1998.

p. 120   "an eternity of Instamatics," Janet Maslin, "Altman's Ophelia," *The Village Voice,* June 23, 1975, p. 116.

p. 121   "The characters couldn't be more disparate," Gibson, AI, September 14, 1999.

p. 123   "I put on a red shirt," Barbara Harris, phone interview, April 6, 1999.

p. 123   "I think Scotty was more the woman," Geraldine Chaplin, AI, January 7, 1999.

p. 123   "She was the end of Altman," Kelly Marshall Fine, AI, September 12, 1998.

p. 123   "She was one of those squirrels," Altman, AI, April 5, 1998.

p. 123   "Evil," Tommy Thompson, AI, March 11, 1999.

p. 125   "Bob said to me, 'You go back,'" Tomlin, AI, September 14, 1998.

p. 126   "We're all equal," Chaplin, AI, January 7, 1999.

p. 127   "There's food and drink," Beatty, AI, March 12, 1999.

Chapter Seven:
Action

p. 128   "Altman throws it up in the air," Karen Black, AI, September 20, 1998.

p. 128   "Give me a group of people," Altman, AI, April 19, 1999.

p. 129   "The tension was so thick," Gibson, AI, September 14, 1999.

p. 130   "Oh, that's fine, Opal would be pregnant," Chaplin, AI, January 7, 1999.

p. 131   "logistical nightmare," Thompson, AI, May 26, 1999.

p. 132   "Bob was there setting up," Nicholls, AI, January 13, 1999.

p. 132   "Tough love," Carradine, AI, April 19, 1999.

p. 133	"Paul was an odd case," Rudolph, AI, October 16, 1998.
p. 133	"Since we were dealing," Altman, AI, April 19, 1999.
p. 133	"He said, 'Well, am I in a close-up,'" Glenn, phone interview, October 28, 1998.
p. 134	"Goddammit, I've having the kid drive," Gibson, AI, September 14, 1998.
p. 134	"Just don't contradict me," Blakley, AI, September 13, 1998.
p. 136	"Everybody was charged up," Rudolph, AI, October 16, 1998.
p. 137	"I was expecting a Henry Mancini," Wayne Simpson, phone interview, June 18, 1999.
p. 137	"He seemed to thrive," Carradine, AI, April 19, 1999.
p. 137	"It was the kind of thing," Altman, AI, April 16, 1999.
p. 139	"Bob hates extras," Chaplin, AI, January 7, 1999.
p. 139	"I don't know why there is such a big *chazerai*," Altman, AI, April 19, 1999.
p. 139	"The night we watched the dailies," Gibson, AI, September 14, 1998.
p. 139	"Finally we gave up," Altman, AI, April 16, 1999.
p. 140	"Okay, now, you're a field man," Harry Haun, AI, October 30, 1998.
p. 141	"It was giving audiences equal exposure," Rudolph, AI, October 16, 1998.
p. 142	"There wasn't anyone in Hollywood," Richard Portman, phone interview, January 18, 1999.
p. 142	"Well sure," Jim Webb, AI, September 16, 1998.
p. 144	"In the big scenes I had to talk," Nicholls, AI, January 13, 1999.
p. 145	"I tried patching in phone calls," Webb, AI, September 16, 1998.
p. 146	"We felt that there was a lot of jealousy," Portman, phone interview, January 18, 1999.
p. 147	"This is where graft and corruption surface," Webb, AI, September 16, 1998.
p. 150	"He hauled a lot of people," Philips, AI, March 22, 1999.
p. 152	"one of those street-artist sketches," Tewkesbury, *Nashville* screenplay, first draft.

p. 152   "We were playing one of the stronger," Beatty, AI, March 12, 1999.

p. 153   "What you had to do with each of the actors," Tewkesbury, AI, April 6, 1999.

p. 153   "You guys talk all you want," Murphy, AI, March 15, 1999.

p. 153   "That's when I thought I was going to be fired," Chaplin, AI, January 7, 1999.

p. 155   "He'd always say, 'Harris, you gotta be crazy,'" Harris, phone interview, April 2, 1999.

p. 155   "We could not find her," Tewkesbury, AI, September 15, 1998.

p. 156   "At one point she wanted to leave," Baskin, AI, March 8, 1999.

p. 156   "I think Barbara became that flaky, flighty character," Thompson, AI, March 11, 1999.

p. 156   "Me and Barbara Baxley," Harris, phone interview, April 6, 1999.

p. 156   "If you had the moxie," Carradine, AI, April 19, 1999.

Chapter Eight:
Dailies: The Agony and the Ecstasy

p. 159   "She was a wonderful woman," Tomlin, AI, September 14, 1998.

p. 159   "He loved to be touched and hugged," Beatty, AI, March 12, 1999.

p. 159   "I was worried about the kids," Tomlin, AI, September 14, 1998.

p. 160   "The day I was to get married," James Calvert, letter, June 22, 1999.

p. 160   "When an actor is looking for something," Altman, AI, April 16, 1999.

p. 161   "Nashville without the music," Beatty, AI, March 12, 1999.

p. 162   "The actors become infatuated," Altman, AI, April 19, 1999.

p. 162   "What if I don't feel like coming," Glenn, phone interview, October 28, 1998.

p. 162   "I had no drinking restrictions then," Altman, AI, April 16, 1999.

p. 162   "He was capable of tongue lashings," Barton, phone interview, April 20, 1999.

p. 163   "Barbara sat down front," Altman, AI, April 16, 1999.

p. 163   "That was almost a knock-down drag-out," William Myers, AI, March 24, 1999.

p. 164   "I placated him and bit my tongue," Altman, AI, April 19, 1999.

p. 164   "That's not how Coppola," Haun, AI, October 30, 1998.

p. 164   "Henry was Method-ing all over the place," Raines, AI, March 9, 1999.

p. 166   "I deliberately packed that container," Gibson, AI, September 14, 1999.

p. 166   "I had to discover what my relationship," Robert Doqui, AI, September 17, 1998.

p. 166   "Allen Garfield *was* Barnett," Murphy, AI, March 15, 1999.

p. 167   "Bob gets us all together in this room," Beatty, AI, March 12, 1999.

p. 167   "Ronee was in left field," Thompson, AI, March 11, 1999.

p. 167   "Bob was interested in seeing," Beatty, AI, March 12, 1999.

p. 168   "Ronee brought the balls," Tewkesbury, AI, March 12, 1998.

p. 168   "It almost seems to follow," Beatty, AI, March 12, 1999.

p. 168   "They couldn't just five of them get into a car," Gibson, AI, September 14, 1999.

p. 169   "It's just a general contempt," Nicholls, AI, January 13, 1999.

p. 170   "Alan, could you pass me the salt?," Haun, AI, October 30, 1998.

p. 170   "MY NAME IS DAVID ARKIN," Gibson, AI, September 14, 1999.

Chapter Nine:
Summer and Smoke

p. 171   "Robert Altman is a very moral man," Harris, phone
          interview, April 6, 1999.

p. 173   "*Nashville* was really the beginning," Kathryn Altman,
          AI, April 20, 1999.

p. 177   "As I approached them," Beatty, AI, March 12, 1999.

p. 177   "It was like we belonged to this country club," Hay-
          ward, AI, March 8, 1999.

p. 179   "It wasn't rude but it was very startling," Goldblum, AI,
          April 20, 1999.

p. 180   "Don't worry, I own the block," Hayward, AI, March 8,
          1999.

p. 180   "Bob regaled us the next day," Carradine, AI, April 19,
          1999.

p. 180   "At that point, T.G.I.F.'s was pretty impressive,"
          Nicholls, AI, January 13, 1999.

p. 180   "That was a lot of money in 1974," Gibson, AI, Septem-
          ber 28, 1998.

p. 181   "It stood about this high," Carradine, AI, April 19,
          1999.

p. 181   "I started singing," Gibson, AI, September 14, 1998.

p. 181   "He took his coat," Carradine, AI, April 19, 1999.

p. 182   "I don't think fantasies hurt us," Gwen Welles, Para-
          mount press release, 1973.

p. 183   "I remember Barbara Baxley when she was young,"
          Harris, phone interview, April 6, 1999.

p. 183   "He got the D.T.'s right in the middle," Remsen,
          November 15, 1998.

p. 183   "We had a sequence on where to find him," Kelly Mar-
          shall, AI, September 12, 1998.

p. 183   "They said I was the only one," Rudolph, AI, October
          16, 1998.

p. 184   "As Bob said, 'Keenan doesn't do knitting,'" Glenn,
          phone interview, October 28, 1998.

p. 184   "We had a lot of empathy because of 'my father,'"
          Chaplin, AI, January 7, 1999.

p. 185   "That's terrible," James Barron, "Keenan Wynn is Dead at 70," *The New York Times,* October 15, 1986, p. D30.

p. 186   "When he shaved his mustache," Gibson, AI, September 14, 1999.

Chapter Ten:
Invading the Grand Old Opry

p. 190   "I wanted to have my own identity," Brown, phone interview, May 26, 1999.

p. 190   "Christ, what did you do to Bob?" Brown, phone interview, May 26, 1999.

p. 194   "The song and its presentation," "Nashville Smashville," *Time Out,* September 19–25, 1975, p. 10.

p. 196   "It was something she learned in school as a kid," Gibson, AI, September 14, 1999.

p. 196   "The bicentennial thing was sweeping the country," Baskin, AI, March 8, 1999.

p. 196   "I had the very notion," Gibson, AI, September 14, 1999.

p. 197   "Other commitments," Black, AI, September 20, 1998.

p. 197   "Of all the performers, Karen was the most interesting," Baskin as quoted by Shaun Considine, "Hollywood Can Sing Country Just Like Nashville," *The New York Times,* August 24, 1975, Arts and Leisure section.

p. 198   "I was really quite frightened in those days," Black, AI, September 20, 1998.

p. 198   "[I] go out to Bob's place and everybody's smoking dope," Black to Chris Hodenfield, "Zoom Lens Voyeur: A Few Moment's with Bob Altman's 'Nashville,'" *Rolling Stone,* July 17, 1975, p. 64.

p. 198   "It really worked on her behalf," Gibson, AI, September 14, 1998.

p. 198   "A loon," Barton, AI, April 20, 1999.

p. 199   "He developed a crush on me," Black, AI, September 20, 1998.

p. 200   "She adored Michael," Gibson, AI, September 14, 1998.

p. 200   "I had no idea I was going to be put through," Julie Christie, phone interview, January 25, 1999.

p. 201   "I'm so very interested as to why," Christie, phone in-
              terview, January 25, 1999.

p. 202   "He couldn't do a thing without her," Blakley, AI, Sep-
              tember 13, 1998.

p. 203   "Isn't this an incorrect stereotype?" Robb Baker,
              "Incarnating a Superstar," *Soho Weekly News,* June 12,
              1975, p. 23.

p. 204   "Allan was so fucking generous," Tewkesbury, AI, April
              6, 1999.

p. 204   "Ronee was very self-oriented," Altman, AI, April 19,
              1999.

p. 204   "We were cheering," Hayward, AI, March 8, 1999.

p. 204   "That town was in tears," Gibson, AI, September 14,
              1998.

p. 205   "Look at what you've done to our president," Gibson,
              AI, September 14, 1998.

Chapter Eleven
Nothing Sacred, but the Sacraments

p. 206   "People looked forward to it," anonymous source.

p. 209   "We were all in a daze," Rudolph, AI, October 16, 1998.

p. 210   "He was a limo driver," Nicholls, AI, January 13, 1999.

p. 211   "I accused her of not being who she is," Murphy, AI,
              March 15, 1999.

p. 211   "Because they didn't understand," Chaplin, AI, Janu-
              ary 7, 1999.

p. 211   "I never thought she worked for the BBC," Tewkes-
              bury, AI, September 15, 1998.

p. 214   "Baxley's script was this thick," Altman, AI, April 16,
              1999.

p. 215   "Geraldine is a real radical," Altman, AI, April 19, 1999.

p. 215   "I didn't dare interrupt," Chaplin, AI, January 7, 1999.

p. 216   "When I saw the bus yard," Altman, AI, April 19, 1999.

p. 217   "Bob said, 'If you're trying to be Opal,'" Chaplin, AI,
              January 7, 1999.

p. 218   "Geraldine sees the Goyaesque side," Rudolph, AI,
              October 16, 1998.

p. 218   "It was very heavy," Harris, AI, April 2, 1999.

p. 218   "I was hypersensitive," Tomlin, AI, September 14, 1998.

p. 220   "Susan was pretty fragile too," Tewkesbury, AI, September 15, 1998.

p. 220   "She's already fainted once," Blakley, AI, September 13, 1998.

p. 225   "We were getting ready to leave," Altman, AI, April 5, 1998.

p. 226   "We were shooting downtown," Thompson, AI, March 11, 1999.

p. 227   "I was parking Keith's Land Cruiser," Raines, AI, March 9, 1999.

p. 228   "Theirs is the best marriage I've ever seen," "Keith Carradine and Tina Raines Share a House," *People*, May 1, 1978, p.104.

p. 229   "Pan back from the twelfth-floor view," Holdenfield, "Zoom Lens Voyeur," *Rolling Stone*, July 17, 1975, p. 64.

p. 230   "Michael and I were comfortable with improvising," Allan Nicholls, AI, January 13, 1999.

p. 231   "Right before we started shooting," Murphy, AI, March 15, 1999.

p. 232   "It hadn't been that long since," Nicholls, AI, January 13, 1999.

p. 232   "That's the thing about Bob," Raines, AI, March 9, 1999.

Chapter Twelve
Getting Naked, Getting Enough

p. 234   "There was a definite undercurrent of violence," Raines, AI, March 9, 1999.

p. 234   "We're sitting there having our beer," Gibson, AI, September 4, 1998.

p. 235   "I never punched anybody in my life," Altman, AI, April 19, 1999.

p. 236   "At the end of dailies," Barton, AI, April 20, 1999.

p. 237   "I think this had to be the movie," Harris, AI, April 6, 1999.

p. 238   "Stoned and drunk out of his mind," Chaplin, AI, January 7, 1999.

p. 238   "I'd be drinking at night," Altman, AI, April 16, 1999.

p. 238   "It's the key to the movie," Tewkesbury, AI, September 15, 1998.

p. 239   "Romancin' the stone," Doqui, AI, September 17, 1998.

p. 239   "Someone like Linnea would never," Tomlin, AI, September 14, 1998.

p. 240   "Basically she is a woman who is at a crossroads," Tewkesbury, AI, September 15, 1998.

p. 241   "At the dailies, I couldn't figure out," Nicholls, AI, January 13, 1999.

p. 241   "There were real Nashville people," Raines, AI, March 9, 1999.

p. 242   "Lily was in great anguish," Gibson, AI, September 14, 1999.

p. 242   "I knew this was an important scene," Tomlin, AI, September 14, 1998.

p. 243   "We talked and we talked," Beatty, AI, March 12, 1999.

p. 244   "She has chosen," Tewkesbury, *Nashville* screenplay, first draft.

p. 245   "It was very sleazy," Marshall, AI, September 12, 1998.

p. 245   "We couldn't get extras to come," Tewkesbury, AI, September 15, 1998.

p. 245   "I think the winner took the money," Philips, AI, March 22, 1999.

p. 245   "Ned came in and said, 'You know Bob,'" Tewkesbury, AI, September 15, 1998.

p. 246   "This was the most vulnerable period in her life," Richard Perry, phone interview, May 15, 1999.

p. 247   "She knew more about nutrition," Chaplin, AI, January 7, 1999.

p. 247   "On the second verse of the song," Webb, AI, September 16, 1998.

p. 247   "Our assignment was to yell and scream," Myers, AI, March 24, 1999.

p. 248   "It was kind of difficult," Murphy, AI, March 15, 1999.

p. 248   "Gwenny had these gym socks," Tewkesbury, AI, September 15, 1998.

p. 250   "What were we worried about?," Beatty, AI, March 12, 1999.

p. 250   "They took the whole day," Chaplin, AI, January 7, 1999.

p. 250   "I remember how much tension," Marshall, AI, September 12, 1998.

p. 252   "Lily made a significant shift in that scene," Tewkesbury, AI, April 16, 1998.

p. 252   "As a teenager, I had an affinity for bad-women movies," Tomlin, AI, September 14, 1998.

p. 252   "Lily said I would like to try and teach," Tewkesbury, AI, April 16, 1998.

p. 253   "Lily was not always the most trusting," Altman, AI, April 16, 1999.

p. 253   "She told me something about what her feelings," Beatty, AI, March 12, 1999.

p. 254   "I don't think she was anywhere as skittish," Carradine, AI, April 19, 1999.

p. 254   "We would weep every night with our parts," Harris, AI, April 6, 1999.

p. 255   "I think he may have been dealing with his own dislike," Raines, AI, March 9, 1999.

p. 255   "I don't think he's so awful," Altman, AI, April 16, 1999.

p. 255   "He didn't do anything," Carradine, AI, April 19, 1999.

p. 255   "I think Ned suffered a bit, too," Tewkesbury, AI, April 6, 1999.

p. 256   "It was easy to find villainy," Beatty, AI, March 12, 1999.

Chapter Thirteen:
The Assassination

p. 257   "The thing at the Parthenon," Beatty, AI, March 12, 1999.

p. 259   "It was the first time I'd ever seen Bob nervous," Nicholls, AI, January 13, 1999.

p. 259   "We had all these people in position," Altman, AI, April 16, 1999.

p. 261   "That [fight] was really about the script," Tewkesbury,
           AI, April 6, 1999.

p. 261   "Bob said, 'You and Allan go out there and fight,'"
           Murphy, AI, March 15, 1999.

p. 261   "It got a little real there," Murphy, AI, March 15, 1999.

p. 262   "All twenty-four of us are in the hair and makeup
           room," Tomlin, AI, September 14, 1998.

p. 262   "Everybody was so happy," Harris, AI, April 6, 1999.

p. 264   "So I'm standing there and talking to this extra,"
           Beatty, AI, March 12, 1999.

p. 264   "I saw a cliff that I could dive into the river from," Hay-
           ward, AI, March 8, 1999.

p. 265   "At twelve-thirty, they came from everywhere, like
           ants," Thompson, AI, March 11, 1999.

p. 265   "So the crowd is building," Gibson, AI, September 14,
           1999.

p. 266   "This is it, let's go with it," Thompson, AI, March 11,
           1999.

p. 266   "We had like forty-five minutes to shoot the thing,"
           Baskin, AI, March 8, 1999.

p. 266   "From over the radio we hear," Thompson, AI, March
           11, 1999.

p. 268   "I had worn the key to the violin case," Hayward, AI,
           March 8, 1999.

p. 268   "I asked him if I got shot by such and such a caliber,"
           Blakley, AI, September 13, 1998.

p. 269   "In a funny way, this sinister edge all falls apart," Gib-
           son, AI, September 14, 1998.

p. 269   "I had this camera operator from Chicago," Altman,
           AI, April 19, 1999.

p. 270   "I was in danger of losing the crowd," Altman, AI, April
           19, 1999.

p. 271   "Bob and Barbara Harris did not get on at all at that
           point," Chaplin, AI, January 7, 1999.

p. 271   "Bob didn't do that out of vindictiveness," Tewkesbury,
           AI, April 6, 1999.

p. 272   "Bob must have paid his dues to the man upstairs,"
           Webb, AI, September 16, 1998.

Chapter Fourteen:
Nashville *Opens*

p. 273   "I have often hoped that the arts," "Nashville," *Vogue,* June 1975.

p. 273   "I think Altman just had a nightmare," Susan Toepfer, "Nashville Stars on *Nashville,*" *Family Weekly,* December 28, 1975.

p. 274   "Altman had, and always has, an uncanny sense," Dennis Hill, AI, September 16, 1998.

p. 274   "Editors hate him," Carradine, AI, April 19, 1999.

p. 274   "To be an editor with Bob," Hill, AI, September 16, 1998.

p. 274   "The screenings were a way of learning the film," Viertel and Colker, "The Long Road to *Nashville,*" *New Times,* June 14, 1975, p. 57.

p. 275   "I've never thought that way," Altman, AI, April 16, 1999.

p. 275   "I'll ride this sonuvabitch," Hill, AI, September 16, 1998.

p. 276   "He came to me one day," Starger, AI, March 10, 1999.

p. 276   "The screening was at eight o'clock," Rudolph, AI, October 16, 1998.

p. 277   "She came up to me in my office afterward," Altman, April 19, 1999.

p. 277   "The *Citizen Kane* of this generation," Howard W. Koch, letter. July 18, 1975.

p. 277   "A masterpiece," Dominick Dunne, letter, June 16, 1975.

p. 277   "Now I can take things," Sidney Lumet, letter, June 17, 1975.

p. 277   "I'm *from* and *of* Nashville," Dinah Shore, letter, July 7, 1975.

p. 278   "Charlie and Bob were out in front," Hill, AI, September 16, 1998.

p. 278   "An old silent film that had been scratched," Altman, AI, April 16, 1999.

p. 279   "When in hell did you do this?" Myers, AI, March 24, 1999.

p. 279   "I think you've made an unforgettably great movie," Allan Garfield, letter, February 6, 1975.

p. 280   "After I saw it, it occurred to me," Pauline Kael, phone
          interview, May 27, 1998.

p. 281   "Is there such a thing as an orgy for movie-lovers?"
          Kael, *The New Yorker,* March 3, 1975.

p. 282   "Robert Altman has used the camera to produce," Von-
          negut, *Vogue,* June, 1975.

p. 283   "If one can review a film on the basis," Vincent Canby,
          "On Reviewing Films Before They're Finished," *The
          New York Times,* March 9, 1975, II, p. 17.

p. 283   "There is nothing unusual," Kael, phone interview,
          May 27, 1998.

p. 284   "It should be enshrined in the Smithsonian," David
          Sheehan, *CBS Evening News,* July 7, 1975.

p. 284   "The tragedy implicit in *Nashville,*" Frank Rich, *New
          Times,* August 22, 1975, p. 38.

p. 285   "a Chaucerian musical pilgrimage," Andrew Sarris and
          Molly Haskell, "A Critic's Duet on *Nashville,*" *The Village
          Voice,* June 9, 1975, p. 128.

p. 285   "For now, let me say that it is better than most Altman
          films," Rex Reed, *Daily News,* June 13, 1975 p. 80.

p. 285   "Pauline Kael is always foaming at the mouth about
          something," Reed, *The Merv Griffin Show,* July 16, 1975.

p. 286   "*Nashville* is a vicious, malicious," Reed, *Daily News,*
          June 22, 1975.

p. 286   "Far more is *there* than merely the American mobility
          culture," Tom Wicker, "*Nashville*—Dark Perceptions in a
          Country-Music Comedy," *The New York Times,* June 15,
          1975, II, p. 1.

p. 287   "An unglued female star clips her tocnails," George F.
          Will, "Country Music Stars and Politicians," *Nashville
          Banner,* July 1, 1975, p. 6.

p. 288   "As *Ragtime* and *Nashville* are proving," Griel Marcus,
          "*Ragtime* and *Nashville:* Failure of America Fad," *The
          Village Voice,* August 4, 1975, p. 96.

p. 289   "If I put down anything it was me and my impression,"
          Altman quoted in ,"What I Consider America Today,"
          The Tennessean, June 6, 1975, p. 55.

p. 290   "It stinks," Eve Zibart, "*Nashville:* Some Find It Amus-
             ing, Others . . ." *The Tennessean,* June 8, 1975, p. 8A.

p. 291   "I'd rather see *Bambi,*" George Vecsey, "Nashville Has
             Mixed Feeling on *Nashville,*" *The New York Times,* August
             10, 1975, I, p. 41.

p. 291   "It was getting late," Myers, AI, March 24, 1999.

p. 292   "I'll tell you what I liked best about the film," Bill
             Hance, "*Nashville* Premiere Churns South," *The Banner,*
             August 11, 1975, p. 1.

p. 292   "I'm afraid a lot of people who love our music," Susan
             Toepfer, "Nashville Stars on *Nashville:* Too Close for
             Comfort—or Not Close Enough?" *Family Weekly,* De-
             cember 28, 1975.

p. 292   "A rip-off," Toepfer, "Nashville Stars on *Nashville:* Too
             Close for Comfort—or Not Close Enough?"

p. 292   "I was *personally* affronted," Toepfer, "Nashville Stars on
             Nashville: Too Close for Comfort—or Not Close
             Enough?"

p. 293   "I don't think [Altman]'ll ever be able to come back,"
             Toepfer, "Nashville Stars on *Nashville:* Too Close for
             Comfort—or Not Close Enough?"

p. 293   "I'm not a moviegoer," Toepfer, "Nashville Stars on
             Nashville: Too Close for Comfort—or Not Close Enough?"

p. 293   "It's simply not true that *anybody* can write songs,"
             Bruce Cook, "Patronizing the Nashville Sound," *The
             New Leader,* July 21, 1975, p. 29.

p. 293   "However it may irk country buffs," Shaun Considine,
             "Hollywood Can Sing Country Just Like Nashville,"
             The New York Times, August 24, 1975, II.

p. 294   "Great! Fabulous!," Toepfer, "Nashville Stars on
             Nashville: Too Close for Comfort—or Not Close
             Enough?"

p. 294   "I don't care if they have me kinda crazy," Toepfer,
             "Nashville Stars on *Nashville:* Too Close for Comfort—
             or Not Close Enough?"

Chapter Fifteen:
The Sequel: Linnea vs. Godzilla

p. 296   "This is not *Fiddler on the Roof,* babe," Tewkesbury, AI, September 15, 1998.

p. 297   "NASHVILLE BEAUTIFUL FILM DADDY SO MOVED," Oona O'Neill Chaplin, Telegram to Geraldine Chaplin, September 20, 1975.

p. 297   "My father especially loved this film," Geraldine Chaplin, AI, January 7, 1999.

p. 297   "Listen, this is quite a lot of film," Tom Stoppard, phone interview, March 2, 1999.

p. 297   "the American cinema has a genius," Dilys Powell, *Sunday Times,* September 21, 1975.

p. 298   "stupid, charmless, and lacking even basic tact," Hugh Herbert, *The Guardian,* September 20, 1975, Arts, p. 8.

p. 298   "The thing that strikes any traveller in America," Alexander Walker, "Altman's Grand Motel," *Evening Standard,* September 19, 1975.

p. 299   "Robert Altman appears on the verge," "Self-Indulgence to B.O. Click, Trend for 'Difficult' Altman: Kael and Other Critics Aid," *Variety,* June 11, 1975, p. 4.

p. 299   "The lumpen proletariat never got near it," Kael, phone interview, August 17, 1999.

p. 299   "and the end is not in sight for either," "Critics' Laurels vs. Public Support; 'Nashville' Into 300 Situations," *Variety,* January 14, 1975, p. 30.

p. 301   "It is the first time I have ever seen a film that is at the same time an act of prophecy," Eugene Wyatt, "Nashville Garners top Honors in New York Critics' Awards," *The Tennessean,* January 26, 1976.

p. 301   "Doctorow never let us forget that he was an accredited emissary," Andrew Sarris, "Swept Away at Sardi's," *The Village Voice,* February 9, 1976, p. 106.

p. 301   "I don't understand what he said, but I'm sure it'll sell to the kids," Sarris, "Swept Away at Sardi's," p. 106.

p. 302   "The reason given by the executive committee," Altman, Mailgram, January 26, 1976.

p. 303   "I was very pissed," Baskin, AI, March 8, 1999.

p. 303   "She was wearing a lacy cotton thing," Carradine, AI, April 19, 1999.

p. 305   "The prospect of living up to *Nashville* was terrifying," Robert Harders, phone interview, August 24, 1975.

p. 308   "I blanked him out because I never knew," Harders, phone interview, August 24, 1975.

p. 308   "I know how I would do it now," Harders, phone interview, August 24, 1975.

p. 308   "schoolmarmish . . . if it wasn't on the page, it wouldn't go on the stage," Harders, phone interview, August 24, 1975.

p. 309   "Again, I'm not sure it would have been a blockbuster," Starger, AI, March 10, 1999.

p. 309   "I think I was stupid," Tomlin, AI, September 14, 1998.

p. 309   "The commercial dragon roared," " 'Commercial Dragon' KO'd Sequel," *Daily Variety*, July 13, 1990.

Epilogue

p. 312   "I don't know why Bob and I didn't click better," Hayward, AI, March 8, 1999.

p. 312   "For some odd reason which I've never understood," Brown, phone interview, May 21, 1999.

p. 313   "Barbara used to be a letter writer," Remsen, AI, September 15, 1998.

p. 318   "When Michael Ovitz and Ron Meyer started CAA," Altman, AI, April 19, 1999.

p. 319   "He didn't approve of that ad that came out," Blakley, AI, September 13, 1998.

p. 319   "I assisted him with the casting," Altman, AI, April 19, 1999.

p. 320   "She seemed extremely vulnerable," Chaplin, AI, July 7, 1999.

p. 320   "A year later, when Geraldine Chapline and I went to the Oscars," Blakley, AI, March 7, 1999.

p. 320   "My sense was that Bob knew the handwriting was on the wall," Tewkesbury, AI, September 15, 1998.

p. 324   "Some woman walked up the aisle, very butch," Alt-
              man, AI, April 19, 1999.
p. 326   "I'm always shocked," Altman, AI, April 19, 1999.
p. 326   "Don't you feel responsible," Altman, AI, April 5, 1998.
p. 326   "Well, somebody should have paid notice," Altman, AI,
              April 5, 1998.

Index

Page numbers in *italics* refer to photographs.